When God Is Near
On the High Holidays

מגיד
MAGGID

Rabbi Yehuda Amital

When God Is Near
On the High Holidays

ADAPTED AND EDITED BY
Rabbi Yoel Amital

TRANSLATED BY
Kaeren Fish

AFTERWORD BY
Rabbi Yehuda Gilad

Yeshivat Har Etzion
Maggid Books

When God Is Near
On the High Holidays

First Edition, 2015

Maggid Books
An imprint of Koren Publishers Jerusalem Ltd.

POB 8531, New Milford, CT 06776-8531, USA
& POB 4044, Jerusalem 9104001, Israel
www.korenpub.com

The publication of this book was made possible
through the generous support of Torah Education in Israel.

ISBN 978-1-59264-437-7, *hardcover*

A CIP catalogue record for this title is
available from the British Library

Printed and bound in the United States

וְטַהֵר לִבֵּנוּ לְעָבְדְּךָ בֶּאֱמֶת

"Purify our hearts to serve You in truth"

This book is dedicated to the memory of
Moreinu verabbenu, our dear friend
Rabbi Yehuda Amital ***zt"l***
a great teacher and leader
who graced us with his heartfelt prayers
as *sheliaḥ tzibbur* in Yeshivat Har Etzion for decades.
May his memory continue to be a
blessing for us and for *Klal Yisrael.*

With appreciation and longing,
Marcos and Adina Katz
Mexico

Contents

ROSH HASHANA

ROSH HASHANA ON SHABBAT

THE BINDING OF ISAAC

SHABBAT SHUVA

YOM KIPPUR

NE'ILA

Foreword

> "Remember the days of old; consider the years of many generations. Ask your father and he will recount it to you; your elders, and they will tell you" (Deut. 32:7). Each year a new interpretation of the Torah comes into being.... In every generation and in every period a new insight into the Torah descends from the heavens, suited to the generation. And the *tzaddikim* of each generation perceive in the Torah that which is needed to instruct that generation. (*Ḥiddushei HaRim, Haazinu*)

My father, of blessed memory, quoted this on many occasions. One of the distinguishing features of his *siḥot* – discourses or talks – was their relevance, both in terms of what was happening in Israel and the world, and in terms of the *zeitgeist*. Now, as I review and transcribe his *siḥot* for the *Yamim Nora'im*, I return to the original meaning of the verse, "consider the years of many generations" – the years gone by, concerning which I must "ask your father and he will recount it to you."

This is a collection of *siḥot* delivered by my father and teacher, Rav Yehuda Amital *zt"l*, over the course of forty years during which he served as *rosh yeshiva* of Yeshivat Har Etzion, from its founding in 5729 until he passed away on the 27th of Tammuz 5770.

The special flavor of a *siḥa* delivered by a *rosh yeshiva* to his students in the *beit midrash* – especially on the *Yamim Nora'im* – is familiar to anyone who has studied at a yeshiva. My father's voice, opening the *siḥa* for *Seliḥot* each year with the verse, "Righteousness is Yours, O Lord," or opening the *siḥa* preceding *Ne'ila* each year with the verse, "I rose to open up for my beloved," continues to echo in the memory of those who heard his *siḥot* at those climactic moments. For us, the words of the verse are enough to bring back his warm but powerful voice and to transport us into the atmosphere of the *Yamim Nora'im*. It is my hope that this collection of *siḥot* will succeed in conveying these feelings even to those who did not hear them firsthand.

Despite the challenge of translating an oral address into a written essay, I have tried to preserve, as far as possible, my father's style of speaking and to transcribe his words in a way that conveys to the reader the range of ideas that he presented over the years. I hope that readers will sense the unique nature of these *siḥot* in terms of their content, richness of ideas, originality, practical relevance, and the great honesty with which they were uttered. As one expects, many of the ideas repeated themselves over the years, with varying emphases, and I have chosen to repeat them. Every *siḥa* highlights a different dimension or a new context, and this contributes to a deeper understanding and internalization of the message.

Some of the *siḥot* included here have already appeared in various publications of Yeshivat Har Etzion, especially the *Daf Kesher* newsletter for students serving in the IDF, as well as on Yeshivat Har Etzion's Israel Koschitzky Virtual Beit Midrash (etzion.org.il). The chapter entitled "Studies in the *Akeda*" appeared in *Alon Shvut Bogrim*, Tishrei 5762. It was reworked from handwritten notes for *siḥot* that my father entrusted to the capable hands of Prof. Aviad Hacohen.

The *siḥot* delivered on the first night of *Seliḥot* were reworked and edited from tape recordings. The other *siḥot* have been transcribed from manuscripts and notes for *siḥot* that were found among my father's writings. In my editing of the *siḥot* I have tried to remain faithful to the manuscript of the *siḥa*, although sometimes the material consisted of no more than a sheet of paper with headings. I have resisted the urge to elaborate on the material, even though my father would add or subtract as the spirit moved him. Some *siḥot* could be transcribed as they were, requiring only minor editing and the addition of sources. Other *siḥot* appearing here are composites created from manuscripts of several *siḥot*. I was aided in this work by reference to a collection of my father's *siḥot* from different publications, gathered at the initiative of Dr. Beni Gesundheit. His promise to my father during his final days that his *siḥot* would be published was a source of great comfort to him.

When my father spoke about the in-depth halakhic essays in his book *Resisei Tal,* which I had the privilege of transcribing and editing, and wanted to comment on my work, he would say, "About what you wrote...." It was no use protesting that it was not I who had done the writing, but he. The same thing happened when, after Yom Kippur of 5769, I handed him a printed version of the *siḥa* for *Ne'ila* which I had transcribed from his dictation over the telephone just prior to Yom Kippur. It was never clear to me whether he meant this as a compliment or criticism for something that was not altogether accurate, and therefore he viewed it as having been written by me, rather than himself. It was therefore with great trepidation that I embarked on this project, in honor of my father.

I received great encouragement in this project from my beloved mother, may she live a good and long life, who offered her own illuminating comments and was a great support to my father throughout his life.

My brother-in-law, Rabbi Yehuda Gilad, was a full partner in the reworking of the *siḥot,* offering many helpful comments and corrections, and he also contributed the Afterword at the end of this volume. Rabbi Avihud Schwartz meticulously edited the original Hebrew edition, and Rabbi Reuven Ziegler contributed valuable advice throughout the process.

I wish to thank Yeshivat Har Etzion, its *rashei yeshiva,* and its administration for taking upon themselves the commitment to publish my father's writings.

Thanks also to Matthew Miller, Rabbi Reuven Ziegler, Tomi Mager, and the dedicated staff of Maggid Books for giving this book its final form. Kaeren Fish skillfully rendered the book into English, Rabbi Eli D. Clark artfully edited it, and David B. Greenberg carefully proofread it.[1]

A heartfelt thanks to the family of Marcos and Adina Katz (Mexico) for generously enabling the publication of this book.

My father's *siḥot* are distinguished by their ability to penetrate the heart while at the same time appealing to the intellect. My father would often quote the comment of the Maharal of Prague (*Netzaḥ Yisrael* 23) on the mishna in Tractate Avot: "May it be Your will that the Temple be rebuilt speedily in our days, and grant our portion in Your Torah": we ask for the rebuilding of the Temple, which is the "heart," and at the same time we seek a "portion in Your Torah" – the intellect. My father knew how to integrate emotion and intellect in his life and in his teachings, as we see in the *siḥot* presented here.

I hope that this collection of *siḥot*, so animated by my father's spirit, will preserve the special ideas and the special atmosphere of the *siḥot* that caused us, his students, such spiritual uplift during the intense period of the *Yamim Nora'im*. It is my prayer that this collection will help open our hearts as we approach the *Yamim Nora'im* and allow us to engage in sincere prayer and repentance.

Yoel Amital
Shaalvim

1. Kaeren Fish translated forty-two of the book's fifty chapters. The remainder were translated by: Elli Fischer (79), David Silverberg (31, 129, 193), David Strauss (133), Alex Tsykin (199), Gila Weinberg (35), and Jonathan Ziring (75).

Elul

The Themes of Elul

The following midrash appears in *Pirkei DeRabbi Eliezer*:

> On Rosh Ḥodesh Elul, God said to Moses, "Come up the mountain to Me and sound a shofar throughout the camp." Because Moses was ascending the mountain, the shofar was sounded in order that the people not repeat the error of idol worship.... For this reason, *Ḥazal* decreed that the shofar be blown on Rosh Ḥodesh Elul every year, in order to remind Israel that they should repent, as it is written, "Will the shofar be blown in the city and the nation not be afraid?" (Amos 3:6). (*Pirkei DeRabbi Eliezer* 45)

The Rosh (*Piskei HaRosh,* Rosh HaShana 4:14) and *Tur* (*Oraḥ Ḥayim* 681) cite this same passage as binding law.

On the first of Elul, Moses ascended Mt. Sinai to receive the second tablets. The accompanying shofar blast served two purposes: first, notifying the people that Moses was ascending to receive the Torah; second, warning them not to repeat their error of worshipping an idol.

Why was it necessary to notify them that Moses was receiving the Torah? The shofar blast was meant to tell the nation, "The road is long and difficult. You have to prepare yourselves. You need to know that you are about to receive the Torah." This is our first task in the month of Elul: to mark our destination, the goal toward which we are aiming.

In *Parashat Ki Tetzeh*, we read of the *ben sorer umoreh* – the stubborn and rebellious son. According to Nahmanides, this passage teaches us our true aim in life. The *ben sorer umoreh* is guilty of two sins: he rebels against his father and mother and rejects their authority, and he is a glutton and a drunkard. Regarding this second sin, we are taught something curious: the death penalty is imposed on the *ben sorer umoreh* only if he consumes vast quantities of kosher meat, but if he eats non-kosher meat, or meat that the Rabbis prohibited, the laws of *ben sorer umoreh* do not apply to him. Nahmanides explains that the sin of the *ben sorer umoreh* is that he violates the norms of proper behavior, and thereby transgresses the command of the Torah, "You shall be holy" (Lev. 19:2). We see that the Torah demands that even an adolescent boy of thirteen live a life of sanctity, and if he fails to do so, he may fall into the category of the *ben sorer umoreh*.

The Torah's imperative, "You shall be holy," means that our performance of mitzvot is not sufficient. We are required to aspire to a higher level whose very essence consists of being holy. The Torah limits our consumption of meat because man needs to become more spiritual, to ensure that carnal desires not be the central focus of his life. Even when young, a person must strive for a life that is more spiritual, more moral, more balanced, more pure. Every one of us is expected to strive to achieve closeness to God, to develop a personality that is more authentic, more moral. Failure to do so makes a person into what Nahmanides calls a *naval bireshut haTorah*, "a scoundrel with Torah approval," even if, like the *ben sorer umoreh*, he scrupulously observes the finest details of the laws of *kashrut*.

The sounding of the shofar in Elul defines our goal in life. We who learn in yeshiva have an obligation to translate this goal into a single aim: the aspiration to become a *talmid ḥakham*, to attain Torah knowledge and to engage completely in Torah study. Today more than ever, it is imperative to become a *talmid ḥakham*. *Ḥazal* asserted that "an ignoramus cannot be pious" (Mishna Avot 2:5), but nowadays even a simple Jew is required to be a *talmid ḥakham*. In the past it was possible to be a good Jew even without being a *talmid ḥakham* and engaging in Torah study. In previous generations there were simple Jews, manual laborers, with no pretensions in the area of Torah study, who were nevertheless "good Jews." In our day, this is virtually impossible for a number of reasons, which I would like to explore with you.

The first factor is the nature of the period we live in. We live in a time when the outside culture seeps into our consciousness from every possible direction. Once upon a time, a Jew could live in a small town and never be exposed to anything that ran contrary to his way of life. His community was homogenous. Every day, he would go to synagogue, return home, go out to work. He was never exposed to the things we see every day. We, on the other hand, want to know what is going on in the world; we read newspapers and connect to different sources of news and information. As a result, we are exposed to a different culture. Therefore today we need a different standard of *yirat shamayim* and Torah study from that required in earlier generations.

The second factor is our lifestyle. Today, people have a lot of free time, and a whole culture of leisure time has developed to fill the vacuum. People no longer work from sunrise to sunset. We have substantial amounts of leisure time, and one of our main problems is what to do with so much free time. As technology advances, the problem of leisure time has become more pronounced. And one thing is certain: whatever time one does not spend on Torah will be filled with other things. There is no middle ground. No one can claim, "I'm just not meant to learn Torah." If you don't learn, you'll end up wasting your time.

The third factor relates to the intellectual debate in which we are engaged every day and every minute, often unconsciously. We are surrounded by a secular culture, a secular world which day and night declares its supremacy. Our struggle with this world animates our every step and generates challenges to our faith, our *yirat shamayim,* and our performance of mitzvot. The most dangerous thing is that we aren't always aware of this influence. For this reason we need to arm ourselves intellectually, with a firm grounding in Torah.

The fourth factor concerns the contemporary job market. Let's be honest: most of us connect the term "job" with some kind of intellectual pursuit, with a career involving thought and analysis. Obviously this applies not only to those who are planning a future in the rabbinate or teaching, but to anyone who intends to enter a profession. What will we become if we dedicate our most important faculty – our brain – solely to making a living, to advancing our career, and not to serving our Creator? Our *avodat Hashem* will be limited to physical activities, eating matza, washing hands, walking to the synagogue, but will not engage our minds. How can the intellect, the pinnacle of human achievement, not be central to our *avodat Hashem*? In the past, people's livelihoods were not connected with intellectual pursuits – they worked as a carpenter, a shoemaker, or some other unskilled labor. But we, who are accustomed to engaging our minds to meet our basic needs, can we neglect to do so for our spiritual needs?

The fifth factor involves the events we have witnessed in our day. We have seen hundreds of thousands of Russian Jews immigrating to Israel.[1] I doubt that a thousand of them knew what Torah is or heard of Abraham. Their move to Israel will change the country's social fabric. If Jewish knowledge becomes the province of a minority of the population, there is a real danger that the Jewish people will split between those who know and those who don't. We need to embody the uniqueness of Torah in our daily lives, but also make it known to others. We cannot leave all those hundreds of thousands of people who have never heard of Torah in the hands of those who are Jewishly ignorant. We need to create an educational elite to reach these people, and this will require intensive Torah study.

The last factor concerns our position in Israeli society. We do not seek to cut ourselves off from the national conversation. We are deeply involved in what is happening around us. The very concept of a *hesder* yeshiva reflects this involvement. But I believe that it is impossible to be involved in a secular society without a strong Torah basis. Without Torah we will be left with nothing.

The basis of the Torah is the Oral Law. "The Holy One, blessed be He, made a covenant with Israel only for [the sake of] the Oral Law"

1. Rav Amital here refers to the wave of immigration to Israel from the former Soviet Union between 1990 and 2000.

(*Tanḥuma, Bereshit* 58). Everything is built on the disputes of Abbaye and Rabba and, in descending order, Tanakh, then Jewish philosophy. But the Oral Law has a special aspect, a magic of its own. By studying the Oral Law a person hears the word of God Himself. In the words of the Midrash:

> "Let them take for Me a contribution" (Ex. 25:2) – To what can this be compared? To a king who had an only daughter. Another king arrived and married her. The king said to him, "I cannot tell you not to take her, for she is your wife. On the other hand, I cannot be separated from her, for she is my only daughter. I ask only this favor of you: wherever you go, build me a small chamber so that I may dwell with you." Similarly, God said to Israel, "I gave you the Torah. I cannot be separated from the Torah, but I cannot ask you not to take it with you. Wherever you go, build Me a small structure so that I may dwell there." (Exodus Rabba 33:1)

The study of Torah brings you closer to God. No one understands how this works. But if you focus your study on Jewish philosophy, Tanakh, or other subjects – you will fail. The Oral Law is the basis for everything – faith, Torah, *yirat shamayim*, love of mitzvot. Afterwards, of course, it is necessary to supplement with aggada and mussar, Tanakh and philosophy. But the foundation of all foundations is the Oral Law.

The second reason for sounding the shofar on Rosh Ḥodesh Elul, according to *Pirkei DeRabbi Eliezer*, is to prevent further idol worship. Let us imagine how the people felt following the debacle of the golden calf. They were surely weighed down by a feeling of failure as they prepared to receive the second set of tablets. Indeed, "My sin is before me constantly" (Ps. 51:5) is one of the principal themes of Elul.

This verse does not refer to a specific sin. We need constantly to examine ourselves: How deep is our faith really? How scrupulous is our performance of mitzvot? How do we treat others? Do we exercise responsibility toward society as a whole? What are our priorities? What is our level of *yirat shamayim*? How committed are we to Torah? These are the issues that demand introspection and self-evaluation.

We also need to examine the quality of our prayer. How many times a day do we repeat the words, "who sanctified us with His commandments"? This is not mere words, but an expression of the power of mitzvot to sanctify us. "He pours out his heart before the Lord" (102:1). Are we truly capable of pouring out our hearts before God?

Do we appreciate the great benefit of studying Torah and fulfilling mitzvot? The prophet Malachi (3:13) says, "'Your words have been strong against Me,' says the Lord. Yet you say, 'What have we said against You?'" God accuses the people, "You have spoken harshly against Me." The Jews do not understand: "What did we say? Heaven forbid! We've said nothing against You!" The prophet responds, "You have said, 'It is useless to serve God; what have we gained by keeping His charge, and by walking in abject awe of the Lord of Hosts? And so, we account the arrogant happy: they who have performed wickedness have endured; they have indeed dared God and escaped.'"

"It is useless to serve God." People say, "What difference does it make whether or not we observe the mitzvot? What do we gain? God commanded us to do, and so we do. Just as it says in the *Mishna Berura*."

If we do not constantly feel, every hour and every minute, the great value of putting on *tefillin*, keeping Shabbat, or performing mitzvot generally, then our actions fall under the category of "Your words have been strong against Me…'It is useless to serve God.'"

This is the second lesson from Moses' climb to the top of Mt. Sinai and the second foundation of Elul. Our quest for self-improvement begins, as we said, with an awareness of failure, and the desire to bridge the distance between where we want to be – and need to be – and where we actually find ourselves.

A third principle relating to Moses' ascent of Mt. Sinai to receive the second tablets is, "Carve yourself two tablets of stone like the first ones" (Ex. 34:1). The second tablets were inscribed with divine writing, just as the first tablets were, but Moses was required to hew the second tablets from stone. Speaking of the *yetzer hara*, *Ḥazal* say, "If this *menuval*, this contemptible creature, confronts you, drag him into the *beit midrash*" (Sukka 52b). Rabbi Menaḥem Mendel of Kotzk explained that the phrase "this *menuval*" refers to the one outside the *beit midrash*. But in the *beit midrash* another *menuval* waits for you, the same *yetzer hara* in a different form. The *yetzer hara* sometimes fools you into thinking that "the *beit midrash* will make everything right." You don't need to make an effort; the *beit midrash* will create the right atmosphere and will have the desired influence on you.

But we need to remember that the true experience of Elul doesn't just happen; it results from an effort of "Carve yourself," of hard work. Certainly, the atmosphere of the *beit midrash* adds something, but anyone who builds his life on atmosphere is wasting his time. A person has to apply himself, to overcome shifts in mood and interest. Being a student in yeshiva requires rousing oneself to engage in *avodat Hashem* whether one feels like it or not. One has to get to the *beit midrash* on time, and open the Gemara, no matter his mood. Constantly applying oneself is hard work. In other areas – preparing for an examination, for example – one knows that the moment will come when he has reached the finish line, the task is complete. This isn't true of *avodat Hashem*. The effort is constant and unrelenting.

One's years in yeshiva can be the most productive years of your lives. I envy you. But you have to make proper use of this time. If a person is presented with such possibilities, can he possibly be forgiven for not making the most of the opportunity?

When Moses prepares to receive the second tablets, he is told, "And no one will ascend with you" (Ex. 34:3). Rashi comments on this verse that the first tablets attracted the evil eye as a result of the fanfare and thunder and throngs accompanying their transmittal, whereas, for the giving of the second tablets, "modesty is the most worthy trait."

Not creating a big impression; not making a big noise; not the superficial but the substantive. Whoever feels that appearances are primary needs to correct this. Fear of Heaven requires going beneath the surface.

Performance of mitzvot also demands that we turn inward. Many mitzvot require little effort – going to synagogue, buying kosher food, etc. But even with respect to these, we need to add another dimension, to deepen our fulfillment of these commandments.

That is why we have gathered in the *beit midrash*. Sometimes, we may feel despair, we may lose faith in our own abilities. But one must strengthen his faith in himself too, as *Ḥazal* taught: "Open for Me an opening the size of the eye of a needle" – that alone is sufficient – "and I will make an opening for you as wide as the entrance to the Holy Temple." The mussar masters explain: If one makes a hole in some fabric the size of a needle, it can easily be lost. It's there, but he cannot see it. God here is promising that, even if we pry open a tiny opening, it will remain open, it won't be lost. And then we are promised that God will expand for us the opening "as wide as the entrance to the Holy Temple."

Elul: Repentance and Repair

On Rosh Ḥodesh Elul Moses climbed Mt. Sinai to receive the second tablets and a shofar was sounded throughout the camp. The rabbinic decree to blow the shofar during Elul is based on that original shofar blast, which called the people to repent (*Tur, Oraḥ Ḥayim* 571).

Let us try to imagine the atmosphere during that month in the Israelite camp, in the wake of the smashing of the tablets. A very short time separated the heights of "You shall be chosen unto Me" and the depths of the golden calf and God's threat, "Leave Me, that I may annihilate them." A sense of failure hung over the camp.

Then Rosh Ḥodesh arrived, and God told Moses to climb Mt. Sinai once again. But the doubts persisted. Had God forgotten the golden calf? If so, had He also forgotten the great revelation of "I am the Lord your God"? In the words of *Ḥazal*:

> [Zion] said to Him, "Master of the universe – if there is no forgetfulness before Your Throne of Glory, perhaps You will never forget the golden calf?"
>
> [God] answered, "These too shall be forgotten" (Is. 49:15).

> Then she said to Him, "Master of the universe – if there is indeed forgetfulness before Your Throne of Glory, perhaps You will forget the Revelation at Sinai?"
>
> He answered, "And I shall not forget you" (ibid.). (Berakhot 32a)

According to the midrash in *Pirkei DeRabbi Eliezer*, the shofar was sounded to warn the nation not to repeat their sin of idol worship. But why should this be a concern? Forty days had passed, and the people had already repented. Why, then, was it necessary to sound the shofar to prevent them from relapsing into idolatry?

To understand this midrash, we need to understand the causes of the sin of the golden calf. According to many authorities – especially Rabbi Yehuda HaLevi – the Children of Israel were certain that they were on the correct path, but felt a need to act. How could they sit idly for forty days after the Revelation at Sinai? The giving of the Torah was a visceral experience, transmitted in awe and terror, and they felt an urgent need to respond in a tangible way.

Moses understood the nation. He knew they would not fashion another calf, but he worried that their desire to translate their feelings into action might lead to some other form of idolatry. Therefore God commanded that the shofar be sounded, to remind them: Any kind of worship that is not commended by God is like idolatry! Do not seek the passion of religious experience, just the faithful fulfillment of God's word.

The Torah's description of the giving of the second tablets teaches us how to go about correcting past failures. The process involves two stages. First, God told Moses, "Carve for yourself two tablets of stone" (Ex. 34:1). While the first tablets were fashioned by God Himself – "the tablets were the work of God" (32:16) – here Moses is told to carve them himself. The same applies to repentance. You cannot rely on your surroundings to inspire you. Carve them yourself, with effort and determination! As with the second tablets, we can no longer expect to receive God's handiwork as a gift. If you want to change direction, to alter your behavior, chart a different course, you need to carve into bedrock.

The second stage is, "No one shall ascend with you, nor shall anyone be seen anywhere about the mountain" (34:3). At the giving of the first tablets, God commands, "You shall ascend, and Aaron too" (19:24), and He revealed Himself amidst thunder and lightning. For the second tablets, Moses stands alone and receives them in a quiet, private experience.

Moses climbs Mt. Sinai, thinking that the people's sin has been forgiven. But before God gives him the tablets, He teaches him the Thirteen Attributes of Mercy:

> "The Lord passed before him and proclaimed" (Ex. 34:6) – R. Yoḥanan said, "Were it not written in the Torah, it would be forbidden to say! This verse teaches us that the Holy One wrapped Himself like a *sheliaḥ tzibbur* and showed Moses the order of prayer. He told him, 'Any time that Israel sins, let them do this before Me, and I shall forgive them.'" (Rosh HaShana 17b)

What does it mean, "Let them do this before Me"? It is not enough to say the words; one needs to actively imitate God's attributes. The Attributes of Mercy need to be translated into practice in our daily lives, in our interaction with our fellow man.

The Children of Israel thought that repairing their relationship with God was the remedy for the golden calf. But it is impossible to achieve full atonement and forgiveness from God if the Thirteen Attributes do not animate our relationship with others.

Concerning R. Yishmael's dictum, "Receive every person with joy" (Mishna Avot 3:12), Maimonides teaches, "One must receive every person – whether small or great, free man or slave, every member of the human race – with joy."

Repentance begins between man and his fellow, in the home and the *beit midrash*, in the way one receives other people. All of us are excellent at criticizing and judging others. On the other hand, we are adept at justifying and rationalizing. Generally, we apply our criticism to others, while we justify our own behavior. At this time of repentance, we need to do the reverse: We need to be critical of ourselves, and look for the best in others. We must receive others with joy. The Gemara teaches:

> R. Yoḥanan said, "One who shows the whites of his teeth [i.e., smiles] to his fellow is superior to one who gives him milk to drink, as it is written: 'teeth whiter than milk' (Gen. 49:12). Say not 'white teeth' but 'showing the white of one's teeth.'" (Ketubot 111b)

We live in a world of alienation, and we need to end the disregard of others here and now.

During these days of divine compassion, we need to relive that first Elul after the giving of the Torah – the collective awareness of failure, the hewing of the tablets, the active improvement of our own conduct. For this reason, we begin the *Seliḥot* with the Thirteen Attributes, which teach us how to treat our fellows.

Allow me to share with you a personal experience. In my life I have lived through three very different periods. During the first period, Jews in the Diaspora lived in peace and quiet. No one worried about the future. There were some Zionists who spoke about Jewish nationalism, but not out of fear. When people prayed, they worried mainly about themselves – who would live and who would die, who in his time and who before his time.

Then came the Holocaust, when every individual had only one concern: personal survival. No one spoke about the Jewish people, only how to survive from one day to the next.

Now we live in a period when people are not so concerned about personal survival. Despite the constant threat of terrorism – may God protect us – most people in Israel are not worried about their personal safety. Our main worry is: What will happen to the Jewish people? What will happen to the State of Israel, the Land of Israel?

In such a period, a person may say to himself: When the fate of the nation is at stake, what does it matter if little me behaves a little better or a little worse? How important are my personal problems compared to those of the state? Maybe we should put aside ourselves in favor of the concerns of the Jewish people.

We need to remember the Gemara that teaches:

> R. Yonatan said, "Repentance is great, because it brings redemption, as it is written (Is. 59:20), 'A redeemer shall come to Zion, and to those who turn from sin amongst Jacob': What is the reason that 'a redeemer shall come to Zion'? Because of 'those who turn from sin amongst Jacob.'" (Yoma 86b)

The redemption of which R. Yonatan speaks is not the full and final redemption, but the everyday redemption which results from the personal repentance of each and every one of us. Our personal repentance is not isolated from what happens to the Jewish people; it is related and has an effect on the nation as a whole.

We see that our personal self-improvement is in no way divorced from the fate of the Jewish people. Maimonides writes:

> Every person needs to see himself as if his merits and demerits are evenly balanced and as if the entire world's merits and demerits are evenly balanced. If he commits a single sin, he will tilt the balance of judgment against him and the entire world, sentencing it to destruction. But if he performs one mitzva, he will tilt the balance of judgment in his favor and in favor of the salvation of the entire world, as it says, "The righteous is the foundation of the world" (Prov. 10:25). He who acts righteously will bring about the world's vindication and salvation. (*Mishneh Torah*, Laws of Repentance 3:5)

May we merit this in our lifetime!

Seliḥot

Heed the Praise and the Prayer

On this Saturday night, we begin to say the *Seliḥot,* and we plead that God "heed the praise (*rina*) and the prayer." This phrase comes from Solomon's prayer at the dedication of the Temple:

> Receive the prayer of Your servant and his supplication, O Lord my God, heed the praise (*rina*) and the prayer which Your servant prays before You this day." (I Kings 8:28)

The reason we invoke praise as well as prayer is that praise is an essential part of prayer. As *Ḥazal* teach, "One should always organize his praise of God first and then go on to pray" (Berakhot 32a). But the term *rina* has another meaning, as we read in Psalms:

> Heed my cry (*rina*), for I am brought very low; deliver me from my persecutors, for they are too strong for me. (Ps. 142:7)

From the depths of his prayer, David cries out, "Heed my cry (*rina*)." There is no doubt that this does not refer to praise, but to the cry that is the essence of prayer. *Rina* in this sense refers to the prayer of the person who believes that only God can save him, of "I lift my eyes to the mountains; from where shall my help come?" (121:1). This is how David felt when Saul entered the cave in which he and his men hid (I Sam. 24). David faces two untenable options – raising his hand against Saul, God's chosen one, or falling into Saul's clutches. At this moment, David cries out to God, "With my voice I cry to the Lord; with my voice I petition the Lord" (Ps. 142:2). David is asking: Is it Your will that Saul fall into my hands or that I fall into his? Only You know what is in my best interest and therefore only You can aid me!

This prayer turns into praise, into a paean to God, who alone is all-knowing and who is the only source of salvation. When one realizes that his only hope is the Lord, the King, the Redeemer and Savior, his prayer turns into praise. For this reason, we begin the *Seliḥot* with a prayer that is a kind of praise (*rina*).

> "God passed before him and proclaimed" (Ex. 34:6) – R. Yoḥanan said, "Were it not written in the Torah, it would be forbidden to say! This verse teaches us that the Holy One wrapped Himself like a *sheliaḥ tzibbur* and showed Moses the order of prayer. He told him, 'Any time that Israel sins, let them do this before Me, and I shall forgive them.'" (Rosh HaShana 17b)

Ḥazal are saying that God playing the role of *sheliaḥ tzibbur* is something that would be forbidden to say were it not written in the biblical text. Maimonides (*Mishneh Torah,* Laws of the Foundations of the Torah 1:7–9) demonstrated that God has no body or corporeal form and the visions of the prophets were merely an allegory. Maimonides proves this from the fact that even Moses sees God as a great warrior at the Red Sea and as a *sheliaḥ tzibbur* at Sinai. The question is, why does R. Yoḥanan say that seeing God as a *sheliaḥ tzibbur* is "forbidden to say"?

The answer lies in the contrast between the verses we say at the beginning of the *Seliḥot* service and the Thirteen Attributes of Mercy. The verses emphasize the loftiness of the Lord. Yet, we move from these expressions of God's grandeur to the Thirteen Attributes of Mercy. This reminds us that, even though God is great and grand, when the Thirteen

Attributes were said, He wrapped Himself in a tallit like the *sheliaḥ tzibbur*. In so doing, He was saying to Moses: Even though I am lofty and grand, I put Myself in the midst of the Jewish people, I pray with them as their *sheliaḥ tzibbur*. When I reveal Myself, I take a human form and exhibit human attributes. This is why *Ḥazal* teach us that this would be forbidden to say were it not written explicitly in the biblical text. When God dwells in our midst, it is as if He joins us in prayer.

In the wake of the sin of the golden calf, God tells Moses, "I will send an angel before you…for I will not go up in your midst, for you are a stiff-necked people, lest I consume you on the way" (Ex. 33:2–3). But after God reveals the Thirteen Attributes to Moses, and thereby reveals His closeness to the People of Israel, Moses permits himself to request the following: "If now I have found grace in Your sight, Lord, let the Lord, I pray You, go in our midst, for they are a stiff-necked people, and pardon our iniquity and our sin" (34:9).

If God is so close to us that He can serve as our *sheliaḥ tzibbur*, He can certainly travel in our midst despite our stubborn nature.

The Gemara continues as follows:

> "Lord, Lord" – I am He before one sins and I am He after one sins and repents. (Rosh HaShana 17b)

The divine attribute of *ḥesed* is guaranteed to us both before we sin and after. Why does one need the attribute of mercy before he sins? This is an important message for every Jew, even one who has not sinned. The attribute of *ḥesed* provides that a person can follow the ways of the Lord, even though He is lofty and elevated. The Torah commands us, "Walk in His ways" (Deut. 28:9). But we are so far beneath Him, how can we approach Him and follow His ways? This problem is solved by God's appearance as *sheliaḥ tzibbur*. God is saying: I am in your midst. I am with you and I am your *sheliaḥ tzibbur*. It follows that each of us can follow in His path. We see that the day that God related to Moses the Thirteen Attributes was a banner day for the Jewish people!

The Thirteen Attributes are human attributes, yet God adopts them. We learn from this that even we mortals are capable of following in God's path. In fact, the Torah commands us to walk in God's path and cleave to Him:

> After the Lord your God shall you walk, and Him shall you fear, and His commandments shall you keep, and His voice shall you heed, and Him shall you serve, and to Him shall you cleave. (13:5)

The Gemara (Sota 14a) explains that cleaving to God means imitating His attributes. But everyone needs to know: This is not easy to achieve! There are people looking all over for mystical experiences. But these strange and unusual experiences have nothing to do with the cleaving required by the Torah. True closeness to God comes from "walking in His path." Maimonides (*Mishneh Torah,* Laws of Personal Development 1:5–7) explains that this means following the golden mean.

"Righteousness and justice are the foundation of Your throne; mercy and truth go before You" (Ps. 89:15). This verse, said at the beginning of the *Seliḥot,* refers to God's attributes. But it also teaches us what path we need to follow: the path of righteousness and justice, mercy and truth.

Truth is an important attribute of the Divine. What is truth? How can we achieve it? The answer appears in the *Seliḥot*: "Yours, O Lord, is righteousness, while we are shamefaced." If we look at ourselves in an honest and straightforward manner, and experience shame, then we can achieve truth.

A popular practice attributed to the *Shelah* calls for one to say at the end of the *Amida* a verse that begins with the first letter of his name and ends with the last letter. The aim is to remember one's name on the Day of Judgment. Why is this necessary? On the Day of Judgment, a person confronts the gulf between his self-image and his true self. This disparity can cause him to forget his own name. Standing before the heavenly Judge, you ask yourself: Who am I really? If I don't know who I am, I also don't know my name. On the Day of Judgment the truth comes out, no longer obscured by the masks that hide one's true self during his lifetime.

"Purify our hearts to serve You in truth." We pray that God will assist and accept us, will give us the ability to see our true selves and sincerely turn to Him in our prayers. We pray that, like David of old, we will understand that we have nowhere else to turn, that only God can help us. Once we realize this, our prayer will become a cry (*rina*). And God has promised that He will heed the cry and the prayer.

Hearer of Prayers

"You who hear a prayer – to You shall all flesh come." (Ps. 65:3)

Although the Holy One, blessed be He, hears many prayers, the editors of the *Seliḥot* chose to begin them with this verse, formulated in the singular – just "prayer." In the Midrash (*Pesikta Rabbati* 21), *Ḥazal* compare this to a portrait which many people see, and each one is convinced that the face in the portrait is looking back at him. *Ḥazal* explain that at Mt. Sinai, God looked at the multitudes of Jews and said to each one, "I am the Lord your God." In the same way, the Midrash goes on, God hears the prayer of every person as if he was the only worshipper in the world. "The verse does not say 'prayers,' but rather 'You who hear *a* prayer – to You shall all flesh come.'"

We are approaching Rosh HaShana, the Day of Judgment. In the Mishna (Rosh HaShana 1:2), we learn that on this day all creatures pass before God "like *benei maron*." The Gemara proposes three different images to explain this expression:

> This is translated, "like a flock of sheep" [Rashi: like lambs counted for the animal tithe, which are counted one by one as they pass through a small opening which does not allow them all to emerge at once].

> Resh Lakish said, "As in the ascent of Beit Maron" [Rashi: a narrow pass where wayfarers had to proceed in single file, since the valley was deep on both sides].
>
> Rav Yehuda said in the name of Shmuel, "Like the troops of the House of David" [Rashi: who pass in review one by one as they go out to battle]. (Rosh HaShana 18a)

These images are different from one another. According to the first image, each individual stands alone, but is also part of the whole. When the sheep are counted, each animal passes individually, but each also belongs to a larger group from which the tithe must be taken. Thus, every person in the world is judged as an individual, but viewed also in relation to his environment.

According to Resh Lakish, every person stands on a narrow pass, with the abyss on either side and no room for another person to pass. On the Day of Judgment a person stands alone before the Master of the world and is judged solely according to his own actions, not in relation to others. Resh Lakish teaches that there is no point in comparing my behavior with that of other people. Each of us stands alone, and if he has done his utmost and repented, then he can climb the narrow steps without fear.

The third image evokes the fear of judgment. A soldier of the House of David does not stand alone; he belongs to a larger group of soldiers. At the same time, every soldier knows that, Heaven forbid, he may not return from battle. The fact that he is part of a whole will not necessarily save him from judgment. So it is concerning all the people of the world, who pass before God like "*benei maron.*"

It is important to emphasize we stand in judgment before God as individuals. The thought that I might be judged favorably simply because I have observed more mitzvot than someone else is totally wrong. *Ḥazal* teach us that the prohibition against murder is not set aside if one's own life is in danger. In the words of the Gemara (Sanhedrin 74a), "Who says that your blood is redder? Perhaps his blood is redder." Rashi explains:

> Because when the Torah said to violate a mitzva because "you shall live by them," it means because a Jewish soul is precious to

> Him. But in the case of a murderer, in the end a Jewish soul will be extinguished, so why should it be permitted to violate [the prohibition against murder]: who knows whether one's soul is dearer to his Creator than the soul of his fellow?

Unfortunately, some people think they are more beloved to God than others because they belong to a community that is more religious, more spiritual, more exacting in its fulfillment of the commandments. They believe that by virtue of their mitzva observance their "blood is redder." This is simply unspeakable. We cannot know another person's history, where he came from, or where he began. Maybe I received a better religious education than he did; maybe if he had grown up where I did and in the same circumstances, he would have achieved far more than I have done.

At the heart of the *Seliḥot* are the Thirteen Attributes. The Gemara teaches:

> R. Yoḥanan said, "Were it not written in the Torah, it would be forbidden to say! This verse teaches us that the Holy One wrapped Himself like a *sheliaḥ tzibbur* and showed Moses the order of prayer. He told him, 'Any time that Israel sins, let them do this before Me, and I shall forgive them.'" (Rosh HaShana 17b)

Two important messages are conveyed here. The first is the incomprehensible idea that God Himself wraps Himself in a prayer shawl, as it were, and stands with us in prayer. One of the greatest sources of anxiety in prayer is the feeling that I may not be worthy of standing before the Master of the world: "Who shall ascend the mountain of the Lord, or who shall stand in His holy place?" (Ps. 24:3). The Gemara gives us confidence that when we stand in prayer we are standing in His Presence, as it were, and He prays along with us. This image also helps us to explain the verse, "Of You my heart has said, 'Seek My face.' Your face, O Lord, I seek" (27:3). The worshipper feels like the emissary of God, who stands with him in prayer and tells him, "Seek My face."

Second, in the Gemara *Ḥazal* create a unique combination of revelation and concealment. God wraps Himself like a *sheliaḥ tzibbur* after promising Moses, "I shall cause *all My goodness* to pass before you"

(Ex. 33:19). Pay close attention: "all My goodness" – all of creation – is spread before Moses, and at precisely that point God wraps Himself like a *sheliaḥ tzibbur*, concealing Himself. A person in prayer is also required to "conceal himself," to subdue his ego. At the same time, by concealing one's ego, one uncovers the full extent of his personal and communal responsibility. A person who is mired in concealment may sink to a state of complete self-abasement, which prevents him from acting, advancing, and influencing his environment. We are commanded to emulate the Holy One, blessed be He: "Just as He is compassionate, so you shall be compassionate; just as He is merciful, so you shall be merciful." The *sheliaḥ tzibbur*, then, must understand that his wrapping himself in his tallit requires the assumption of responsibility. In order to stand and ask for forgiveness on behalf of the community, he must conceal his own personal identity, while at the same time feeling responsibility for those he represents.

Can a person really be expected to "imitate God?" We must remember that this imitation does not relate to God's essence, but to some of His attributes. We are required to imitate His compassion, His kindness, but not His zealousness or vengeance. The imitation of God involves only those Thirteen Attributes that were transmitted to Moses, and only in relation to them does the command to emulate the King of kings apply.

Needy and destitute paupers we come before God, ashamed and embarrassed. At the same time, we are required to emulate His ways. To this end we need to really understand how it feels to stand before God – during our daily prayers and all the more so as the Day of Judgment approaches. We stand before God despite all of our human failings. This inspires great fear, on one hand, but also a feeling of strength and power, for God desires that we stand before Him, and even "joins" with us in our prayers. We are not pushed away, Heaven forbid, but desired by God. All year long a person tries to draw near to God, eagerly anticipating any hint of rapprochement from His side. At this time, during the period of *Seliḥot* and divine mercy, God promises that He will forgive us if we stand and say the Thirteen Attributes, wrapping ourselves so as to conceal our personal desires, emphasizing instead communal needs.

We need to use this time to draw near to God and to return to Him with humility, love, and fear. "You stand this day, all of you, before the Lord your God" (Deut. 29:9), and we must appreciate the privilege of being able to stand before Him.

May it be His will that we to turn to Him with a sense of closeness, that He hear our prayers, and bless us with a good year during which we will truly feel close to Him, and sense the responsibility that this confers upon us.

"How Can We Justify Ourselves?"

> How can we complain, what can we say, how can we speak, and how can we justify ourselves? We will examine our ways and scrutinize them, and we will return to You, for Your hand is outstretched to accept returnees. Not with abundance and not with deeds have we come before You; needy and destitute we knock on Your door. (from the *Seliḥot* prayers)

Throughout the year, we try to appear to ourselves and to others as richly endowed with religious virtue, blessed with the ability to confront the outside world and full of religious merit and good deeds. But when we begin saying *Seliḥot* and the moment of truth comes, it becomes clear that "needy and destitute we knock on Your door." Not only have we little in the way of real spiritual achievements, but the little that we have is not ours; it is a direct result of the education we received from our parents. If we make a true accounting of the education we received and the blessings of God against what we have added on our own, we recognize that we are, indeed, needy and destitute.

We read in the Torah:

> You stand this day, all of you, before the Lord your God – your tribal heads, your elders, and your officials, all the men of Israel, your children, your wives, even the stranger within your camp, from woodchopper to water-drawer – to enter into the covenant of the Lord your God and its sanctions, which the Lord your God is concluding with you this day. (Deut. 29:9–11)

There was no greater event than this one, because God relates to every person individually. From the woodcutter to the water-drawer, everyone merited to stand before God.

In these verses, the Torah establishes that the relationship between God and Israel is a covenant, which means the relationship is mutual. A person who commits a sin faces the threat of punishment, but, in the context of a covenant, there is also the possibility that the sin is an affront to the other party. A covenant is the most demanding form of commitment and, as such, any deviation or violation represents a breach of the relationship, Heaven forbid. If a person turns his back on the covenant, the immediate response is a sense of "Yours, O Lord, is righteousness, while we are shamefaced."

"What can we say, how can we speak, and how can we justify ourselves?" When we feel shame, we feel the urge to justify our behavior. But we really have only one option: "We will examine our ways and scrutinize them, and we will return to the Lord." This is not easy. We need to work hard on ourselves if we wish to get to a state of "I will go and I will return to my first husband, for it was better for me then than now" (Hos. 2:9). Only once the individual truly recognizes that "it was better for me then than now" can he achieve full repentance. Our task over the days ahead is to reach this recognition: "We will examine our ways and scrutinize them."

During the *Seliḥot* period, we take advantage of the special opportunity that we have to say the Thirteen Attributes of Mercy. All of the rest of the *Seliḥot* service is just a preface to the Thirteen Attributes.

We learn from the Gemara (Rosh HaShana 17b) that we can invoke the special prayer that God bestowed on Moses only if we act as a *sheliaḥ tzibbur*. Without an awareness of being an emissary, a person cannot hope to enjoy the divine promise that God will not turn away the Thirteen Attributes empty-handed.

Every Jew in every generation is a *sheliaḥ tzibbur*. Nearly all of the High Holiday prayers speak not of the individual, but of Israel, the world, the restoration of Jewish monarchy, and so on. If we said only those prayers composed by the Members of the Great Assembly, we would not say a single personal prayer. Fortunately, the Sages over the years added such prayers as *Avinu Malkenu* and *UNetaneh Tokef*, which also give expression to personal concerns. But the primary prayers speak exclusively about Israel as a people. As a result, an individual must stand in prayer as a *sheliaḥ tzibbur*.

If this principle has always been true, how much more so for us, who sit in the *beit midrash* and set the tone for the entire nation? Students of Torah are *sheliḥei tzibbur*, and we bear a greater responsibility than others, because we preserve the Jewish character of the State of Israel. All of the Jews who crowd into synagogues and say *Seliḥot* without a feeling of being a *sheliaḥ tzibbur* are praying as mere individuals. We must pray for everyone. Without a sense of communal responsibility, one cannot say the Thirteen Attributes of Mercy. This has always been true, and is especially so nowadays.

That gemara in Rosh HaShana teaches us that a *sheliaḥ tzibbur* must wrap himself. In so doing, he suppresses his ego, his sense of self. He himself becomes invisible and what remains is only his role as agent and emissary. This sense of a calling, of communal responsibility which obscures the ego, is an absolute condition to God's promise not to turn our prayers away empty-handed.

One of the most difficult challenges we confront on the High Holidays is that God judges us as a group, and I am far from the worst of the bunch; there are worse than me. On the other hand, if I am judged by myself, what chance do I have of acquittal? The solution is to view oneself as a *sheliaḥ tzibbur,* who stands before God as an individual, but is also the emissary of a community. Even if I am not worthy, the community is.

The Thirteen Attributes describe God's ways which we are commanded to emulate. As He is merciful, so must we be; as He is compassionate, so must we be. On the first attribute, Rabbi Moshe Cordovero writes:

> This refers to God as a tolerant King who bears insult in a manner beyond human understanding. Indeed, nothing is hidden from His view. Yet, there is not a single moment when man is not nourished and sustained by virtue of the divine power bestowed upon him. Thus, no man ever sins against God without – at that very moment – God bestowing upon him the very spirit of life and the strength to move his limbs. Yet even though a person uses this vitality to sin, God does not withhold it from him. Rather, He suffers this insult and continues to give him strength to move his limbs. Even though the person at that very moment uses that power for iniquity, sin, and rebellious deeds, still God bears the insult. (*Tomer Devora*, ch. 1)

A person who puts himself first makes innumerable demands on others and is easily insulted and offended. Therefore, we need to adopt the attributes of the Almighty and abandon our own traits.

The Gemara in Rosh HaShana tells about the time Rav Huna b. Rav Yehoshua fell critically ill and was visited by Rav Papa. Rav Papa sensed that the end was near and ordered the preparation of shrouds. In the end, Rav Huna recovered, much to the embarrassment of Rav Papa. Rav Huna told him that he had been correct and Rav Huna's death had been decreed. But this decree was cancelled because Rav Huna did not stand on his honor. If one lives with the sense that he is undeserving and that he bears responsibility for the community, he will be judged favorably.

This is the feeling with which we need to say *Seliḥot*. In this way, we can take advantage of the Thirteen Attributes of Mercy and prepare ourselves to repent wholeheartedly. "We will examine our ways and scrutinize them." We need to internalize the feeling of responsibility for the community and our sense of being "needy and destitute," with no expectation of reward. We will pray first of all for the Jewish nation and Land of Israel, and for each person individually. May we all merit a year of good life, a *ketiva vaḥatima tova* to us and all of Israel, amen!

"Needy and Destitute, We Knock at Your Door"

The *Shulḥan Arukh* (*Oraḥ Ḥayim* 581:1) states, "The custom is to rise before dawn and beg God for forgiveness." *Shaarei Teshuva* criticizes people who say the *Seliḥot* before midnight, then adds, "But one is permitted to say *Viduy*, except on Saturday night, when saying *Viduy* is forbidden before midnight, because of the sanctity of Shabbat." A puzzling statement. *Havdala* has been said, all work is permitted – why then is saying *Viduy* forbidden?

Perhaps we can find the answer in the following midrash:

> "I am black but comely, daughters of Jerusalem" (Song 1:5). "I am black" – on weekdays. "But comely" – on Shabbat. "I am black" – all year long. "But comely" – on Yom Kippur. "I am black" – in this world. "But comely" – in the World to Come. (*Yalkut Shimoni* 11:982)

According to the Midrash, our personalities include different – and conflicting – aspects: light and dark, Shabbat and weekday, Yom Kippur, and the World to Come. There are many points of light: morality, spirituality, purity. However, we also embody profane elements: materialism, envy, hatred, lust, selfishness, and exhibitionism. Elements of darkness and shadow co-exist with the light of Shabbat.

We are forbidden to confess our sins on Shabbat, because it is a day dedicated to enhancing the Shabbat-like qualities within us. In contrast, *Viduy* highlights those points of weakness which require confession. When we are still imbued with the sanctity of Shabbat, the taste of Shabbat, we may not be able to see those failings that we must confess. Therefore, the halakhic authorities ruled that *Viduy* be said on Saturday night only after midnight, lest the "comeliness" of Shabbat blind us to the "I am black" of the weekdays.

A central motif of the *Seliḥot* is that we stand before God: "Needy and destitute, we knock at Your door." What does the phrase "needy and destitute" mean?

The Hasidim tell the story of a beggar who came to complain to a rebbe: "How can you justify such favoritism? When I come to you, you see me for only a few short moments, yet you entertain some rich person for hours on end!" The rebbe responded, "My dear boy, when you come before me, I can immediately identify you as a beggar. The rich man who appears wealthy sat with me for two hours until I realized that he was a beggar just like you!"

Sometimes a person who prays immediately recognizes that he is needy and destitute, but other times he must examine himself for a long time until he realizes that he is indeed needy and destitute. At first glance, we have performed many mitzvot over the course of the year, which means we are not "needy and destitute." But on further reflection, how can we approach God with the false claim that our conduct is rich with meaning?

The Gemara says:

> R. Yehoshua b. Levi said, "Why were they called the 'Men of the Great Assembly'? Because they restored things to their former glory.
>
> "Moses came and said, 'The great, mighty, and awesome' (Deut. 10:17).

> "Jeremiah came and said, 'Gentiles are high-stepping in His temple; where are His awesome deeds?' He did not say God was 'awesome.'
>
> "Daniel came and said, 'Gentiles are subjugating His children; where are His mighty deeds?' He did not say God was 'mighty.'
>
> "Then came the Men of the Great Assembly and said, 'The greatest expression of His might lies in His self-control, that He is patient with evildoers. And His awesome deeds are that, were it not for the awe of the Holy One, blessed be He, how could one nation continue to exist among the other nations?'"
>
> And how could the Rabbis [Rashi: Jeremiah and Daniel] deviate from a decree set down by Moses? R. Elazar said, "Because they know that God is truthful, so they would not be false with Him." (Yoma 69b)

Ḥazal teach us an important principle in worshipping God: God's attribute is truth, so we can only approach Him by way of this attribute. Therefore, even though Moses described God as "great, mighty, and awesome," Jeremiah and Daniel did not follow his example, because they knew that God is truth and He can only be approached in truth. Beset by the question, "Where are His awesome and mighty deeds?" they knew God would not welcome them calling Him "the awesome," "the mighty."

We too cannot be false in our prayers. So, even if we performed many mitzvot during the year, we cry out, "Needy and destitute, we knock at Your door!" The spiritual value of a mitzva is measured by the degree of awe and love of God which inspired it. As a result, we cannot know the true worth of the mitzvot we performed. If we examine our deeds based on their spiritual value, we may conclude that "their fear of Me is a commandment of men learned by rote" (Is. 29:13). We may have performed many mitzvot, but what is their true worth?

We are like a person who has a great deal of paper money, but it has lost all its value and he is left with a pile of worthless paper. In this respect, even though we have performed mitzvot, we are still "needy and destitute."

In the Musaf prayer of Rosh HaShana, we say, "The memory of every being comes before You, each person's acts and his purpose." What does "his purpose" mean? It means one's role, his mission. God determines whether a person has fulfilled his purpose in the world. We need to ask ourselves whether we have fulfilled our God-given assignment.

Sometimes the task is imposed by the circumstances of a specific day and age. One hundred thousand Jews have immigrated to Israel this year, Jews who are needy and destitute in relation to Judaism. Is it conceivable that God's demands of them are the same as His demands of us? We are obligated to ask ourselves, what is our responsibility toward them?

One's purpose in life is also affected by the environment in which he was raised and educated. According to Maimonides, "We cannot evaluate; only God judges our traits and He alone knows how to weigh good deeds against sins" (*Mishneh Torah,* Laws of Repentance 3:2). One cannot compare the mitzva performed by one who received a strong religious education to the mitzva performed by someone else. We were fortunate enough to imbibe from infancy Torah, fear of Heaven, faith, and mitzvot. We got used to keeping mitzvot from the surroundings in which we grew up. So we need to ask ourselves honestly, without comparisons to others: was there an added dimension that we brought to our service of God?

This week I read about the annual balance sheet of one of the largest enterprises in Israel. Its operating profit was twelve million dollars, but the net results were a loss of nineteen million dollars. Where did this loss come from? The explanation is simple: the enterprise had enormous debts to pay. So it is with us. We keep the mitzvot, we made some "profit," but how much of that profit do we owe to those who invested in us? How much is actually the fruit of our own labor?

The Torah tells us that Moses was "exceedingly humble, more than any other person on the face of the earth" (Num. 12:3). How to understand this humility? Did Moses, the greatest of the prophets, believe that there were people greater than he? Perhaps we can say that Moses, the humblest of men, had doubts about his own greatness. He thought to himself: Could this simple Jew, crying out for his portion of meat, be on a higher spiritual plane than me? He was not raised in Pharaoh's palace, but in servitude. He did not see the revelation at the burning bush nor did he commune with God at Sinai. Perhaps, if this same Jew had enjoyed all of the privileges that I grew up with, he would have reached a higher spiritual level than me, and would certainly not hunger for meat. That was Moses' unique humility.

If this was true for Moses, how much more so are we, with all of our good deeds, still needy and destitute? We will be judged according to "each person's acts and his purpose." Who can know what mission God has imposed on him? So we begin the *Seliḥot* and proclaim, "Needy and destitute, we knock at Your door," "Yours, O Lord, is righteousness, while we are shamefaced."

And yet, our awareness that we are needy and destitute can also teach us about God's mercy. The Midrash states:

> "And I shall be gracious to whom I shall be gracious" (Ex. 33:19) – At that time God showed him all the treasure houses of reward that await the righteous.
>
> He said to Him, "For whom is this treasure house designated?"
>
> He answered him, "For those who perform mitzvot."
>
> "For whom is this one designated?"
>
> "For those who raise orphans." And so on, for each and every treasure.
>
> Eventually he saw one great treasure house and asked, "For whom is this designated?"
>
> God told him, "Those who have earned their reward – I give them from that which is theirs; those who have not earned any reward – I give them for free," as it is written, "I shall be gracious to whom I shall be gracious." (Exodus Rabba 45:6)

When a person stands before God with a sense of not having earned a reward, when he says, "Lord of the universe, I have nothing. I come before You empty-handed" – he will ultimately recognize God's kindness, which He bestows upon His creations from the treasure house of free gifts.

Our self-awareness must be genuine and lead to practical consequences. If we are indeed destitute of mitzvot, we need to perform them. What are the consequences of this sense of not having earned a reward? If the feeling is genuine, it can serve as the springboard for change.

We have said that mitzvot are measured by their spiritual value, by the degree of fear of Heaven that animates them. For this reason, we stand needy and destitute, because we doubt the true value of the mitzvot we performed. But I have some advice for you. Certain mitzvot have intrinsic worth regardless of one's intentions. Regarding mitzvot between you and your fellow, *Ḥazal* teach that if a person gives charity "in order that my son will live," he is considered a totally righteous person (Pesaḥim 8a).

Here is another example. The Talmud deals with the ceremony of *egla arufa* in response to the discovery of a corpse outside a town, where the local elders declare, "Our hands did not spill this blood and our eyes did not see":

> Did anyone imagine that the elders spilled blood? Rather, they are saying, "It is not the case that the victim came to us and we sent him away without food; it is not the case that we saw him but did not accompany him on his way." R. Meir would teach, "It is permissible to require that visitors be accompanied on their way, for the merit of such a mitzva has no limit, as it is written (Judges 1:24–25), 'And the watchmen saw a man leaving the city, and said to him, "Show us the city gate and we will be kind to you".... And he showed them the city gate.' What was the kindness? That they slew the entire city, and sent this man and his family to safety....
>
> "This Canaanite, who never spoke nor walked a single step, saved himself and his family for generations. How much more worthy is the man who exerts himself to accompany another!"
>
> How then did he show them the gate? Ḥizkiya said, "He signaled with his mouth." R. Yoḥanan said, "He showed them with his finger." (Sota 46b)

This Canaanite received a handsome reward for assisting in the capture of Beit El by showing kindness to soldiers who were not familiar with the locale; he merely "signaled with his mouth" or "showed them with his finger." *Ḥazal* learn from this that, when a person finds himself in strange surroundings, and someone helps him, even in a small way – there is no greater mitzva than this. The modern equivalent of accompanying a stranger on his way is to show kindness to a visitor. This, *Ḥazal* teach, is a mitzva which brings reward without measure.

In our day, there are many people who qualify as "visitors," people who find themselves in unfamiliar surroundings. All they need is a nod of the head, a little bit of attention. The Gemara teaches:

> R. Yoḥanan said, "One who shows the whites of his teeth [i.e., smiles] to his fellow is superior to one who gives him milk to drink, as it is written, 'teeth whiter than milk' (Gen. 49:12). Say not 'white teeth' but 'showing the white of one's teeth.'" (Ketubot 111b)

Smiling at someone is equivalent to giving him a glass of milk to drink. People need a little attention paid to them and we can give it to them.

This is true even within the yeshiva itself. There are new students who are not familiar with their surroundings, who do not yet feel at home in the yeshiva. *Ḥazal* tell us: there is no limit to giving someone a little attention, guidance, a smile, even pointing the way with a finger.

None of us can know "each person's acts and his purpose," what is one's God-given mission in this world. But one thing is certain: part of our mission is the obligation to help the newcomers in our midst.

If we are looking for points of merit before the Day of Judgment, this is one that is easy to perform. We do not need lofty spiritual intentions. One just needs to do it.

"Needy and destitute," we approach the Throne of Glory. We need to make every effort to come prepared. As we approach the Day of Judgment, each one of us must come with a true sense of being spiritually "needy and destitute," of "those who have not earned any reward."

At the beginning of the *Seliḥot,* we say, "The Lord is close to all who call Him, to all who call Him sincerely." With this firm belief, with confidence that God is close to all who call Him sincerely, we prepare to stand before Him. We prepare to say the *Seliḥot*, to ask for mercy for ourselves and for every Jew wherever he may be. In particular, we pray for this holy land of ours, that God grant us a year of life and peace, material and spiritual, peace from our enemies without and harmony within, for ourselves and all of Israel, amen.

Between Routine and Renewal

> At the departure of the day of rest, we have come before You for the first time. (from the first night *Seliḥot* service)

Our custom, dating from the period of the *Geonim*, is to say *Seliḥot* nightly during Elul and up until Yom Kippur. The innovation of the *Geonim* was not merely the recitation of *Seliḥot*, but the times they fixed for saying them: on Motza'ei Shabbat, or early in the morning. These are not regular times for prayer, which indicates that their intention was that we break from our routine. The awe of the Day of Judgment demands that we shake ourselves from our complacency, that we not continue with business as usual. Breaking from routine is required of us all the time, but especially during the High Holidays. *Ḥazal* taught:

> Bar Hei-Hei said to Hillel, "Why the repetition in the verse, 'Then you shall again discern between the righteous and the wicked, between him who serves God and him who does not serve Him' (Mal. 3:18)? Surely, 'the righteous' is 'him who serves God,' and 'the wicked' is 'him who does not serve Him.'"
>
> He answered him, "Both 'him who serves' and 'him who does not serve' refer to the perfectly righteous, but one who has

> reviewed his studies a hundred times cannot be compared to one who has reviewed a hundred and one times."
>
> Bar Hei-Hei said to him, "And because of this one extra time he is called 'him who does not serve Him'?"
>
> He answered, "Yes! As we know from those who hire donkeys: the price for ten parsangs is one *zuz*, but for eleven parsangs – two *zuz*." (Ḥagiga 9b)

A person who reviews his studies a hundred times is not the same as someone who reviews a hundred and one times. That one extra review shows that the student is not simply following routine, complacent with his progress. The extra effort reflects that none of his study was routine.

Ḥazal tell us that one who serves God out of routine is considered as if he "does not serve Him." How can they make such a harsh judgment? In order to understand their statement, we must examine the context of the verse cited in the Gemara:

> "Your words have been strong against Me," says the Lord. Yet you say, "What have we spoken against You?" You have said, "It is useless to serve God; what have we gained by keeping His charge, and by walking in abject awe of the Lord of Hosts? And so, we account the arrogant happy: they who have performed wickedness have endured; they have indeed dared God and escaped." Then those who fear the Lord spoke to one another; and the Lord listened, and heard it, and a Book of Remembrance was written before Him for those who fear the Lord, and take heed of His name. "And they shall be Mine," says the Lord of Hosts, "on that day which I appoint as My particular day; and I will spare them, as a man spares his own son who serves him. Then you shall return, and see the difference between the righteous and the wicked, between him who serves God and him who does not serve Him." (Mal. 3:13–18)

The prophet claims that Israel spoke harshly about God – "'Your words have been strong against Me,' says the Lord." They claim that they have not benefited in any way from their observance of the commandments: "It is useless to serve God; what have we gained by keeping His charge, and by walking in abject awe of the Lord of Hosts?" Furthermore, "so we account the arrogant happy" – we see that the wicked prosper; we envy them and consider them fortunate. The evildoers, for their part, have tested God to see if He would punish them, and they have evaded retribution: "They have indeed dared God and escaped."

These are indeed serious charges: "your words have been strong against Me." Yet, the people say to the prophet, "What have we spoken against You?" This response is difficult to understand: Do they not understand the severity of what they have said? How can they not be aware of the harshness of their own words?

The prophet's answer to them is also hard to understand: "Those who fear the Lord spoke to one another; and the Lord listened, and heard it, and a Book of Remembrance was written before Him for those who fear the Lord and take heed of His name." The prophet calls those who complain against God "those who fear the Lord," although they say, "It is useless to serve God." Moreover, the prophet declares, "And they shall be Mine, says the Lord of Hosts, on that day which I appoint as My particular day; and I will spare them, as a man spares his own son who serves him." In other words, despite their claims against God, He will spare those who fear Him.

We must try to understand how it is that people who fear God ask what benefit they receive from serving Him. From *Ḥazal*'s words it seems that the statement of the people – "It is useless to serve God" – is not spoken out of defiance, but out of sadness and pain. The people are frustrated because they serve God routinely. Because of this, the prophet considers them as "him who does not serve Him." They claim "it is useless to serve God" because for them it has lost its vitality and freshness. We can understand why they ask, "What have we gained by keeping His charge?" What is gained from such service, when it has no vitality, no freshness?

To contend with this problem, the *Geonim* established the practice of breaking routine, and reciting *Seliḥot* not during regular prayer times, but rather on Motza'ei Shabbat or early morning.

What makes Motza'ei Shabbat special is that it falls somewhere between the sacred and the profane. The Midrash comments on the verse: "'I am black' (Song 1:5) – on weekdays. 'But comely' (ibid.) – on Shabbat" (*Yalkut Shimoni* 11:982). This applies not only to the weekdays and Shabbat in the literal sense, but also to times that are figuratively "Shabbat times" and "weekday times." The tragedy of man is that he has a dimension of "blackness" and a dimension of "comeliness." We all experience moments of inspiration and elevation and times that are gray and bleak. Sometimes this can be frustrating, but other times it is comforting: even when immersed in routine, we remember that we have Shabbat, special moments, times of sanctity.

Sometimes a person becomes so enamored with the "comeliness" that he no longer sees the "blackness." Whether consciously or not, we can forget the need to deal with the routine and the mundane aspects of our being. This is one of the problems of living in two worlds: Shabbat and the weekday, blackness and comeliness.

In *Parashat Ki Tavo* we read:

> Moses called to all of Israel, and said to them, "You have seen all that the Lord did before your eyes in the land of Egypt to Pharaoh and to all his servants, and to all his land. The great trials which your eyes have seen, the signs and those great miracles. Yet the Lord has not given you a heart to perceive, and eyes to see, and ears to hear, until this day." (Deut. 29:1–3)

The Children of Israel lived through powerful experiences and witnessed tremendous miracles. They had seen the divine revelation. Nevertheless, "the Lord has not given you a heart to perceive, and eyes to see, and ears to hear, until this day." Rashi explains: "to recognize the mercies of the Holy One, blessed be He, and to cleave to Him." You have seen great things, but you were blind to recognizing God's grace. The fact that there are special times, great days, does not guarantee anything for the day after. Therefore, *Ḥazal* teach, one has to remember that there is "blackness" and "comeliness," weekdays and Shabbat. Throughout the week we must remember that in addition to the blackness, we also have elements of Shabbat within us. The times of spiritual elevation should cast their aura over the routine times.

We start *Seliḥot* specifically on Motza'ei Shabbat, not at a regular time for prayer. As we emerge from Shabbat and look to the weekdays ahead, our initial reaction is, "Yours, O Lord, is righteousness, while we are shamefaced." A person usually feels shame when things become known that he did not want people to know about. A person who feels shame tries to hide his thoughts and desires from God, but often it turns out that he is trying to hide things from himself, to forget them. For a person to be honest with God, he has to be honest with himself. We often hide ourselves from ourselves – but for how long? When a person realizes that he thought – even subconsciously – that he could hide himself from God, Heaven forbid, he is overcome with shame. Ezra declares, "I said, 'My God, I am ashamed and blush to raise my face to You, my God, for our iniquities are increased over our head, and our guilt has mounted to the heavens'" (Ezra 9:6).

How can a person judge himself? The Gemara sets down two requirements:

> Our Sages taught, "For two and a half years there was a dispute between the School of Shammai and the School of Hillel. The former said it would be better for man not to be created than to be created; the latter said it is better for man to be created than not to be created. They took a vote and decided that it was better for man not to be created than to be created. But now that he has been created, let him examine (*yefashpesh*) his deeds." Or, as others say, "let him look over (*yemashmesh*) his deeds." (Eiruvin 13b)

What is the difference between the two verbs used for reviewing his actions? Rabbi Moshe Ḥayim Luzzatto, in *Mesillat Yesharim* (ch. 3), explains that "*yefashpesh*" means he should evaluate all his actions, especially his sins. In addition, it is necessary that he "*yemashmesh*" – scrutinize his good deeds, and ask: Were they really good deeds? Was there no taint to them?

Ramḥal's interpretation recalls the biblical rebuke: "Because you would not serve the Lord your God with joyfulness, and with gladness of heart, for the abundance of all things" (Deut. 28:47). This means: even though you served God, you did not feel any joy in this service, you did not feel freshness in performing mitzvot, you found no meaning in them. Spiritual problems stem from lack of interest, lack of feeling, and lack of enthusiasm. Force of habit in performing mitzvot makes them stale. When our service of God becomes rote and routine, then we need to plead for divine mercy.

In conclusion, I would like to quote a passage from a book of mussar to which I feel a special attachment. My grandfather of blessed memory, Rabbi Tzvi Klein, was a simple Jew, neither a rabbi nor a scholar of note. At the end of his life, he bequeathed to me his copy of *Pele Yo'etz*. On the first page of the book he inscribed the dates on which he finished reading the book – once every year and a half or two years. Over the course of thirty-five years, he finished the book twenty times. Every evening before he went to sleep, he studied it. I have not reached his level, but once in a while I study the book. Under the heading "Advocacy," the *Pele Yo'etz* writes:

> It is known that God desires that we argue in defense of the Jewish people, on both the communal and the individual level.... Thus, preachers must be very careful, especially during the High Holidays, not to indict the audience in their sermons by mentioning communal sins, Heaven forbid. Rather, they should say, "This is what should be done, and this should be avoided," and the audience will understand. And if one finds himself in a congregation of unlearned people, and hears the preachers saying harsh things about the Jewish people, he should summon the courage to speak in their favor, even using arguments that he is not certain about. He should say, "What shall a son do to keep from sin? Poverty does not produce good traits, nor does exile. They become assimilated among the nations and learn their ways, and the inclination of man's heart is evil. Therefore they are not to be held responsible. Everyone acted unintentionally, for they do not know that such-and-such is forbidden," and so on. One should judge them favorably. And anyone who judges others favorably, God will judge him favorably too.

Especially nowadays, with the public in Israel so sharply divided, we need to avoid condemnations, and instead to argue in defense of the

Jewish people. The author of *Pele Yo'etz* warns that a person who judges others strictly brings strict judgment on himself on the Day of Judgment. We need to emphasize the "comeliness" of the nation of Israel, not the "blackness." We need to pray that all of Israel repent, and as a result, as we seek to judge others favorably, perhaps we will succeed in changing ourselves as well.

Let us pray to God at this time that He have mercy on His people, in the Land of Israel and elsewhere, and may the heart of Israel return to their Father in heaven. We are in need of great mercy. We must consider ourselves as emissaries of the community, feel responsibility for the nation, feel their pain – even if the community itself does not feel it. Just as an individual may be sick without being aware of it, so it is with the community: there is sickness of which the community is unaware. Let us – who are fortunate enough to sit in the *beit midrash* – turn to God and ask that at this time He have mercy on His people Israel, and that we merit a year of life and peace. May we and all of Israel be inscribed and sealed for a good year.

Standing Before the Almighty

The *Levush* (681:1) writes that the structure of the *Seliḥot* service parallels that of the weekday morning prayers. According to this, the central portion of the *Seliḥot* is the equivalent of the *Amida* prayer.

Within this section, the two most important texts are the Thirteen Attributes and *Viduy*. The Gemara (Rosh HaShana 17b) calls the Thirteen Attributes a "prayer service" which God revealed to Moses. *Viduy* forms an intrinsic part of the process of repentance, which is the central concern of the period of *Seliḥot*.

The question is, what do the *Seliḥot* add? After all, we say the Thirteen Attributes and *Viduy* at least twice a week all year round, and some even say them twice daily. The answer is that the most distinctive element of the *Seliḥot* is that we say them at night. Moreover, if we look closely at the Ashkenazi version of *Seliḥot*, we will see a unique aspect that distinguishes them from the daily prayers.

After *Ashrei* and Half-Kaddish, we say a brief prayer that serves as a sort of introduction: "Righteousness is Yours, O Lord… for You hear our prayers." Thereafter, we say about fifty verses that describe the loftiness and greatness of God. Finally, we call on every living creature, "Come, let us sing to the Lord; let us call out to the Rock of our salvation!"

What is the connection between these verses and the *Seliḥot* service? Maimonides, in his preface to *Mishneh Torah,* Laws of Repentance, writes: "This contains one positive commandment: that a sinner should turn away from his sin before God and make confession." He expands on this as follows:

> With regard to all the commandments of the Torah, whether positive or negative – if a person violates one, whether intentionally or not, when he repents he is required to confess before God, blessed be He, as it says, "When a man or a woman shall commit any sin…they shall confess their sin which they have committed" (Num. 5:67) – this refers to verbal confession. This confession is a positive commandment. How is one to confess? He says, "Please, O Lord – I have sinned, I have transgressed, I have committed evil before You; I have done such-and-such, and behold, I regret and am ashamed of my deeds, and I will never go back to doing them." This is the essence of *Viduy*. (*Mishneh Torah,* Laws of Repentance 1:1)

Maimonides teaches us that one should open *Viduy* with "Please, O Lord" ("*Anna Hashem*"). This is also the phrase with which the High Priest begins each of the three confessions that he is required to say on Yom Kippur. The Gemara (Yoma 37a) brings biblical verses as precedent for saying "Please" and "O Lord." Maimonides applies this requirement to every *Viduy* that is said. In his view, the commandment to repent requires one to confess before God. The phrase, "Please, O Lord," establishes that one is confessing before God.

But in practice we do not follow this view, and do not begin *Viduy* with the phrase, "Please, O Lord." Maimonides himself writes that the customary formula for *Viduy* begins, "But we have sinned" (*Mishneh Torah,* Laws of Repentance 3:8). The reason why we don't say, "Please, O Lord," may be our fear of saying something that isn't true. As Maimonides rules:

> One who confesses verbally without having resolved to abandon his sin is like one who immerses in a *mikve* while holding vermin in his hand. (2:3)

In the *Viduy* of Yom Kippur we specifically mention confessing falsely: "For the sin that we have sinned before You in our verbal confession." Perhaps out of this concern, the custom developed not to begin *Viduy* with the words, "Please, O Lord."

Nevertheless, the fundamental principle remains unchanged: repentance and confession must be performed out of a sense of standing before God.

What does it mean to sense the Divine Presence in this context? Regular people like us tend to think of God in a very limited way, mainly in terms of God as a source – for the individual or the community – of assistance and support, as a healer and savior or – Heaven forbid – the God who metes out punishment and suffering or cuts short the lives of ordinary people.

It is only natural that people's perception of the Divine Presence in their lives is likewise limited to God's generous gifts to us. This is the reason we start the *Seliḥot* with a plea: "Righteousness is Yours, O Lord… for You hear our prayers."

But this limited sense of God's Presence is inadequate. The High Priest, in his *Viduy* on Yom Kippur, pronounces God's ineffable name in order to inspire a sense of God's loftiness, splendor, greatness, and awesomeness. And all of this while bowing and prostrating himself before Him.

And this is why the Ashkenazi sages chose to begin the *Seliḥot* service with verses that express this sense of the Divine Presence, at its loftiest and grandest level.

The giving of the Torah at Sinai teaches us an additional emotion that needs to accompany the *Seliḥot*:

> The entire people saw the thunder and the lightning, and the sound of the shofar, and the mountain smoking, and the people

> saw it and were shaken and stood at a distance. And they said to Moses, "You speak to us, and we will hear; let God not speak to us lest we die." And Moses said to the people, "Do not be afraid, for God has come in order to test you, and in order that His fear be upon you, so that you will not sin." (Ex. 20:15–17)

Ḥazal teach (Nedarim 20a), "In order that His fear be upon you – This refers to shame." When a person senses the Presence of God and judges his actions, he is filled with shame, as it is written (Ezra 9:6), "My God, I am ashamed and confounded to lift my face towards You." No other reaction is conceivable. That feeling of shame washes over the person, and from the depths of his heart he looks up to God and declares, "Yours, O Lord, is righteousness, while we are shamefaced."

But after all this we still have only scratched the surface. We have not yet considered another extremely important dimension of God – His attributes. Moses requested of the Almighty, "Please teach me Your ways" (Ex. 33:13).

On Yom Kippur, we read the following in the haftara:

> For thus says the High and Lofty One that inhabits eternity, whose name is Holy: "I dwell in the high and holy place, with him also that is of a contrite and humble spirit, to revive the spirit of the humble, and to revive the heart of the contrite ones." (Is. 57:15)

On this verse, the Gemara says:

> R. Yoḥanan said, "Wherever you find God's might, you also find His humility. This is written first in the Torah, second in the Prophets, and a third time in the Writings. In the Torah it is written, 'For the Lord your God is God of gods and Lord of lords' (Deut. 10:17), and then, 'He executes justice for the orphan and widow.' Second, in the Prophets it is written, 'For thus says the High and Lofty One that inhabits eternity, whose name is Holy,' and then, 'of a contrite and humble spirit.' The third time, in the Writings it is written, 'Extol Him who rides upon the skies, whose

> name is the Lord' (Ps. 68:5), and then, 'A Father of the fatherless, and a Judge of widows.'" (Megilla 31a)

It is impossible to distinguish between God's greatness and His attributes. Our Sages instructed us to cleave to His attributes: "As He is merciful, so shall you be" (*Sifrei*, Deut. 11:22). This is the import of the Thirteen Attributes of Mercy, which teach us both God's ways and our obligation to follow their example. If we fail to internalize the Thirteen Attributes of Mercy, our experience of God's Presence can never be complete.

Moreover, if we stopped after saying the verses relating to God's absolute majesty, without continuing to say the Thirteen Attributes, we could lapse into total self-abasement before God. This could, Heaven forbid, paralyze a person and prevent him from trying to imitate the Almighty. A person might think, "I am nothing but a tiny, insignificant speck. Who am I to sing out praises to the Rock of our salvation?" Such self-abasement runs contrary to the great calling of "You shall walk in His ways" (Deut. 28:9). The requirement that we emulate the attributes of the Almighty demands that we take stock of the spiritual and moral progress that we achieved during the year. But self-abnegation and kneeling serve merely to temper feelings of superiority and self-satisfaction.

When we say the verses that describe the grandness of God, we are expressing our readiness to prostrate ourselves before Him. But we need to remember that this self-abasement is not paralyzing but elevating. We gape in wonder at God's wondrous deeds and His control over all of creation. We feel so inspired that we turn to the creatures in the wild and cry out: "Come, let us sing to the Lord, let us call out to the Rock of our salvation" (Ps. 95:1).

The requirement that we "walk in His ways," that we imitate His attributes, must issue from an awareness of everything that is special in our personality. We derive spiritual sustenance from His Torah and the wonders of His creation. These spiritual gifts are from God; He has allocated them to those who seek Him and study His Torah. Therefore, we should not be abasing ourselves, but striving to imitate Him to the best of our ability.

I pray that, animated by a sense of God's greatness, we will confess wholeheartedly and repent truthfully, so that we will walk in His ways, giving of ourselves to those who are in distress and hallowing His name.

“The Holy One Wrapped Himself like a *Sheliaḥ Tzibbur*”

> “The Lord passed before him and proclaimed” (Ex. 34:6) – R. Yoḥanan said, “Were it not written in the Torah, it would be forbidden to say! This verse teaches us that the Holy One wrapped Himself like a *sheliaḥ tzibbur* and showed Moses the order of prayer. He told him, ‘Any time that Israel sins, let them do this before Me, and I shall forgive them.’” (Rosh HaShana 17b)

God does not merely make a statement or proclamation, but “passes before” Moses and shows him how to pray. According to *Ḥazal,* Moses had trouble grasping the procedures for the sanctification of the new moon and collection of the half-shekel until God showed him these things directly. It seems that Moses also had trouble with the order of prayer, until God wrapped Himself like a *sheliaḥ tzibbur,* physically demonstrating the prayer service.

Why does the *sheliaḥ tzibbur* wrap himself? The tallit of the *sheliaḥ tzibbur* serves to de-emphasize and conceal his individuality. There is no requirement that a worshipper cover his head during prayer, but a *sheliaḥ tzibbur* is required to wrap himself, so that his personal identity is not at the center of the prayer. Only in this way can he serve as the emissary of the congregation.

Sometimes, self-concealment serves to silence the act of prayer. This is concealment in the sense of "Enter into the rock and hide in the dust for fear of the Lord and for the glory of His majesty" (Is. 2:10). A person who hides in the underground tunnels amongst the rocks for fear of facing God stands totally helpless before Him. The concealment of the *sheliaḥ tzibbur* is different. He obscures his individual personality and emphasizes his complete dedication to serving as emissary of the community, his sense of responsibility towards the collective. Only then is he worthy of reciting the Thirteen Attributes of Mercy.

The kabbalists drew a connection between the Thirteen Attributes and the prophecy of Micah:

> Who is a God like You, who pardons iniquity, and forgives the transgression of the remnant of His heritage? He does not maintain His anger forever, because He delights in mercy. He will again have compassion upon us; He will suppress our iniquities. And You will cast all their sins into the depths of the sea; You will show truth to Jacob, loyal love to Abraham, as You have sworn to our fathers from days of old. (Mic. 7:18–20)

Let us consider the first divine attribute cited by the prophet. Rabbi Moshe Cordovero writes:

> "Who is a God like You" – This refers to God as a tolerant King who bears insult in a manner beyond human understanding. Indeed, nothing is hidden from His view. Yet, there is not a single moment when man is not nourished and sustained by virtue of the divine power bestowed upon him. Thus, no man ever sins against God without – at that very moment – God bestowing upon him the very spirit of life and the strength to move his limbs. Yet even though a person uses this vitality to sin, God does not withhold it from him. Rather, He suffers this insult and continues

> to give him strength to move his limbs. Even though the person at that very moment uses that power for iniquity, sin, and rebellious deeds, still God bears the insult.
>
> This, then, is a virtue man should emulate – namely, tolerance. Even when he is insulted to the degree mentioned above, he should not withdraw his benevolence from those upon whom he bestows it. (*Tomer Devora*, ch. 1)

The Thirteen Attributes should be said with this sort of understanding of each individual attribute. This is possible only when a person wraps himself like a *sheliaḥ tzibbur*: when his own personality, his ego, is submerged. The Gemara teaches:

> "Mighty, merciful, and gracious" (Ex. 34:6) – Rav Yehuda said, "A covenant has been made that the Thirteen Attributes are never turned away empty-handed, as it is written, 'Behold, I make a covenant…' (v. 10)." (Rosh HaShana 17b)

At the same time, along with this sense of being a *sheliaḥ tzibbur* whose individual personality is concealed, every person is also required to remember that in this time of year he stands in judgment as an individual. The Mishna (Rosh HaShana 1:2) states that on Rosh HaShana all people pass before God "like *benei maron*." The Gemara offers three different explanations of this expression:

> This is translated, "like a flock of sheep" [Rashi: like lambs counted for the animal tithe, which are counted one by one as they pass through a small opening which does not allow them all to emerge at once].
>
> Resh Lakish said, "As in the ascent of Beit Maron" [Rashi: a narrow pass where wayfarers had to proceed in single file, since the valley was deep on both sides].
>
> Rav Yehuda said in the name of Shmuel, "Like the troops of the House of David" [Rashi: who pass in review one by one as they go out to battle]. (Rosh HaShana 18a)

Resh Lakish arouses our fear of judgment by invoking the "ascent of Beit Maron" – or, according to a different textual variant, "Beit Ḥoron." This was a narrow, steep ascent with a frightening abyss stretching down on both sides: a truly dangerous path. Rav Yehuda goes further, comparing our judgment on Rosh HaShana to the troops of the House of David, who go out to war knowing that there is no battle without casualties.

What is common to all three interpretations is the idea that man stands alone before the Throne of Glory. Sometimes a person reassures himself that he is part of a community. When he looks at the community as a whole, he thinks that maybe he is not so bad: he is part of the group, not significantly worse than anyone else. But on Rosh HaShana each of us passes "like *benei maron*" – one by one – and a person must recognize that he will be judged as an individual, including all the dark corners where he himself has no wish to look, all those aspects of himself which he tries to conceal. As the prophet declares, "'Can anyone hide himself in secret places, that I shall not see him?' says the Lord" (Jer. 23:24).

Yet there is also a communal aspect to God's judgment. The Gemara continues:

> Rabba b. Bar Hanna said in the name of R. Yoḥanan, "They are all reviewed with a single glance." Rav Naḥman b. Yitzḥak said, "We also have learned the same idea: 'He who fashions their hearts alike, who considers all their deeds' (Ps. 33:15)." (Rosh HaShana 18a)

The communal judgment is one of mercy, in the sense of "The Holy One, blessed be He, wrapped Himself like a *sheliaḥ tzibbur*." If a person is capable of wrapping himself, submerging his individual personality, concealing his ego, and assuming responsibility for the community, then "a covenant has been made that the Thirteen Attributes are never turned away empty-handed."

Another feeling that gives rise to a sense of responsibility toward the community is based on the Gemara in Kiddushin:

> A person should always see himself as if his merits and demerits are evenly balanced. If he performs a single mitzva, happy is he – for he has tilted the balance of judgment in his favor and in

> favor of the salvation of the entire world. If he commits a single sin, woe is he – for he has tilted the balance of judgment against him and the entire world, as it is written, "...but he who sins once destroys much good" (Eccl. 9:18): because of a single sin, he loses many good things. (Kiddushin 40b)

A person needs to live with a sense of ultimate responsibility, that a single act on his part can tilt the fate of the entire world. It is with this awareness that the Thirteen Attributes should be said.

> "Lord, Lord" – I am He before one sins and I am He after one sins and repents. (Rosh HaShana 17b)

The commentators struggled to understand this statement. Why does one need mercy before he sins? The Rosh writes:

> And if one should say, "What need does a person have for the divine attribute of mercy before he sins?" the answer may be that even though it is already known and revealed before God that he is going to sin in the future, He nevertheless behaves towards him now with the divine attribute of mercy, "where he is at." (*Piskei HaRosh,* Rosh HaShana 1:5)

A person might say: Am I capable of being a *sheliaḥ tzibbur*? Am I able to bear responsibility for the entire world? After all, I am a sinner and transgressor! According to the Rosh, our answer is: God was there before you sinned, and your sin is known and revealed to Him. Nevertheless, God acts in accordance with His attribute of mercy, and makes certain that a Jew's sins will not create too much distance, such that repentance will no longer be possible. This is the meaning of the words in the Gemara, "I am He before one sins."

We are approaching the Day of Judgment, knocking on the doors of heaven; "needy and destitute we knock on Your door." In the first *Seliḥot* service we say, "At the departure of the day of rest, we have come before You for the first time. Lend Your ear from on high, You who are throned on praise, to heed the joy (*rina*) and the prayer." There is prayer in the sense of "joy," and there is prayer that is "the prayer of the pauper." Prayer of joy includes thanks for the past and requests for the future: "Keep this forever in the imagination of the thoughts of the heart of Your people, and direct their hearts to You" (II Chr. 29:18); "may the Lord our God be with us, as He was with our fathers; let Him not leave us, nor forsake us…" (I Kings 8:57). But there is also a different sort of prayer: "A prayer of the afflicted, when he faints, and pours out his heart before the Lord" (Ps. 102:1). The Zohar (*Balak* 195) describes King David as removing his crown and his royal robes, covering himself with sackcloth, sitting on the ground, and declaring, "Master of the universe, I am poor and lowly!" This is not praise; this is the prayer of the afflicted, the destitute.

There are times when our prayer is that of "the pauper when he faints"; "I am poor and lowly"; "what is man, that You are mindful of him, and the son of man, that You visit him?" (Ps. 8:5). This "prayer of the afflicted" arises from our sense of mortality, our awareness that man is like a fleeting breath. He is "like a broken shard and like a passing dream." However, there is another cause of "prayer of the afflicted," and that is frustration. Last Rosh HaShana one looked forward to the year ahead filled with optimism, but now that year has passed and he takes stock of what he has done and what he has achieved. Has he accomplished even half of what he hoped?

Moses was overcome with frustration after the episode of the golden calf. The *Tur* (*Oraḥ Ḥayim* 586) quotes from *Pirkei DeRabbi Eliezer* that the sounding of the shofar during the month of Elul is connected to the sounding of the shofar when Moses ascended Mt. Sinai for the last time, which was meant to assure that the Children of Israel would not stray again into idol worship. At the giving of the Torah, the angels were jealous of the people's declaration, "We shall do and we shall hear," and a heavenly voice called out, "Who has revealed this secret to My children – an expression that is used by the ministering angels?" Despite all this, the nation needed the shofar to remind them not to worship idols. This unquestionably gave rise to frustration and heartbreak. The People of Israel, who stood at the pinnacle of spiritual heights, had fallen to the lowest depths. But despite this, Moses ascends the mountain once more. He undoubtedly remembers the exaltation and joy of his ascent to receive the first set of tablets, and the profound disappointment after the sin of the golden calf. Nevertheless, he ascends once more. This is how the Jewish people feel during the month of Elul.

Wrapping oneself as a *sheliaḥ tzibbur* is required not only during prayer, but also during Torah study. *Ḥazal* describe R. Eliezer and R. Yehoshua engaging in study:

> They began with Torah and from Torah to the Prophets, and from the Prophets to the Writings, and the words were as joyful as at their giving at Sinai, and a fire raged around them, for the essence of their transmission at Sinai was also with fire, as it is written, "and the mountain burned with fire to the heart of heaven" (Deut. 4:11). (Ruth Rabba 6)

One who engages in Torah study while submerging his ego, who does not see himself in everything, will be able to experience the giving of the Torah from Sinai from amidst the fire. But we are not always able to see the connection between our own study and the fire of Sinai. In our daily prayers we say, "Enlighten our eyes with Your Torah and cause our heart to cleave to Your commandments," and before that we say, "Our Father, merciful Father who acts mercifully, have mercy upon us; instill in our hearts to understand…." There is no other prayer in which we invoke all the powers of mercy. Only the prayer "*Ahava Rabba*" ("Abundant love…"), the prayer of "Enlighten our eyes with Your Torah," requires such a great measure of mercy.

It is important to remember that prayer and Torah are bound up with one another. If, Heaven forbid, a person's prayer separates from his study, and on a day when he merits understanding in Torah, he fails to see the connection between that Torah insight and his prayer, then he is not truly enjoying the experience of "He who teaches Torah to His nation Israel." God gives the Torah and teaches it to Israel, and as a result, we are able to experience its sweetness. Severing the connection between prayer and study means that the person has failed to keep his ego submerged and he has removed the *tallit*, as it were, from over his head.

Our prayer must be "the prayer of a pauper when he faints"; "needy and destitute we knock on Your door." If, in our prayers, we feel truly destitute, if we "wrap" ourselves so that we feel the responsibility of being a *sheliaḥ tzibbur,* then our prayers will be accepted. There has never been a time when every individual, every household, and the entire nation of Israel more desperately needed a leader, and no one can evade the obligation of wrapping himself and living his life as a *sheliaḥ tzibbur*.

Let us live with this sense of praying as paupers, and knock on the heavenly gates; let us consider the Thirteen Attributes and fulfill the directive, "Just as He is compassionate, so you shall be compassionate; just as He is merciful...." Then, the covenant of the Thirteen Attributes will assure that we will not be turned away empty-handed. When we say the *Seliḥot* and the Thirteen Attributes, let us plead for divine mercy for ourselves and all of Israel. Let us engage in genuine soul-searching: Have we achieved the objectives that we set for ourselves? Have others truly seen us as *benei Torah* in every step that we took, at home, in the army, in the *beit midrash,* in the street?

If our prayer is accompanied with introspection, then we are assured that our prayers will not go unanswered, and God will grant our petitions and grant us forgiveness and mercy, and a year of life and peace for us and all of Israel.

A Treasure House of Humility

In the *Seliḥot*, we proclaim:

> It was You who descended in the cloud of Your glory upon Mt. Sinai and showed the ways of Your goodness to Moses Your servant. You revealed to him the ways of Your kindness and made known to him that You are a merciful and compassionate God, long-suffering and abundant in lovingkindness, greatly beneficent and directing the entire world with the attribute of mercy, as it is written, "And He said, 'I shall cause all My goodness to pass before you, and I shall proclaim the name of the Lord before you, and I shall be gracious to whom I shall be gracious, and show mercy to whom I shall show mercy.'" (Ex. 33:19)

God promises Moses that He will cause all His goodness to pass before him. This means that Moses will achieve a total understanding of God's providence over the world and His attributes of mercy and kindness. God showed Moses how He would guide the world until the end of time, under His everlasting mercy.

God also showed Moses the reward in the World to Come. The Midrash teaches:

> "And I shall be gracious to whom I shall be gracious" (Ex. 33:19) – At that time God showed him all the treasure houses of reward that await the righteous.
>
> He said to Him, "For whom is this treasure house designated?"
>
> He answered him, "For those who perform mitzvot."
>
> "For whom is this one designated?"
>
> "For those who feed orphans." And so on, for each and every treasure.
>
> Eventually he saw one great treasure house and asked, "For whom is this designated?"
>
> God told him, "Those who have earned their reward – I give them from that which is theirs; those who have not earned any reward – I give them for free," as it is written, "I shall be gracious to whom I shall be gracious." (Exodus Rabba 45:6)

The last treasure house that Moses sees is one that gives out free – a treasure house set aside for "those who have not earned any reward," and to whom God gives "for free." The first time I read this midrash, I imagined tens of thousands of people standing at the gates of this treasure house. Who would not want a free reward?

But on second thought, the reality may be just the opposite. Perhaps the line in front of the free treasure house is not so crowded. Very few Jews in *kippot* are there – after all, the treasure is meant for "those who have not earned any reward," and we do not imagine that we fall into that category. What does it have to do with us? Just take an occasional look at our literature and our newspapers: the tone is one of smug self-satisfaction. See how much we have, how spiritually and culturally rich we are! "Those who have not earned any reward" must surely come from some other sector of the population; we belong to a community who "have earned their reward." These views have taken hold in our community.

At one level, this view seems justified: we study Torah, we put on *tefillin* and observe Shabbat. Compared to other communities, we are entitled to claim that we have earned a reward. However, it is specifically here that we must exercise humility and undertake genuine self-introspection. Such humility is not only a virtue in itself, but a fundamental condition for any *Viduy,* any prayer with genuine intent. A person who wishes to elevate himself, or even just change himself slightly, must be humble. Some people bring about truly revolutionary change in their lives, like R. Elazar b. Dordaya (Avoda Zara 17a), who realized that "it depends only on me." But even smaller, easier, more modest changes require true humility.

What is humility? Ramḥal explains that even though we possess intelligence, we should not take pride in what is our "inborn nature":

> Wisdom, more than anything, is responsible for a person's coming to feel arrogance and pride. This is because wisdom is a quality that resides in the highest faculty of the person, his intelligence. But there is no person so wise that he cannot err and will not need to learn from his fellows and often from his students. How, then, can one take pride in his wisdom? In truth, anyone who is honest, even if he is extremely wise, will see that there is no place for pride and arrogance. For a man of intelligence, who knows more than others, is simply acting according to his nature, like a bird that flies, or an ox that pulls heavy burdens. So one is wise only because his nature makes him so. (*Mesillat Yesharim,* ch. 22)

Ramḥal's statement goes to the heart of what we said above. All of us are observant Jews because we were born into religious families and received a religious education. Do we deserve credit for this? Have we added anything of our own? Are we not simply following our "nature"? Someone who is born into a religious family is not right to think that he is assured a place in Paradise. If one is fortunate enough to have a religious background, then more is expected of him! As Ramḥal explains, this requires true humility.

The Torah tells us that Moses was "exceedingly humble, more than any other person on the face of the earth" (Num. 12:3). Apparently, Moses did not view himself as greater than his brethren. He understood that he had been privileged to grow up in Pharaoh's palace, and to witness God's revelation at the burning bush. Had someone else been through the same experience, Moses thought, he surely would have been even greater than me! Such humility is an essential condition for divine service.

> A psalm unto David: Lord, who shall reside in Your tent; who shall dwell in Your holy mountain? He who walks uprightly and acts justly, and speaks the truth in his heart. He who does not slander with his tongue, nor cause any evil to his fellow, nor take up a reproach against his neighbor. A vile person is despised by him, but he honors those who fear God; he swears to his own hurt and does not change. He does not lend out money with interest, nor take a bribe against the innocent; he who does these things will never be moved. (Ps. 15)

The Gemara (Makkot 24a) teaches that Rabban Gamliel would weep when he read this psalm. Why? Did he ever lend money with interest? Did he not "walk uprightly and act justly"? The Gemara explains that Rabban Gamliel was indeed endowed with fine attributes, but he did not develop these attributes to their fullest: he did not "walk uprightly" as Abraham did, he did not "act justly" as Abba Ḥilkiya did, he did not "speak the truth in his heart" as Rav Safra did, etc. Concerning this last, Rashi comments:

> This is what happened: Rav Safra had a certain item for sale. A person appeared while he was reciting *Shema,* and said, "Sell me that item for such-and-such sum." He did not answer, because he was reciting *Shema*. The buyer believed that he was unwilling to sell for that price, so he said, "Give it to me for such-and-such additional amount." After he finished reciting *Shema,* Rav Safra said to him, "Take it for the original price, for I intended to give it to you for that price."

This story illustrates how high the standards are. We tend to define such concepts as justice, truth, and integrity in terms of our social norms. But what is actually required of us is the tears of Rabban Gamliel, who wept when he feared that he was not considered to be "walking uprightly" and "acting justly."

The Gemara goes on to say that Rabban Gamliel's colleagues tried to console him, pointing out that the psalm concludes, "He who does these things," but is not limited to "he who does *all* these things" – meaning, it is enough to possess one of these virtues. However, even this – to fully realize even one virtue – is not something that most people achieve.

There is another aspect to humility, which relates specifically to prayer. When we address God in prayer, we need to approach with humility, asking that He do whatever is right in His eyes, whatever He knows to be good, rather than asking Him to help us as we believe is right. The Talmud Yerushalmi relates concerning Bar Kokhba:

> When he would go out to battle, he would say, "Master of the universe – do not help us, and do not hinder us!" (Y. Taanit 5:5)

Bar Kokhba coarsely tells God, "Stay out of things." He was completely sure of himself in the battle against the Romans. He was so convinced of his abilities that he believed that divine intervention could only make things worse, Heaven forbid.

A prayer such as that of Bar Kokhba has no value. If when we pray we are completely certain of ourselves, then we are not really praying but showing disrespect toward God.

Outside of prayer, it is good to have a personal approach to life, a philosophy which guides our actions. But when it comes to prayer, we must say, "Master of the universe – do what is right in Your eyes!" Do we really know what is truly good for the Jewish people? Sometimes we accomplish something that we set as a goal, but ultimately it turns out to be a great disappointment. On the other hand, sometimes our greatest fear becomes a reality, and it turns out to be the best thing that could have happened. The shorter road often turns out to be the longer one, and the longer road is the shorter. For this reason, we need to be humble in our prayers before God.

The destiny of the Jewish people and the destiny of the State of Israel are not like those of other nations. Zechariah declares:

> So says the Lord of Hosts, "Old men and old women will again dwell in the streets of Jerusalem, each with his staff in his hand for old age. The streets of the city will be filled with boys and girls playing in its streets." (Zech. 8:4–5)

What is so special about this vision? After all, the presence of boys and girls, old men and women, is a normal phenomenon everywhere in the world. However, the prophet continues:

> So says the Lord of Hosts, "If it is marvelous in the eyes of the remnant of this nation in those days, shall it also be marvelous in My own eyes?" says the Lord of Hosts. (v. 6)

This is truly amazing! What is altogether natural in Switzerland, France, or anywhere else in the world is not natural for us. Our entire history shows that the Land of Israel and the People of Israel follow a wondrous and unique course.

Therefore, we pray to God and tell Him that He knows what is best for our people. We, for our part, pray with humility, and with the hope that God will heed our prayers.

May it be God's will that we merit a good year, a year of life and peace, a year of spiritual awakening. May we be able to stand at the gates of the "treasure house of free gifts" and say to God, "We have not earned a reward." May we pray with humility. Perhaps then God will grant us a spiritual awakening and salvation for each individual and for the nation as a whole, and inscribe and seal us and all of Israel for a good year.

A Letter to the Soldiers on the Front Lines

BS"D, 18 Elul 5762 (2002)

To all our dear students in the Israel Defense Forces, wherever you may be, peace and blessing and God's pleasantness upon you!

> Look to Me and be saved, all the ends of the earth, for I am God, and there is none other. (Is. 45:22)

This call is directed to everyone in the world. Concerning Israel, we read, "For what nation is there so great, that has God so near to them, as the Lord our God is in all things that we call upon Him for?" (Deut. 4:7).

The Gemara (Rosh HaShana 18a), in its discussion of God's response to our prayers, draws a distinction between the congregation and the individual. Concerning the congregation, the Torah says, "in all things that we call upon Him for"; in other words, God responds at all times, in all situations. But when it comes to the individual, we are told, "Seek out the Lord when He is found; call upon Him when He is near" (Is. 55:6), meaning, not at all times and in all situations, but only when He is found, when He is near. The Gemara then adds, "These are the ten days between Rosh HaShana and Yom Kippur." It is during these days that God is near and attends even to the cry and call of the individual.

This period, which includes Rosh HaShana, Yom Kippur, and the days in between, has always been the occasion of communal gatherings in synagogues and *battei midrash*. Even many who keep to themselves throughout the year join in the services in the synagogue during the *Yamim Nora'im*.

Who, then, are the individuals who pray to God at this time in solitude? Apparently, *Ḥazal* anticipated situations in the future when Jews seeking closeness to God would be forced to pour out their hearts to their Father in heaven as individuals, with no possibility of joining a *minyan* – even a small one, let alone a vast congregation in a *beit midrash*.

My dear students, my friends! You, who are engaged at this time in defending our security in all kinds of different ways and circumstances, your merit is multiplied many times over. On one hand, God is present and close to you – as individuals. On the other hand, you have the merit of belonging to a community to which God is near "in all things that we call upon Him for," because you are acting as emissaries of the community in your security assignments. May the Holy One, blessed be He, watch over you, guard you, and protect you from all trouble and anguish.

My dear friends, you and I – on the battlefront and on the home front, in the field and in the yeshiva – know how happy we would be to see each other in the *beit midrash* during these High Holidays. But do not allow your spirits to fall! God will connect your prayers with ours in the *beit midrash*, and will heed our cry together with the prayers of all of Israel, and we will merit to be included in the grant of salvation and mercy, for us and for all of Israel.

With best wishes for a *ketiva vaḥatima tova*, in love and friendship,
Yours,
Yehuda Amital

Rosh HaShana

Sounds Without Words

> Happy is the people that know the *teru'a*; they shall walk, O Lord, in the light of Your countenance. (Ps. 89:17)

The Torah does not say explicitly that the shofar be sounded on Rosh HaShana. We are told only, "a day of sounding the shofar (*teru'a*) shall there be for you" (Num. 29:1), and "a remembrance of sounding the shofar, a holy gathering" (Lev. 23:24). "A day of sounding the shofar" means, simply, a day that is characterized by that sounding; the blowing of the shofar leaves its mark on the day as a whole. Nahmanides, in his commentary on the Torah, explains that the "memorial of sounding the shofar" means that the Children of Israel are remembered before God, as it is written, "and you shall sound the trumpets… that they may be for you a memorial before your God" (Num. 10:10). Bringing the memory of the Jewish people before God on Rosh HaShana is achieved through the shofar, and this is part of the mitzva.

The Baḥ (*Oraḥ Ḥayim* 625) asserts that the rationale of the mitzvot of sukka, *tefillin*, and tzitzit is an integral part of its fulfillment. Concerning tzitzit we read, "In order that you will remember…" (Num. 15:40); concerning *tefillin* we read, "And it shall be a sign for you upon your hand and as a remembrance between your eyes, in order that the Lord's Torah may be in your mouth" (Ex. 13:9); and concerning sukka we read, "In order that your generations may know that I caused the Children of

Israel to dwell in sukkot..." (Lev. 23:43). Understanding the reason for the mitzva is necessary for its proper observance.

The same principle applies to the mitzva of shofar. Both the shofar blower and his audience are required to think about bringing the memory of the Jewish people before God.

This insight may resolve a question of Nahmanides'. Rashi interprets the term, "a remembrance of sounding the shofar" (v. 24) – "Mentioning the verses of *Zikhronot* and *Shofarot*." Nahmanides asks: But the verses of *Zikhronot, Malkhuyot,* and *Shofarot* are not biblically ordained! It may be that, while there is no obligation from the Torah to mention these verses, saying them nevertheless fulfills the mitzva of remembering and the mitzva of "a day of sounding the shofar shall there be for you."

Why did the Torah dictate that we be remembered through the sounding of the shofar? Why use the language of sounds and symbols rather than words and speech (such as, for example, our retelling of the Exodus story)? The answer is that the shofar adds breadth and depth to the human voice. A person invests all his energy into the shofar, and the shofar emits a sound that is far more powerful than the human voice.

The sounds of the shofar express more than one can convey in words. At the giving of the Torah we read, "The sound of the shofar grew louder and louder; Moses speaks and God answers him with a voice" (Ex. 19:19). It is said that this sound refers to the unlimited spread of Torah over the course of time.

A person who turns to God faces a problem. In general, prayer is verbal. But human language was created as dialogue between people, between one limited creature and another. There is something tragic in the fact that a person is forced to use human speech when he approaches God. Human speech is limiting, constricting, and distorting; it cannot express what lies in the recesses of one's heart. The sounding of the shofar helps somewhat to solve this problem.

Rabbi Saadia Gaon listed ten reasons for sounding the shofar, and these appear in some editions of the Maḥzor. We can study these reasons, think about them, and put them in order – but do they really express what we feel in the depths of our heart? In the heart, things are not organized systematically; images, feelings, and thoughts explode and fill our consciousness. Sometimes we manage to bring order to our thoughts. But in our heart, everything is scrambled together: ancient memories of the creation of the world, of the Revelation at Sinai, the destruction of the Temple, the coronation of God, the fear of judgment, and the voices of the prophets. The heart is a jumble of thoughts and feelings, and we struggle to convey to God what we really feel in words and speech. God gave us the mitzva of shofar, and through it we transmit to God the emotions of our heart: "for You listen to the sound of the shofar and heed the *teru'a* and there is none like You."

According to the Gemara, we learn that the *teru'a* is a sobbing sound from the mother of Sisera (Rosh HaShana 33b). Rabbenu Natan, author of the *Arukh* (under the entry "*erev*") takes this comparison further, noting that the custom of sounding a hundred notes mimics the one hundred sobs sounded by the mother of Sisera.

The question is, what do we have to do with the mother of Sisera? How can it be that the laws of sounding the shofar are derived from a gentile who was the mother of a wicked enemy?

We see that a person can grow up in a completely pagan, idolatrous culture, but even there, nothing is more natural than a mother's concern for her child. Sarah, our matriarch, and the mother of Sisera are two women who could not be more different from one another. But despite coming from very different worlds, there is a common denominator between the one hundred sobs of Sisera's mother and the six screams that Sarah screamed on hearing of the binding of Isaac (Leviticus Rabba 20:2). What connects them is the deep-seated maternal concern for the welfare of her child – and this is also the force of the sounding of the shofar, which rises from the depths.

The source of the shofar is the ram that was caught by its horns in the thicket. It is remarkable that Abraham is silent throughout the binding of Isaac. Other than answering "*Hineni*" ("here I am") to God's initial summons; some technical instructions to the young men accompanying him; and his response to Isaac, "God will provide Himself a lamb for a burnt offering," he says absolutely nothing. At the climax of the story, the angel tells him, "Do not lay your hand upon the lad." What goes through Abraham's mind at that moment? What writer or poet could hope to describe it? Rabbi Yehuda HaLevi writes (*Kuzari* III:5) that a pious person should try to imagine great moments such as the *Akeda* (binding of Isaac) – but one cannot help but wonder, who has the imagination to picture that scene?

Abraham, seeking expression for what he feels, does not utter a sound.

> Abraham lifted his eyes and saw, and behold, behind him a ram caught in the thicket by its horns, and Abraham went and took the ram and offered it as a burnt offering in place of his son. (Gen. 22:13)

Abraham's gaze, focused on the horns caught in the thicket, conveys great tension. It is that same horn that we sound, thereby expressing what we cannot express in words: "for You listen to the sound of the shofar and heed the *teru'a* and there is none like You."

An Inner Voice

> On your day of joy, your appointed seasons, and your new moons, you shall blow the trumpets over your burnt-offerings, and over the sacrifices of your peace-offerings; and they shall be for you a memorial before your God: I am the Lord your God. (Num. 10:10)

> R. Abahu said, "Why do we blow a ram's horn? God said, 'Blow a ram's horn before Me so that I will remember for you the binding of Isaac.'" (Rosh HaShana 16a)

Both the Torah and *Ḥazal* emphasize the importance of invoking our memory before God.

This is difficult to understand: Does God, the Master of the world, need to be "reminded" about the nation of Israel? Does He not "remember the covenant," "remember all deeds ever done," and "recall all past creatures"? Do we not say that "nothing is forgotten before His Throne of Glory, and nothing hidden from His eyes"? Furthermore, we say the following in our prayers:

> The memory of every being comes before You, each person's acts and his purpose… and the memory of all actions comes before You, and You seek out all their deeds. (Musaf of Rosh HaShana)

It seems that the real meaning of invoking our memory before God is that *we* should know and remember who we are and what our purpose in life is. The foundation of *Akedat Yitzḥak* was Abraham's statement, "Here I am":

> The angel of the Lord called to him from the heavens, saying "Abraham, Abraham"; and he said, "Here I am." (Gen. 22:11)

Abraham responded when God called him by name.

As with the *Akeda,* so it was in the Garden of Eden. After the Original Sin, on the very first Rosh HaShana, God called to Adam:

> And God called out to Adam and said, "Where are you?" And he said, "I heard Your voice in the garden, and I was afraid, because I was naked; and I hid myself." (3:9–10)

In God's question, "Where are you?" we see the tragedy of the human condition. Man hides from his God, so God, as it were, has to search him out.

The question posed to Adam – "Where are you?" – is addressed to every person, wherever and whenever he may live. But sometimes it carries a special power; the Day of Judgment is one of those times. The essence of Rosh HaShana is the question, "Where are you?"

Sometimes a person may run and hide, but there is something that is more awful and more frightening: the possibility of forgetting. A person can forget his own name and his own self, even on the Day of Judgment:

> They asked R. Eliezer, "What is the judgment of the grave?"
>
> He responded, "When a person dies, the Angel of Death comes to his grave; strikes him with his hand; and says, 'Tell me your name!' He replies, 'The One who spoke and created the world knows that I do not know my name.' At that moment, his soul returns to his body, he rises and goes to his judgment." (Semaḥot, *Ḥibbut HaKever* 1:6, cited in *Reishit Ḥokhma, Shaar HaYira,* end of ch. 12)

Sometimes a person's self-image is based only on actions and experiences, not his inner thoughts and feelings. Somehow a person's name, which reflects the real "I" of the person, gets forgotten. There is a custom to read daily verses that mention one's name. The *Shelah* adds (*Kitzur Shelah* 101b) that this bears special protection against forgetting one's name on the day of final judgment. The meaning of this is that every person must find his unique place within the Torah, as we ask God, "Give us *our* portion in Your Torah." Until this happens, until one discovers his "special letter" in the Torah, he remains in a kind of exile.

This idea also relates to the shofar. The shofar expresses one's deepest feelings, the most inward, profound, and unique point in a person's heart. The Gemara states:

> If one placed a shofar within a shofar: if he heard the sound of the inner one, he has fulfilled his obligation; if he heard the outer one, he has not fulfilled his obligation. (Rosh HaShana 27b)

"If he heard the sound of the inner one" – God longs to hear our inner voice. This is the true sound that we must make heard on Rosh HaShana. This idea is implied by another rule that appears there:

> If one coated a shofar with gold on the inside – it is unfit. If the coating is outside, then if the sound is different from what it was – it is unfit; if not – it is fit.

An artificial sound is unfit for performing the mitzva. Only the inner voice, the sound which is not affected, is fit for the mitzva. We learn something similar in the laws pertaining to the Temple:

> Our Sages taught, "There was an oboe in the Temple that was smooth, thin, made of reed, and dated from the time of Moses. The king ordered that it be coated with gold, but then its sound was no longer sweet. They removed its coating, and its sound was as sweet as ever." (Arakhin 10b)

On the Day of Judgment, God wants to hear our real voices, not something "coated," artificial, whose natural sound has been altered. May we find our special letter in the Torah and discover our true voice. Only then, when we make that voice heard in its pure form, will we fulfill our obligation.

The Simplicity of Prayer

> R. Levi said, "The mitzva on Rosh HaShana and Yom Kippur is performed with a bent shofar, and the rest of the year with a straight shofar."
>
> But we learn, "The shofar of Rosh HaShana is a straight antelope's horn"!...
>
> What is the basis of this dispute?
>
> One view holds that on Rosh HaShana the more one bends himself, the better.... The other view holds that on Rosh HaShana the more one straightens himself, the better. (Rosh HaShana 26b)

Rashi comments:

> "The more one bends himself" during his prayer, his face directed towards the ground, the better, because "My eyes and heart shall be there perpetually" (1 Kings 9:3); therefore, since the shofar on Rosh HaShana is sounded in prayer and for the purpose of arousing the memory of the binding of Isaac, a bent shofar is required.
>
> "The more one straightens himself, the better" – because "let us lift up our heart with our hands" (Lam. 3:41); therefore, the mitzva is performed on Rosh HaShana with a straight shofar, because it is for prayer.

From here we learn a fundamental principle of prayer. Sometimes, it is actually the straightness, the cry from the heart, that adds a deeper dimension to prayer. "Their heart cried to the Lord" (Lam. 2:18). The heart is the seat of a person's inner truth, and that is where prayer comes from.

Rabbi Simḥa Bunim of Peshischa explained the phrase, "who chooses songs (*shirei*) of praise" as "who chooses the remnants (*sheyarei*) of praise," to teach us that God desires those remnants that remain deep in the heart of a person, which is where the truth resides within him.

The Talmud Yerushalmi states, "Why do we blow the shofar using horns? To say, 'Think of us as if we are bellowing like animals before You'" (Taaniyot 2:1). The animal-like bellowing represents the natural cry that bursts straight from the heart.

We find the same idea in the redemption from Egypt. The verse, "and their cry rose up to God from the bondage" (Ex. 2:23), is explained by the *Or HaḤayim*:

> "From the bondage" – Not that they cried out to God to save them, but that they cried out from anguish, like a person who cries out in pain. The verse informs us that this cry of theirs reached God, as it says, "their cry…from the bondage," i.e., the cry was from the pain of their toil.

A similar idea is inherent in the different sounds we blow with the shofar. The rule that "the length of a *teru'a* is the equivalent of three sobs" is learned in the Gemara from the cries of Sisera's mother:

> It is written, "a day of sounding the shofar shall there be for you," and the Targum translates, "a day of wailing," and it is written of the mother of Sisera, "Sisera's mother looks forth through the window and wails [through the lattice]" (Judges 5:28). (Rosh HaShana 33b)

The Tosafot (s.v. *shiur teru'a*) add in the name of the *Arukh* that the requirement to hear one hundred sounds of the shofar is also learned from this same text, corresponding to the "one hundred sobs that Sisera's mother cried." This is actually very surprising. Could the Sages not find a better source for the sound of our cry before God on the Day of Judgment than the voice of a gentile mother?

Perhaps the Sages are telling us that, even within the culture of Sisera, of lies and falsehood, it is possible to find – after searching and sifting – the "voice from the heart," a sincere voice, natural and true, that arises from the heart, and there is no better example than the voice of a mother worried about her child. The Midrash relates that Isaac returns after the *Akeda* and reports to his mother that he was nearly slaughtered: "At that moment, she emitted six cries, which parallel the six shofar blasts. They said, 'Before she was able to accept it, she died'" (Leviticus Rabba 20:2). It is not surprising that the Sages compared the voices of two mothers: Sisera's mother, and our matriarch Sarah. Despite the innumerable differences between them, they shared that special maternal voice that emerges from the depth of the heart.

The blowing of the shofar expresses that most basic element of prayer: *pashtut*, simplicity. Rashi, as quoted above, connects the dispute regarding the shape of the shofar to one's posture during prayer. This too is the subject of a dispute between the Sages:

> R. Ḥiyya and R. Shimon b. Rabbi sat together; one said, "One who prays must cast his eyes downwards, for it is said, 'And My eyes and heart shall be there perpetually' (I Kings 9:3)."
>
> The other said, "His eyes should be directed above, for it is said, "Let us lift up our heart with our hands [to God in the heavens]' (Lam. 3:41)."
>
> They were joined by R. Yishmael b. R. Yossi. He asked them, "What are you discussing?"
>
> "Prayer," they replied.
>
> He said to them, "My father ruled, 'One who prays must cast his eyes downward and his heart upward so as to fulfill both verses.'" (Yevamot 105b)

Looking downwards, toward one's heart, represents simplicity, the sincerity and integrity of the heart that is required in prayer. "The heart knows the bitterness of his soul" (Prov. 14:10). Prayer is the seat of pain and the voice of emotion.

But Rashi explains differently: "'His eyes downwards' – towards the Land of Israel, because the Divine Spirit dwells there, as it is written, 'And My eyes and heart shall be there' (1 Kings 9:3)." Rashi explains that prayer requires directing one's eyes toward the Land of Israel and the Temple, as God said to Solomon: "I have sanctified this building that you built to bear My name forever, and My eyes and heart shall be there perpetually," "there" referring to the Temple of Solomon.

The Temple represents the public, the community as a whole. The Temple was where the entire nation would gather, no matter the person's social standing or family background. The individual was simply absorbed into the crowd and became a part of the group.

This belonging to the community provides an additional benefit: maintaining the proper balance between what is important and what is secondary. When a person is part of the community, he compares his own troubles to those of his fellows, which allows him to put his needs and concerns into perspective.

The *Ḥiddushei HaRim* (on Rosh HaShana) quotes the Ari as saying:

> On the first day of Rosh HaShana, one needs to request and pray only for spiritual matters; on the second day of Rosh HaShana, one makes requests for worldly needs. (Levine edition, p. 253)

This difference between the two days of Rosh HaShana requires further clarification. Is it really appropriate on the second day to submit requests for personal needs? Rabbi Tzadok HaKohen of Lublin writes in the name of *Tikkunei HaZohar*:

> However, all shout in their prayers on Yom Kippur like dogs, "Give us, give us (*hav hav*) food, etc."... This is like the Gemara that says (Bava Batra 8a), "Sustain me like a dog." (*Peri Tzaddik,* Rosh HaShana, p. 172)

When a person prays on the High Holidays for his own, personal needs, he is like a "barking dog."

But it is totally different when a person's prayers are directed towards the community as a whole. In that case, even if the request is couched as a personal one, for his own benefit, its ultimate purpose is to help the community at large. I pray for myself so that I will be able to help others. Similarly, as long as the ultimate goal is spiritual, there is nothing wrong with requesting food, so that one can advance spiritually. "Where there's no 'flour,' there's no Torah" (Mishna Avot 3:17).

Contrary to what you sometimes hear, it is impossible to separate spiritual problems from physical ones. When a person is sick, and his life is in danger, his Torah study and spiritual world are also affected. The same is true in the communal realm. When an existential threat hovers over the nation of Israel, this also affects our relationship to God.

For this reason, everyone needs to see himself as part of the community and pray for the spiritual and physical needs of himself and his community. During the High Holidays we need to pray for the welfare of the Jewish people and the manifestation of God's sovereignty on Earth.

Remember Us with Favor

> The Holy One, blessed be He, said, "Pour water before Me on Sukkot so that you will be blessed with rain throughout the year. And say before Me on Rosh HaShana the *Malkhuyot, Zikhronot,* and *Shofarot*: *Malkhuyot* – so that you proclaim Me King over you, and *Zikhronot* – so that your remembrance will rise favorably before Me, and how will you say them? With the shofar." (Rosh HaShana 16a)

In our Rosh HaShana prayers we ask, "Remember us with a favorable remembrance before You." This request is difficult to understand: God forgets nothing. What, then, is this "favorable remembrance" that we ask for? It certainly does not mean that God should remember only the positive things we have done, while disregarding the acts for which we are deserving of punishment. "The memory of every being comes before You – each person's acts and his purpose and the path that he chooses and follows, the thoughts and the plans of all mankind." God remembers everything!

The truth is, even though we say, "Nothing is forgotten before the throne of Your glory, and nothing is hidden from Your eyes," it seems that sometimes God does, in fact, "forget." This is not the act of forgetting of ordinary mortals, but rather a form of forgiveness. The Gemara

(Berakhot 32b) teaches that God promises Israel that He will forget the golden calf: "These too shall be forgotten" (Is. 49:15).

But if this divine "forgetting" really means forgiveness, then it would be more appropriate to say, "Forgive us," rather than, "Remember us with a favorable remembrance before You." It seems, then, that when we ask, "Remember us with a favorable remembrance," we are speaking of God's way of running the world. To understand this better, let us consider the words of Maimonides:

> Every person has both merits and sins.... This reckoning is not based only on the number of merits and sins, but also on their magnitude.... This reckoning is carried out according to the wisdom of the Knowing God. He knows how to weigh the merits against the sins." (*Mishneh Torah,* Laws of Repentance 3:1–2)

An individual's personality is not expressed only through his good deeds or his sins; there is more to a person than that. Other elements affect his conduct, and they should also be considered when he is judged. God remembers man and his actions; He remembers and judges "each person's acts and his purpose and the path that he chooses and follows." But He also knows everything that influences a person's behavior: his childhood, his environment, his family, the challenges he faces, etc. This would appear to be the "remembrance" that we refer to when we say, "Remember us with a favorable remembrance before You."

In Gemara Rosh HaShana we find:

> Why does the High Priest not wear his golden garments when he enters the Holy of Holies to perform the service? Because a prosecutor cannot become an advocate for the defense.... But he wears the golden garments outside [the Holy of Holies]! We are speaking of the service in the inner Sanctuary. But is the shofar not also sounded outside [the Holy of Holies]? Since its purpose is to awaken remembrance, it is as if it were used within. (Rosh HaShana 26a)

What do *Ḥazal* mean here when they call the sounding of the shofar "service within the inner Sanctuary," where "a prosecutor cannot become an advocate for the defense"?

The Temple sacrifices are brought for the purpose of atonement, but there is more. The Temple service is meant to purify the souls of Israel from their taint, to unwrap them from their "husks." The sacrifices purify a person's negative tendencies and traits, the sources of sin, in addition to atoning for certain sins.

Similarly, the offering of the incense on Yom Kippur adds sanctity and purity, and increases a person's integrity and pleasantness. The service of the High Priest is meant to affect the deepest recesses of a person's psyche, the source of his wrongful actions and misdeeds. The High Priest enters the Holy of Holies not only to atone for the defilement of the Temple, but also to mend a person's spirit, the "inner sanctuary" of his personality. Sin does not befit the human soul. *Ḥazal* teach:

> "But the soul is not filled" (Eccl. 6:7) – To what may this be compared? To a regular person who marries the daughter of a king. If he brings her everything in the world, it will not impress her at all. Why? Because she is the daughter of a king. So it is with the soul: even if you were to offer it all the delicacies of the world, it will not make an impression. Why? Because the soul comes from the upper worlds. (Ecclesiastes Rabba 6:6)

The service performed in the Holy of Holies on Yom Kippur serves to intensify the inner sanctity – that inner essence of a person which registers in his consciousness only on rare occasions. We say each morning, "The soul that You have placed within me is pure." That inner purity is so delicate that even the hint of a foreign thought can disturb it. We can compare this to playing music: when an entire orchestra plays together, an outside noise will not be noticed. But when a single instrument emits a thin, delicate sound, even the slightest noise will disrupt.

The remembrance in the sound of the shofar echoes that service in the Inner Sanctuary. The sound of the shofar is a simple sound that cannot be expressed in words. It evokes man's inner essence that cannot be expressed outwardly. This is the meaning of the statement that "since its purpose is to awaken remembrance, it is as if it were used within." Thus, God remembers a person's actions, but we ask, "Remember us with a favorable remembrance before You" – remember the innermost parts of our personality, the pure soul that You have placed within us.

This request for remembrance strengthens our connection with God, so that our inner soul radiates sanctity and purity to all the layers of our psyche, whether consciously or unconsciously. "Remember us with a favorable remembrance before You" means that the remembrance of God increases our own attachment to Him and sanctifies us. By the same token, we too are required to remember God: "Happy is the man who does not forget You, the child of man who takes courage in You."

The primary aim of our prayer on Rosh HaShana is to increase sanctity and purity. Therefore, the Men of the Great Assembly and the *Tanna'im* formulated prayers for Rosh HaShana which express God's sovereignty, not for our needs. This is not limited in time: the prayer service that they instituted is suitable for all generations and for all times, just as the Torah is eternal (see *Nefesh HaḤayim* II:13).

According to Maimonides, the eternity of the Torah is bound up with the eternity of Israel. Against the background of Isaiah's prophecy, "So shall your seed and your name remain" (Is. 66:22), Maimonides writes:

> Sometimes the seed remains, while the name has perished. For example, there are many nations that are descendants of the Persians or Greeks, but they are not known by a particular name; rather, they were absorbed into another nation. To my mind, this is another proof of the eternity of the Torah, by virtue of which we received our special name. (*Guide of the Perplexed* II:29)

In other words, the eternity of Israel is derived from the eternity of the Torah.

The eternity of the Torah means that the Torah remains valid forever; more than that, it is relevant in each and every generation. Although generations change, the "plain understandings renew daily" (see Rashbam, Gen. 37:2; *Ḥiddushei HaRim, Haazinu*); every generation finds a new interpretation, new insights, relevant to that time and place.

In the same way, the prayer set by the Men of the Great Assembly is relevant to every generation. For instance, in the *Aleinu* prayer we say, "We therefore put our hope in You, O Lord our God, that we may soon see the splendor of Your might, that You remove the false gods from the earth." The "false gods" of our time are not the same as the false gods of two thousand years ago: in our times Nazism, Communism, even democracy and unbridled freedom. Yet, despite the differences, the prayer remains the same. We say, "Grant honor, O Lord, to Your people, praise to those who fear You, and hope for those who seek You." Fifty years ago, during the Holocaust, we could not have imagined how meaningful and relevant those words would be for us, and to what degree they would be fulfilled in our times.

Today[1] too, with the future somewhat uncertain, we need to fulfill in the most literal way the mitzva, "You shall be wholehearted with the Lord your God" (Deut. 18:13). As Nahmanides comments: "that we should dedicate our hearts to Him alone, and believe that He alone does everything, and that He knows what will happen in the future." We say in our prayers, "Happy is the man who does not forget You," and on the other hand we ask of God, "Remember us with a favorable remembrance before You." May it be His will that we merit, through the sound of the shofar, to be remembered for good before God – amen.

1. This *siḥa* was delivered on Rosh HaShana of 5755 (1994). During the preceding year, dozens of Israelis had died in a number of major terror attacks; a bomb exploded at the AMIA Jewish Community Center in Buenos Aires, killing 85; and the Israeli soldier Nachshon Wachsman was kidnapped and murdered by Hamas.

King over All the Earth

> The Holy One, blessed be He, said: "…Say before Me on Rosh HaShana the *Malkhuyot*, *Zikhronot*, and *Shofarot*: *Malkhuyot* – so that you proclaim Me King over you, and *Zikhronot* – so that your remembrance will rise favorably before Me, and how will you say them? With the shofar. (Rosh HaShana 16a)

In our Rosh HaShana prayers we say the verses of *Malkhuyot*, and the blessing concludes, "King over all the earth…." What is the significance of this theme of kingship on Rosh HaShana? After all, we refer to God as "King of the universe" in every blessing that we say all year round; the halakha even states (Berakhot 40b) that a blessing that does not mention God's kingship is not considered a blessing at all.

The answer lies in understanding the meaning of the "kingship" that we mention in our blessings. The word blessing (*berakha*) means an addition – just like someone who bends a vine (*havrakha*) down to the ground and covers it with dirt with the intention of having it strike roots and grow a new plant. The person who makes a blessing adds to the strength of God's heavenly retinue. Of course, God does not require this "added strength"; He is Master of all worlds. But in this world He determined that a blessing has an effect in the heavens, and thereby draws down divine abundance onto the entire world. This principle was fixed at the time of Creation: God's goodness is brought down through the blessing of mankind (see Responsa of the Rashba v:50–51). Thus, every blessing expresses God's dominion and His kingship over the world.

The verses of *Malkhuyot* on Rosh HaShana emphasize a different aspect of God's dominion over the world: His control over free will. The course of human history appears, on its face, independent of God's rule, Heaven forbid. The casual observer sees God's hand only where He intervenes dramatically in nature, in earthquakes, floods, and so on. But on Rosh HaShana we declare that God's dominion extends over those events that are dependent on man's free will. We declare that God's involvement that began at the creation of the world continues to operate throughout history, even where man is given free will.

"Like water courses is the king's heart in the hand of the Lord, He directs it wherever He wishes" (Prov. 21:1). Even the heart of the king falls under the absolute dominion of God. The Midrash teaches:

> The account of Creation alludes to Israel's subjugation to the nations, and to the redeemer, the King Mashiaḥ. "In the beginning God created … and the earth was without form and void, and darkness was upon the face of the deep, and a wind from God moved over the surface of the waters" (Gen. 1:1–2). "Without form" refers to the kingdom of Babylonia; "and void" refers to the kingdom of Media; "and darkness" refers to the kingdom of Greece, which issued harsh decrees; "upon the face of the deep" refers to the wicked kingdom of Edom; "and a wind from God moved" refers to the King Mashiaḥ. (*Pesikta Rabbati* 33)

Although the rule over every state lies in the hands of human beings, it is God who dictates the course of history, including the rise and fall of empires. God rules the world, and He brings about the removal of false gods from the world and the perfection of the entire world under God's sovereignty.

However, it is important to remember that despite God's global sovereignty, every person is judged on those areas subject to his free will. It is not only with regard to nations and countries that we say, "which are inscribed for the sword, and which for peace," but also concerning individuals: "And all creations are regarded on this day, remembered for life, or for death... the thoughts and the plans of all mankind, and the impulses behind each person's acts."

We believe that God's hand guides the central events of history, especially those events that have an impact on the Jewish people. In general, we do not see God's hand as events unfold, and only at the end of the process God's plan becomes apparent. Only in the Time to Come, when God is King over the entire world, will His sovereignty be fully revealed, as we ask in our prayer: "Reveal the glory of Your kingdom to us swiftly."

Ḥazal emphasize the divine guidance of the world that is concealed from us:

> R. Shmuel b. Naḥman said, "'For I know the thoughts' (Jer. 29:11) – The sons of Jacob were busy with the sale of Joseph, Joseph was busy with his sackcloth and fasting, Reuben was busy with his sackcloth and fasting, Jacob was busy with his sackcloth and fasting, and Judah was busy taking a wife – while the Holy One, blessed be He, was busy creating the light of the King Mashiaḥ." (Genesis Rabba 85:1)

Sometimes, we glimpse God's guiding hand, in the sense of "Behold, He stands behind our wall, observing through the windows, peering through the lattices" (Song 2:9). This year we merited two such glimpses: the Gulf War[1] and the disintegration of the Soviet Union.[2] In his *Epistle to Yemen*, Maimonides writes:

> From the giving of the Torah until today, every idolatrous king who has risen to power, be he violent or ignoble, has made it his first aim and his final purpose to destroy our Torah, and to

1. The First Gulf War, in which coalition forces led by the US attacked Iraq, took place in 1991. During the war, Israel was attacked with missiles which – despite the fears and forecasts – turned out not to be armed with chemical warheads, but nevertheless caused significant damage.
2. The year 1991 saw the fall of the Communist regime in the USSR, which subsequently broke up into a number of independent states.

> negate our religion, by force, through violence, by the sword… and to overturn our Torah by means of arguments which they raise against it, and by questions that they invent, their intention being to contradict the Torah and to erase every trace of it through their writings, just as the despots intend with the sword. But neither the one nor the other shall succeed. For the Holy One, blessed be He, assured us through the prophet Isaiah that any tyrant seeking to destroy our Torah and to terminate our faith through weapons of war – God will break his weapons and they will not succeed. This is only a metaphorical way of saying that he will never accomplish his purpose. Likewise, any disputant who attempts to demonstrate the falsity of our tradition will have his arguments proven to be untenable and ineffective, as it is written, "No weapon that is formed against you shall prosper; and every tongue that shall rise against you in judgment, you shall condemn. This is the heritage of the servants of the Lord and the recompense of their righteousness appointed by Me, says the Lord" (Is. 54:17).

Maimonides speaks of two different wars waged against the Jewish people: a physical assault, "through violence, by the sword," and a spiritual battle, "to undermine our Torah and to annihilate our faith." Our wicked enemy in Iraq, who was armed with very dangerous weapons, sought to unite the sons of Ishmael in a war against Israel, and even stated explicitly that he was fighting against Judaism. To everyone's astonishment, in a most illogical and unexpected way, he incurred the wrath of the United States, the superpower, and its coalition of thirty-four countries. This, then, is how God directs the world against those who seek to destroy us with the sword.

The collapse of the Soviet Union was a surprise of a different kind – on the spiritual front. Never in history was there a nation whose opposition to faith in the Creator of the world equaled that of Communist ideology in scope and in intensity. Christianity, for example, sought to displace the Jewish people and to appropriate the promises about Jerusalem. But the heretical ideology of the Communists sought to displace the Torah itself, and claimed that they could create a worldwide brotherhood of justice and morality devoid of Torah and the prophets, without invoking the name of God. The proponents of this ideology used tools appropriated from Judaism, while ignoring the Torah and the Giver of the Torah. They thought that it was possible to achieve and follow the path of Abraham, the man of kindness, through economic and social equality, but without fear of God.

This year, we saw God "peering through the lattices" on both fronts. This demands that we, and all the world, engage in soul-searching and return to the truth.

> For behold, He who forms the mountains and creates the wind, and declares to man his discourse, who makes the morning darkness and treads upon the high places of the earth – the Lord, the God of hosts, is His name. (Amos 4:13)

The Gemara comments:

> What is the meaning of the phrase, "and declares to man his discourse"? Rav said, "Even a superfluous exchange between husband and wife is told to a person at the time of death." (Ḥagiga 5b)

On one hand, God "treads upon the high places of the earth"; He conducts the entire world. On the other hand, He also "declares to man his discourse." God takes an interest in the tiniest details, as we learn in the Midrash:

> "For the Lord your God is the God of gods and Lord of lords" (Deut. 10:17) – R. Yoḥanan said, "Wherever you find God's might, you also find His humility. ... It is written, 'For the Lord your God is the God of gods and Lord of lords,' and then, 'He executes justice for the orphan and widow.'" (Megilla 31a)

God takes an interest in the tiny details pertaining to each one of us, and desires to hear the prayers of every individual, as the verse states, "My plea is sweet to Him, I will rejoice in the Lord" (Ps. 104:34). On Rosh HaShana, Nehemiah tells the people:

> Go your way, eat sumptuously and drink sweet beverages, and send portions to those for whom nothing is prepared, for this day is holy to our Lord; for the joy of the Lord is your strength. (Neh. 8:10).

The great joy of Rosh HaShana flows from our knowledge that God is interested in each and every one of us, insofar as He guides and watches over the entire world. This knowledge gives us joy, and it is our strength on Rosh HaShana.

Simplicity in a Complex World

The nature of Rosh HaShana is somewhat mysterious. In one place the Torah calls it "a day of sounding the shofar" (Num. 29:1), while elsewhere it is called "a remembrance of sounding the shofar" (Lev. 23:24).

What is this "remembrance"? Is it the remembrance of Israel before the Holy One, as suggested by the verse, "And you shall be remembered before the Lord your God" (Num. 10:9), or is it the remembrance of the Holy One before Israel, in the sense of "Seek out God and live" (Amos 5:6)? Or is it both?

A hint to the answer to this puzzle is provided by Ezekiel: "In the twenty-fifth year of our exile on Rosh HaShana, on the tenth of the month…" (Ezek. 40:1). The prophet connects Rosh HaShana to Yom Kippur. *Ḥazal* make a similar connection regarding Yom Kippur in the Jubilee year, which is called Rosh HaShana (Arakhin 12a). This indicates that Rosh HaShana has an element of atonement, like Yom Kippur. In addition to arousing our memories, the shofar arouses God's remembrance to bring us atonement from on high, as on Yom Kippur.

In the prayer *UNetaneh Tokef,* we say, "And a great shofar will sound and a still, small voice is heard." Just as we blow the shofar on Earth, a great shofar is sounded in heaven.

This idea of two kinds of shofars is echoed in the verses of *Shofarot* that we say in Musaf of Rosh HaShana. *Ḥazal* decided that we say verses from the Torah, then verses from *Ketuvim,* and lastly verses from the Prophets. What is interesting is that the verses from the Torah and the Prophets speak of the sounding of the shofar on the part of God, not on the part of man:

> You appeared to them with the sound of the shofar, as is written in Your Torah, "On the third day when it was morning, there was thunder and lightning, and a heavy cloud on the mountain, and the sound of the shofar was very loud."… And by the servants Your prophets it is written…: "On that day a great shofar will be sounded…." And it is said, "and the Lord God will sound the shofar."

Only the verses from the *Ketuvim* mention the sounding of the shofar by man:

> And in Your holy writings it is written, "God is elevated with the *teru'a,* the Lord with the sound of the shofar." And it is said, "With trumpets and the sound of the shofar, shout for joy before the Lord, the King." And it is said, "Sound the shofar on the new moon, on our feast day when the moon is hidden."

This explains the unconventional order: why the verses from *Ketuvim* are said prior to those from the Prophets. When we blow the shofar, we are required to sound "a simple blast before it, and a simple blast after it." The *teru'a* is sandwiched between two *tekiot.* So too in the order of our prayers: the sounds of God's shofar come before and after, with the sounding of the shofar by man in between.

God's shofar sounds a simple, perfect *teki'a.* But a person, weighed down with broken heart, with disappointments and frustrations, is incapable of blowing a "simple" sound. A person's birth is simple. But the moment after he is born, he cries out from the bottom of his heart. Likewise when a person faces death, his true voice is revealed. But during his lifetime, nothing is simple, and his tortured soul cannot emit a simple sound. The human shofar issues a sob, while God's shofar makes a simple sound.

Ḥazal interpret the verse, "You captured my heart, my sister, my bride; you captured my heart with one of your eyes" (Song 4:9), as hinting at the giving of the Torah: even at that great moment, God noticed that only "one of the eyes" of Israel was really concentrating on the declaration, "We shall do and we shall hear." The other eye was glancing away, toward a voice far from Mt. Sinai – the sin of the golden calf. Only in the Time to Come will the Jewish people gaze heavenward with both eyes.

The world itself is not simple. The Maharal (*Gur Aryeh*, Gen. 48:7, s.v. *aval da lekha*) explains that the prophet's words, "Stop your voice from crying" (Jer. 31:15), were addressed to Rachel, because she recognized that the world is imperfect. According to *Ḥazal*, Rachel volunteered to provide secret signals to her sister, and opened her house to her rival. In a perfect, simple world, Jacob would have only had one wife. But in the real world, he needed more. As a result, Rachel had a strong argument against God: Why do You criticize Your nation Israel for bringing idolatry into their houses? You Yourself created a world full of contradictions, which leads people to worship idols.

Ultimately, there is no harmony in this world; it is full of conflict and division. So the person who blows the shofar makes a broken, sobbing sound, not a simple shofar blast.

This may also explain the controversy among the Sages concerning the "oven of Akhnai," which was constructed from many pieces:

> They cut it into segments and placed sand between them; R. Eliezer declared it pure, while the Sages declared it impure. (Bava Metzia 59a)

According to R. Eliezer, an oven that is not one single piece is not considered a vessel, and therefore cannot contract impurity. Even though sand was placed between the pieces in order to join them together, this does not transform them into a single vessel, a whole entity. R. Eliezer lived in an ideal world, where wholeness is defined in absolute terms. A hodgepodge of stone and sand does not meet this definition.

The Sages, on the other hand, accept an imperfect combination of pieces stuck together with sand as a complete vessel, because they recognize that we live in a complex world that is itself imperfect and incomplete.

This is the essence of the human condition. Sometimes a person actually brings his troubles on himself. "God made man straight, but they have sought many calculations" (Ecc. 7:29). "The foolishness of man perverts his path, and his heart complains against the Lord" (Prov. 19:3).

According to the Midrash (Tosefta Sota 6:5), at the time of the splitting of the Red Sea, infants stopped suckling at their mother's breast to say, "This is my God and I will extol Him!" When things are simple and natural, they need to be expressed even by newborn children!

The purpose of Rosh HaShana is to return to simplicity, to the cry of the infant, before one is caught up in the complications and complexities of life. The Midrash says:

> "With all your heart" – that your heart should not be divided before God. (*Yalkut Shimoni* 1:887)

In prayer, one should aspire to having one heart, simple and straightforward, not "two hearts," full of conflict and complexity.

As students of Torah, we engage in the study of Torah, the "elixir of life." This is the key to achieving simplicity. One of our tasks is to share this with each other.

The Midrash teaches that blowing the shofar changes the attribute of justice to that of mercy. The divine attribute of justice is represented by the name "God" (*Elokim*). "God is elevated with the *teru'a,* the Lord with the sound of the shofar." If we are not worthy, then God will be "elevated with the *teru'a*" – the imperfect, broken sob associated with the attribute of justice. But if we are worthy, we will merit the elevation of "the Lord with the sound of the shofar," the rise of the attribute of mercy through the simple sound of the shofar.

“The Shofar Is Considered Service in the Holy of Holies”

> Speak to the Children of Israel, saying, “In the seventh month, on the first of the month, you shall have a Sabbath, a remembrance of sounding the shofar, a holy gathering.” (Lev. 23:24)

The shofar is closely associated with memory. Usually, the reason for a mitzva does not have halakhic ramifications, but this is not the case with the sounding of the shofar. According to the Mishna, the horn of any animal may be used for a shofar – except for a cow. The Gemara explains that the horn of a cow recalls the sin of the golden calf, and “a prosecutor cannot become an advocate for the defense.” The following discussion then ensues:

> Rav Ḥisda said, “Why does the High Priest not wear his golden garments when he enters the Holy of Holies to perform the service? Because a prosecutor cannot become an advocate for the defense.”…But he wears the golden garments outside [the Holy of Holies]! We are speaking of the service in the inner Sanctuary. But is the shofar not also sounded outside [the Holy of Holies]?

> Since its purpose is to awaken remembrance, it is as if it were used within. (Rosh HaShana 26a)

The negative association with the golden garments applies only inside the Holy of Holies. Generally, gold arouses associations of splendor and majesty. However, the Holy of Holies is an area of special sensitivity. In this place, the golden garments indeed recall the sin of the golden calf, and therefore the High Priest enters wearing linen garments. What the Gemara teaches here is that the shofar too is a kind of "service inside the Holy of Holies"; therefore it may not be made from the horn of a cow.

Ḥazal here are saying something momentous: through the sounding of the shofar on Rosh HaShana, all of Israel are in the Temple, in the Holy of Holies; they are like the High Priest who enters to perform his service wearing linen garments. Rabbi Yehuda HaLevi writes (*Kuzari* III:5) that a pious person should try to imagine great moments such as the *Akeda*, the Revelation at Sinai, or "the Sanctuary built by Moses and its order of service, and the dwelling of the divine glory in the Temple." Regarding the Temple, this means an attempt to feel the exaltation and awe engendered by God's Presence.

The time to do so is during the sounding of the shofar. During these moments we are, as it were, like the High Priest, in his linen robes, in the Holy of Holies. What a special moment! On Yom Kippur, the Jewish people stand in front of the Temple, while the High Priest enters, alone, the Holy of Holies: "And there shall be no one in the Tent of Meeting when he comes to make atonement in the holy place, until he comes out" (Lev. 16:17). On Rosh HaShana, however, anyone who listens to the shofar is standing, as it were, inside the Holy of Holies.

Why does our remembrance before God bring us into that holiest of places? Because when our remembrance comes before Him, it is not a distant recollection, as when a person says, "From afar the Lord appeared to me" (Jer. 31:2), or "Remember the Lord afar off" (51:50). It is a memory in which God accompanies the person, as it were, and brings him into His inner chamber. Then a person really feels God's Presence. This is a remembrance in the sense of "This is my God and I shall extol Him" (Ex. 15:2).

This moment of sounding the shofar should arouse fear and trembling: "Enter into the rock and hide in the dust, for fear of the Lord and for the glory of His majesty" (Is. 2:10). This is a moment of repentance. However, it is a repentance that is not accompanied by confession, for on Rosh HaShana it is forbidden to confess. This is a repentance of both shaking oneself out of complacency and achieving elevation, "like a chicken shaking itself from ashes" (see Genesis Rabba 75).

The High Priest needs to prepare for seven days in anticipation of his entry into the Holy of Holies (Mishna Yoma 1:1). Before sounding the shofar too, there is a need for preparation, as *Ḥazal* taught:

> R. Pinḥas said in the name of R. Yehuda b. Levi, in the name of R. Alexandri, "Why does Israel not sound the shofar during the morning service, but rather only during the Musaf service? So that when they stand in judgment they are full of mitzvot, and will emerge vindicated." (*Pesikta Rabbati* 40)

Perhaps this is how we can explain the custom of two sets of shofar blowing, the "seated blasts" (*teki'ot dimeyushav*) that precede the "standing blasts" (*tekiot dime'umad*). The Gemara teaches that we do this "in order to confound Satan." Rashi explains:

> "In order to confound" – so that he will not indict. When he hears Israel showing affection for the mitzvot, his words will be blocked. (Rashi, Rosh HaShana 16a)

Faithful adherence to the mitzvot is what prepares us for the sounding of the shofar.

Instead of a seven-day period of preparation, our Rabbis prescribed the recital of Psalm 47 seven times prior to the sounding of the shofar (cited in *Siddur Beit Yaakov* of Rabbi Yaakov Emden). This psalm expresses the acceptance of God's sovereignty by all the nations, and this is the best possible preparation for the shofar. The moment when the Jewish people commune with God is significant for the entire world, and therefore we conclude with the words:

Sing out to God, sing! Sing out to our King, sing! For God is the King of all the earth; sing out a psalm. God reigns over the nations; God sits upon the throne of His holiness. The nobles of the peoples are gathered together, the people of the God of Abraham, for the defenses of the earth belong to God; He is greatly exalted. (vv. 7–10)

“I Will Be Exalted Among the Nations”

> God is elevated with the *teru'a*, the Lord with the sound of the shofar. (Ps. 47:6)

The first reason that Rabbi Saadia Gaon gives for the sounding of the shofar is to declare that God is King. He explains that just as trumpets are sounded before a human king on the day of his coronation, so we sound the shofar on Rosh HaShana, “the day of the commencement of Your works,” the day when God began to rule over His world.

The sounding of the shofar serves many purposes. The Gemara teaches:

> Say before Me on Rosh HaShana the *Malkhuyot*, *Zikhronot*, and *Shofarot*: *Malkhuyot* – so that you proclaim Me King over you, and *Zikhronot* – so that your remembrance will rise favorably before Me, and how will you say them? With the shofar.” (Rosh HaShana 16a)

Ritba comments:

> "With the shofar" refers to both *Malkhuyot* and *Zikhronot*. What is the proper way to make Me king and to bring your remembrance before Me? With the shofar.

In other words, we need the shofar to perform both the *Malkhuyot* and the *Zikhronot*. It serves both to coronate God and to raise Israel's remembrance before God with favor.

One can suggest that the shofar that raises our remembrance before God is the shofar that we sound during the *Amida* prayer. We say the *Malkhuyot*, *Zikhronot*, and *Shofarot*; we plead, "Remember us with a good remembrance before You"; and we sound the shofar. In contrast to these shofar blasts that follow the order of the *Amida*, the "seated blasts" have as their purpose the coronation of God. Sounding the shofar is a heralding of royalty: "Sound the shofar and say, 'Long live Solomon the King'" (I Kings 1:34). When we coronate God with the shofar blasts that precede Musaf, we make no supplication for ourselves. But when we raise our remembrance before God with the shofar blasts during the *Amida*, we ask, "Remember us for life," "Inscribe us in the Book of Life."

The Gemara teaches:

> Why do we sound long blasts and broken blasts while seated, and long blasts and broken blasts while standing? In order to confound Satan. (Rosh HaShana 16a)

It may be the special nature of the "seated blasts" (those sounded before Musaf), with no personal supplications, that confuses Satan. When we pray for ourselves and say, "Remember us for life," Satan, i.e., the evil inclination (see Bava Batra 16a), can criticize the way we live our lives. The evil inclination is part of a person, and therefore takes part in the plea that God "remember us for life." The evil inclination plants desires within us other than the desire to fulfill the mitzvot. However, the "seated blasts" are a pure expression of God's sovereignty, with no personal requests, so they offer no place for the evil inclination. Then Satan is confounded and cannot criticize.

The custom is to say Psalm 47 seven times before sounding the shofar. This psalm mentions the sounding of the shofar – "God is elevated with the *teru'a*" – but its real focus is God's sovereignty in the world. This is indeed the most appropriate preparation for the "seated blasts" – the sounding of the shofar that is a coronation of God.

At the beginning of the same psalm we find: "Clap your hands, all you peoples; shout to God with the voice of joy. For the Lord, most High, is awesome; a great King over all the earth" (vv. 2–3). What is the source of this joy that is expressed by all the peoples over God's kingship? Do all the nations appreciate the profound significance of God's kingship? Do they already fulfill the vision, "All the inhabitants of the earth shall acknowledge and know that to You every knee should bow and every tongue should swear?" Has the time arrived when "the Lord will be King over all the world; on that day the Lord will be one and His name – one" (Zech. 14:9)? To this the Midrash replies:

> "To the chief Musician, a psalm for the sons of Koraḥ: Clap your hands, all you peoples" – This is what is meant by the verse, "When the righteous are on the increase, the people rejoice, but when the wicked man rules, the people mourn" (Prov. 29:2). When wicked people rule the world, everyone mourns, and everyone suffers, and no one walks upright.... When one man rules over another unfavorably, it is difficult for the Holy One, blessed be He, and hence we find it written, "There is a time when one man rules over another to his own disadvantage" (Eccl. 8:9). (Midrash Ps., Ps. 47)

The revelation of God's sovereignty in the world brings an end to human rule over men, the end of despotism. All the nations will seek to clap hands and to rejoice in God, so as to remove the reign of evil and tyranny.

The psalm goes on to describe:

> He subdues peoples under us, and nations under our feet. He chooses our inheritance for us, the pride of Jacob whom He loves, Selah! (vv. 5)

This is most surprising: Does the Jewish nation harbor imperialistic aspirations of ruling over the other nations? Is this itself not an example of "one man rules over another to his disadvantage?" Rather, the aim here is establishing God's sovereignty in the world. If no one rules over another, there will be no order in the world. Indeed, *Ḥazal* tell us (Mishna Avot 3:2) to "pray for the welfare of the monarchy, for were it not for the fear of it, man would swallow his neighbor alive." However, the rule that we aspire to is not one of tyranny, not political, economic, or military dominion, but the rule of morality. The prophet Isaiah foretells:

> And it shall be at the end of days that the mountain of the Lord's house shall be established on the top of the mountains, and shall be exalted above the hills, and all the nations shall flow to it. And many people shall go and say, "Come, and let us go up to the mountain of the Lord, to the house of the God of Jacob, and He will teach us of His ways, and we will walk in His paths, for out of Zion shall go forth Torah, and the word of the Lord from Jerusalem." And He shall judge among the nations, and shall decide among many people, and they shall beat their swords into plowshares, and their spears into pruning hooks; nations shall not lift up sword against nation, neither shall they learn war any more. (Is. 2:2–4)

> And there shall come forth a rod out of the stem of Yishai, and a branch shall grow out of his roots; and the spirit of the Lord shall rest upon him, the spirit of wisdom and understanding, the spirit of counsel and might, the spirit of knowledge and of the fear of the Lord; and his delight shall be in the fear of the Lord, and he shall not judge after the sight of his eyes, neither decide after the hearing of his ears. (11:1–3)

It is in this sense that the psalmist speaks of God "subduing peoples under us": spiritual, moral leadership of the entire world.

Rosh HaShana is the Day of Judgment for all of humanity, the day when all people pass before God like sheep. The Day of Judgment is essential to establishing God's sovereignty. God rules over all of His creations, and nothing in the world can deviate from the essence and nature that God has implanted in it: "He assigned them a law and a time, that they not alter their designated task." However, there is one exception, and that is man, who enjoys autonomy through the endowment of free will. It seems that where one has autonomy, the King of kings has no sovereignty. For this very reason there is a need for a Day of Judgment, where the sovereignty of the Creator is felt by those endowed with autonomy. God reviews the deeds of each and every individual; each must give an accounting for his conduct. Thus, judgment is an expression of God's sovereignty over man.

A person might approach his judgment with anxiety, consumed with fear and concern for his personal welfare. On the other hand, we can approach judgment with the joy of accepting God's sovereignty over us. Our personal fears and concerns sometimes cause us to forget a fundamental aspect of the Day of Judgment, concerning which the *Tur* writes:

> R. Ḥanina and R. Yehoshua say, "What nation is like this one, which knows the nature of its God" – meaning, His customs and laws. For throughout the world a person who faces judgment dresses in black and wraps himself in black and grows his beard long and does not cut his nails, for he does not know how his verdict will turn out. But this is not the case with Israel: they wear white, and wrap themselves in white, and trim their beards and cut their nails, and eat and drink and are joyous on Rosh HaShana, because they know that the Holy One, blessed be He, will perform a miracle for them. (*Tur, Oraḥ Ḥayim* 581)

Surely we have no guarantee that God will perform a miracle for us. However, if we put our personal problems second to our acceptance of God's sovereignty, then certainly God will perform a miracle for us in judgment. The traditional interpretation of the verse, "God is elevated with the *teru'a,* the Lord with the sound of the shofar" (Ps. 47:6) is that the shofar blast effects a shift from the divine attribute of justice to that of mercy. When is this true? When the sounding of the shofar carries with it all that is expressed in Psalm 47. A sounding of the shofar that expresses the universal joy of the manifestation of God's sovereignty in the world, and the end of man's dominion over others to their disadvantage, is the shofar blast that transforms divine justice into divine mercy, when God promises to "perform a miracle" for us.

Some years ago we witnessed the shattering of the idol that had brazenly put itself in place of the Sovereign of the world. I refer to the Communist regime established by Josef Stalin, the tyrannical and cruel despot who claimed to be able to repair the world and make people happy without divine involvement. While Christians tried to take the place of the Jewish people, the Communist regime tried to take the place of God. That abhorrent regime murdered millions of people, all in the name of repairing the world. Those who served that despotic god accepted this as necessary.

But this is not the way God rules:

> Righteousness shall go before Him. (Ps. 85:14)

> Come, behold the works of the Lord, who has made desolations in the earth. He makes wars to cease to the end of the earth; He breaks the bow, and cuts the spear in sunder; He burns the chariots in the fire. Be still, and know that I am God; I will be exalted among the nations, I will be exalted in the earth. (46:9–11)

If the sovereignty of Heaven means the end of men ruling over others, let us also examine ourselves to ensure that we are not tainted with the same domineering impulse in our relations with those around us. Let us make God king not only over the whole world, but also over ourselves.

Let us approach the sounding of the shofar as a mitzva and a prayer. As a mitzva – we remember the exaltation of "who sanctified us with His commandments"; and as a prayer – with humble submission, using a bent shofar because "the more a person bends himself, the better."

"A broken and contrite heart, O God, You will not despise" (51:19).

Two Types of Coronation

> The Holy One, blessed be He, said: "... And say before Me on Rosh HaShana the *Malkhuyot, Zikhronot,* and *Shofarot*: *Malkhuyot* – so that you proclaim Me King over you." (Rosh HaShana 16a)

This coronation on Rosh HaShana has two senses which are really one. There is a coronation of God in the realm of consciousness and faith, and a coronation that encompasses all of a person's daily activities, both physical and spiritual.

The coronation in the first sense is mentioned in the *Amida* of Rosh HaShana:

> All who were made will know that You made them, and all who were formed will know that You formed them. And all that have breath in their mouth will say, "The Lord, God of Israel, is King, and His kingship has dominion over all."

The exclusion of any territory, however small, from the realm of God's dominion is not only a reduction of His sovereignty, but in fact heresy, Heaven forbid. God's sovereignty encompasses every place, every time, and every event in the world. To coronate God in this sense requires a broad perspective; penetrating insight; and – most importantly – profound, burning faith.

Therefore, Rosh HaShana is first and foremost a day of faith, when the faith of each and every individual is examined. Faith stands at the center of all of the festivals, whether it is faith in the Exodus from Egypt or faith in the Revelation at Sinai. However, Rosh HaShana is different, because it is not about faith in a one-time event that reflects God's intervention in history and His ability to change the laws of nature, but faith in God's sovereignty. This means believing that His sovereignty is all-inclusive; it is boundless and infinite.

On this day we refresh our faith in God. Even though "no thought can grasp Him," "no place is devoid of Him." "Verily You are a God who hides Himself" (Is. 45:15), and the entire world – the heavens, the earth, and all that they contain – is nothing but a garment within which God conceals Himself. The heavens declare the glory of God, and He set the law and the times for the heavenly host, that they not deviate from their paths. It is God who created the heavenly host for the benefit of man – the greater and smaller stars, nearer and more distant, and all are happy to perform the will of their Creator. The sun, the moon, and the storm wind carry out His word; the mountains and every hill, the creeping things and the birds; concerning all of them the verse testifies, "You hide Your face – they are troubled.... You send forth Your breath – they are created" (Ps. 104:29–30).

God's sovereignty also includes the "kings of the earth and all peoples; princes and all judges of the earth" (148:11). Among these too God's name alone is exalted. It must be emphasized that even the "kings of the earth," who seem to exercise the free will with which man is endowed – the heart of kings and princes is in God's hands. The world is not left to the whims of a cruel despot or of twisted people of weak character with delusions of acting against God, whose sovereignty extends everywhere. "He who sits in the heavens laughs; the Lord holds them in derision" (2:4); if there is peace between God and Israel, He intervenes immediately to deliver them.

The other sense of coronating God on Rosh HaShana is our accepting the yoke of His sovereignty upon ourselves. Even within that sphere of autonomy that is given to man, in which he decides what is good and what is evil, he accepts the yoke of Heaven upon his every limb and sinew.

These two senses of accepting God's sovereignty are connected to each other. On one hand, without accepting the yoke of Heaven, one cannot achieve complete faith and recognition that God's sovereignty is over all, without exception. On the other hand, knowledge of God and His unity is fundamentally bound up with correcting our behavior.

> Be still [literally, let go] and know that I am God; I will be exalted among the nations, I will be exalted in the earth." (Ps. 46:11)

The Midrash comments:

> The Holy One, blessed be He, said to Israel, "Let go of your evil deeds, 'and know that I am God.'" (Song of Songs Rabba 5:2)

Knowing God requires the repair of our character traits and actions, and repairing our traits and actions leads to the revelation of God's sovereignty in the world: "I will be exalted among the nations; I will be exalted in the earth." "The Lord, God of Israel, is King, and His kingship has dominion over all" – when the Holy One, blessed be He, is the God of Israel, then "His kingship has dominion over all."

Our God and God of our forefathers – "reveal the glory of Your kingdom!" The "splendor of Your great might" is still concealed; it still seems to us that wickedness and the rule of tyranny control the world. "He stands and shakes the earth; He beholds, and releases the nations" (Hab. 3:5) – God released the nations and entrusted the role of revealing His sovereignty to the Jewish people. When we fully accept the yoke of His sovereignty, in fulfillment of the verse, "Therefore you are My witnesses, says the Lord, and I am God" (Is. 43:12), then the glory of His sovereignty will be revealed over the entire world. Israel is destined to be the heart of humanity, as Rabbi Yehuda HaLevi teaches: "Israel among the nations is like the heart amongst the other organs" (*Kuzari* II:36). When we fulfill our destiny, then God's sovereignty will encompass all of life, personal, public, and political.

It is because we were chosen to serve as the heart of the nations that we suffer more as a result of our sins. At the same time, however, we know that "we are put to death for Your sake all the day," and we accept this with love. Rabbi Yehuda HaLevi expresses this lofty and wondrous idea:

> Do not consider it strange that it says, "Indeed, he has borne our sickness" (Is. 53:4), that we are in distress while the world is at rest. The troubles that befall us are meant to prove our faith, to cleanse us completely, and to remove all taint from us. Once cleansed and purified, the Divine Influence will infuse the world. (11:44)

If we are worthy, we will fulfill the vision, "Behold, My servant shall prosper, he shall be exalted and extolled and be very high" (Is. 52:13), and "they will crown You, Lord our God, the angels, the multitudes of heaven, together with Your nation Israel, gathering here below." What is demanded of us is not just to observe the 613 commandments, but to imitate God, as Rabbi Moshe Cordovero writes:

> Therefore it is proper that one imitate the actions of the divine "Crown," which are the supreme Thirteen Attributes of mercy. (*Tomer Devora*, ch. 1)

On this day, when God's sovereignty over all is revealed, on this anniversary of the creation of the world, we are commanded to contemplate our actions and to know our obligations.

In *Kiddush Levana* (sanctification of the new moon) we quote the Gemara in Sanhedrin: "If Israel were allowed to greet the countenance of their Father in heaven only once a month – it would be enough for them." If this is so concerning "greeting the countenance of their Father in heaven," how much more fulfilling is this great day on which we are to see God's sovereignty over all of creation.

The nations of the world flee from God's dominion: "The Lord reigns – let the peoples tremble" (Ps. 99:1). At first glance, this fear is surprising, since just two chapters previously we find, "The Lord reigns – let the earth rejoice; let the multitude of isles be glad" (97:1). In fact, the nations see divine sovereignty as confining, so they flee. Out of fear of

God, they submit themselves to all sorts of subjugation, they are full of fears, their hearts are closed. We, on the other hand, pray to God, "Place the fear of You," and because we pray for the fear of God, we do not fear man: "The Lord is my light and my salvation, whom shall I fear? The Lord is my life's strength, whom shall I dread?" (27:1).

On Yom Kippur we say:

> Even though Your dread is upon the faithful angels, / the mighty heavenly hosts, created of ice, / mixed with fire – and Your awe is upon them.
>
> Yet You desire praise from those formed from earth, / denizens of the valleys below, whose actions are meager / and good deeds few in number – and this is Your praise!

The Holy One, blessed be He, the fear of whom is upon all of creation, wants praise from the Jewish people, from those "whose actions are meager." God is near to all those who call upon Him, and we – of "meager actions" – must coronate Him over ourselves and over the entire world.

Rosh HaShana on Shabbat

A Dialogue of Love

> Judah b. Naḥman taught in the name of Resh Lakish, "'God is elevated with the *teru'a*' (Ps. 47:6) – When the Holy One, blessed be He, ascends to sit on the Throne of Justice, He ascends in justice, as it is written, 'God is elevated with the *teru'a*.' And when Israel take up shofars and sound the blasts, the Holy One, blessed be He, rises from the Throne of Justice and sits upon the Throne of Mercy, as it is written, 'the Lord [is elevated] with the sound of the shofar'; and He is filled with mercy for them and is compassionate towards them, and transforms the attribute of justice into the attribute of mercy for them." (Leviticus Rabba 29:3)

Concerning no other mitzva do *Ḥazal* reveal to us, in their divinely inspired wisdom, the effect produced in the heavens by our observance. Only for the sounding of the shofar do *Ḥazal* reveal that, as a result of this mitzva, the Holy One, blessed be He, moves from His Throne of Justice to His Throne of Mercy. The judgment on Rosh HaShana is both a result and a manifestation of God's sovereignty. However, once we sound the shofar and coronate God, He no longer has any need, as it were, to sit upon the Throne of Justice, and therefore He rises from it and sits upon the Throne of Mercy.

The Sages ruled that on Shabbat we are not to sound the shofar. How, then, can judgment be transformed into mercy?

As if the problem were not urgent enough, we learn in the Gemara:

> R. Yitzḥak said, "If the *teki'a* is not sounded at the beginning of the year, a *teru'a* will be sounded by its end." Why is this so? Because Satan was not confounded. (Rosh HaShana 16b)

Ritba comments:

> "A *teru'a* will be sounded by its end" – meaning, as a result of the troubles that will befall them, causing them to fast and sound a *teru'a* on the shofar.

In other words, if Satan is not confounded at the beginning of the year by the blast of the shofar, the community's punishment is to sound the shofar later in the year as they fast over the calamities that will befall them. So what happens in a year when Rosh HaShana falls on Shabbat? How will Satan be confounded? The Tosafot comment:

> "Not sounded at the beginning of the year" – The *Halakhot Gedolot* explains, not referring to Rosh HaShana that falls on the Sabbath, but as a result of circumstance.

Thus, where the shofar was not sounded because of circumstances beyond their control, the shofar will end up being sounded later in the year. But when the shofar is not sounded because of the ruling of the Sages, there is no reason to fear the consequences. Usually, as we know, one who is coerced to sin is not punished, as the Sages derive from the verse, "But to the girl you shall do nothing" (Deut. 22:26). Why, then, is there punishment during a year when the shofar was not sounded at the start owing to some circumstance? To this the *Meshekh Ḥokhma* offers the following explanation:

> The sounding of the shofar is not a positive commandment like any other, where one is punished for failing to perform it, since "God forgives one who is coerced." Rather, it is like a medicine and

> atonement on Yom Kippur.... If someone who is ill is prevented from taking his medication, will he be healed?! Likewise, if there is no remembrance of the shofar, which brings the remembrance of Israel before their Father in heaven, Israel is like a sick person who has no balm or medicine, and the indictment of Satan remains in place. (*Meshekh Ḥokhma*, Lev. 23:24)

The sounding of the shofar is a mechanism which causes the indictment of Satan to be thrown out. We do not understand how this works, but if we fail to sound the shofar – even if we were prevented by outside forces – Satan will indict us. But then, we ask ourselves, how can the *Halakhot Gedolot* write that there is no indictment when the failure to sound the shofar is because of Shabbat? In such a case, surely, Satan has not been confounded?

What we have here is a sort of dialogue between Israel and the Master of the world. When Rosh HaShana falls on Shabbat, God says, as it were, to Israel, "I have given you an antidote, a solution, to confound Satan by means of the shofar. I recommend that you use this remedy even though it may diminish the honor of Heaven, Heaven forbid, if someone carries a shofar four cubits within the public domain, out of enthusiasm to perform this mitzva." But Israel, for their part, respond with the ruling of *Ḥazal*: "Confounding Satan is of secondary importance for us; more important to us is that the honor of Heaven should not be diminished, and that there be no desecration of Shabbat!"

When Rosh HaShana falls on Shabbat, there is indeed concern lest a "simple" Jew carry his shofar four cubits in the public domain. There are deep-seated feelings at the root of Jewish consciousness, and they come to the fore specifically among such Jews. These feelings hold that standing in judgment is inconceivable without sounding the shofar. And we ask ourselves, given that sounding the shofar is not a form of labor, why suspend the mitzva for fear that the shofar might be carried in the public domain? The answer is that while God commanded that we sound the shofar, the Jewish people chose to protect the honor of Heaven, out of concern that someone may violate the prohibition against carrying the shofar.

The dialogue between Israel and God also finds expression in the prayer said on Yom Kippur: "We give You our word, and You give us Yours." This dialogue reflects the great love between us and God. The Gemara expresses this idea as follows:

> Rav Naḥman b. Yitzḥak said to Rav Ḥiyya b. Avin, "What is written in the *tefillin* of the Master of the world?" He answered, "And who is like Your people Israel, a unique nation in the world" (1 Chr. 17:21). Does the Holy One, blessed be He, then sing the praises of Israel? Indeed – as it is written, "You have given your word to the Lord this day.... And the Lord has given His word to you this day" (Deut. 26:17–18). (Berakhot 6a)

We have written in our *tefillin,* "The Lord our God, the Lord is one," while God sings the praises of Israel.

This idea of "we give You our word, and You give us Yours" also plays a role in the interpretation of historical events. Sometimes we interpret events in a way that is the opposite of God's, in the sense of "I am my Beloved's, and my Beloved is mine." We find this in the Torah in relation to the war against Midian. God tells Moses, "Execute the vengeance of the Children of Israel on the Midianites" (Num. 31:2). When Moses transmits this to the people, he says, "Let them go against Midian and avenge the Lord on Midian" (v. 3). In God's eyes, the vengeance belongs to the Children of Israel; in the eyes of Israel, it is God's.

This shows the greatness of Israel and God's love for them. Likewise we find Moses declaring, "Happy are you, O Israel; who is like you, O people saved by the Lord, the Shield of your help, and the One that is the sword of your excellency!" (Deut. 33:29), while God attributes the victory to Israel:

> The Holy One, blessed be He, wages war for Israel, yet the victory is attributed to them. Thus the Torah says, "in all the signs and the wonders...and all of the mighty hand...which Moses performed" (Deut. 34:11–12). It does not say, "which God performed," but "which Moses performed." The Holy One, blessed

be He, sent him to act, and the victory is attributed to Moses. (*Midrash Shoḥer Tov*, Ps. 36)

As we said, there is a dialogue between Israel and God concerning the sounding of the shofar: on one hand, there is the need to confound Satan; on the other hand, the Jewish people are concerned for the honor of Heaven. It seems that this very dialogue of love, whether to sound the shofar on Shabbat or not to, confounds Satan as thoroughly as the shofar blowing would. Israel's dedication to observing Shabbat – even at the price of not having any remedy for judgment and, Heaven forbid, not causing God to move from the Throne of Justice to the Throne of Mercy – is itself an example of the self-sacrifice of the people, which has its roots in the *Akeda*. This itself silences Satan.

If a person identifies with *Ḥazal*'s ruling not to sound the shofar on Shabbat out of concern for the honor of Heaven, and foregoes his personal needs, then he need not be troubled that "the *teki'a* is not sounded at the beginning of the year." As a reward, God will rise from the Throne of Justice and move to the Throne of Mercy, and transform the attribute of justice into the attribute of mercy.

The Sound of a Silent Shofar

> Fortunate is the nation that knows the *teru'a*; they walk, O Lord, in the light of Your countenance. (Ps. 89:16)

Rashi explains the verse as follows:

> Because they know how to please their Creator on Rosh HaShana by blowing the shofar and saying *Malkhuyot, Zikhronot,* and *Shofarot.*

Rashi's source is the following midrash:

> R. Yoshia said, "It is written, 'Fortunate is the nation that knows the *teru'a*' – Don't the gentile nations know how to sound the *teru'a*? Don't they have many horns and trumpets? Rather, fortunate is the nation that knows how to entice their Creator by means of the *teru'a*. When? In the seventh month [i.e., Tishrei]." (*Yalkut Shimoni* 1:645)

If so, then what happens on Rosh HaShana which falls on Shabbat, when we do not blow the shofar? How do we please the Almighty then?

The Gemara (Rosh HaShana 29b) writes that, as far as Torah law is concerned, we are permitted blow the shofar on Rosh HaShana when it falls on Shabbat. The Sages, however, ruled that the shofar not be blown on Shabbat, lest one carry his shofar in the public domain. The Gemara adds that this same concern prompted *Ḥazal* to prohibit taking a lulav when Sukkot falls on Shabbat and to suspend Megilla reading when Purim occurs on Shabbat.

However, there is a difference in this regard between the shofar and lulav. The Mishna states that in the Temple the shofar was blown on Shabbat. After the destruction of the Second Temple, Rabban Yoḥanan b. Zakkai established that the shofar be blown on Rosh HaShana in every locale where a *beit din* sat. Yet no such provision exists with regard to the mitzva of lulav. The Tosafot ask, why did Rabban Yoḥanan rule this way regarding shofar but not lulav? The Tosafot answer:

> Because the shofar serves to bring the memory of Israel before their Father in heaven, they did not want to cancel it entirely. (Tosafot, Sukkot 43a, s.v. *inhu*)

Our original question, then, becomes even more pointed: What about today? Why did Rabban Yoḥanan b. Zakkai not worry about those of us who do not live near a *beit din*? How are we to bring our memory before our Father in heaven when Rosh HaShana falls on Shabbat?

One could perhaps answer very simply that we observe two days of Rosh HaShana, and on the second day we blow the shofar. However, when all is said and done, we observe the second day of Rosh HaShana only as a result of a *sefeika deyoma* – the uncertainty surrounding the correct day of Rosh HaShana. Can our mortal need to bring our memory before our Father in heaven depend on a technical rule for resolving a doubt?

It seems that R. Yehuda HaNasi, who redacted the Mishna, gave us the answer in the order he chose for the *mishnayot* in the third chapter of Tractate Rosh HaShana, which set down rules of shofar blowing. Sandwiched between a mishna dealing with a passerby who overhears the sounds of the shofar and a list of individuals disqualified from blowing, we find a seemingly unrelated mishna:

> "Whenever Moses held up his hand, Israel prevailed [against Amalek]" (Ex. 17:11) – Do Moses' hands make or break the battle?

> Rather, this teaches you that so long as Israel were looking upwards and subjugating their hearts to their Father in heaven, they were victorious; if not, they would fall. Similarly, we find, "Make a seraph figure and mount it on a standard; anyone who is bitten should look at it and shall recover" (Num. 21:8). Does a brass snake kill or cure? Rather, when Israel looked upwards and subjugated their hearts to their Father in heaven, they were cured. If not, they would wither. (Rosh HaShana 29a)

Why did R. Yehuda insert this mishna in the middle of the chapter, between laws concerning the intention required for blowing the shofar? There would seem to be more appropriate places for this mishna, such as the beginning of the second chapter of Berakhot, which discusses the intention required for reciting *Shema*. Why then was this mishna inserted in Tractate Rosh HaShana? Sensing this question, Maimonides writes in his commentary to our mishna, "All this is clear in light of what is required here for the subject that we are dealing with, and in accordance with the book's purpose."

What does this mean? How is the story of Moses' lifting his hands relevant to the laws of blowing the shofar? Furthermore, what does Maimonides think is "the book's purpose?"

The answer seems to be that R. Yehuda HaNasi saw Jews in his day who believed that the shofar has some mystical power, some supernatural quality beyond our comprehension that arouses divine compassion. They thought that the actual sound of the shofar magically brought the memory of Israel before their Father in heaven. R. Yehuda HaNasi contradicted this view: the shofar is no different from Moses' hands and the brass serpent, which did not magically save or heal the Jews. Only when Israel look upwards and subjugate their hearts to their Father in heaven do the gates of heaven open and welcome their prayers. When we do this during the blowing of the shofar, we cause our memory to rise before God. Appropriately, then, the very next mishna teaches, "Whoever is not obligated in a mitzva may not fulfill the obligation on behalf of the public." In other words, total subjugation requires a sense of obligation and acceptance of the yoke of mitzvot upon oneself. Only an individual who feels obligated to his Creator can fulfill the obligation on behalf of others. The Mishna thus teaches us a critical lesson: with regard to shofar, intention to fulfill the mitzva is not a technical requirement; it demands nothing less than absolute acceptance of the yoke of Heaven.

But then fate intervened and the Temple was destroyed. Depression and despair overtook the Jewish people. After the destruction, Rabban Yoḥanan b. Zakkai saw before him a broken, shattered nation. He realized that the people were not ready to accept the message about subjugating one's heart to Heaven. They needed the concrete expression of the shofar blast to restore their hope in repentance and redemption. Therefore, although some authorities were prepared to prohibit shofar blowing on Shabbat, Rabban Yoḥanan overruled them and insisted on sounding the shofar (Rosh HaShana 29b).

In truth, then, it is not the sound of the shofar that confounds Satan, but rather the accompanying subjugation of the heart (see Ran, Rosh HaShana 3a). Indeed, this is the message of the Midrash: "'Fortunate is the nation that knows the *teru'a*' – that 'knows how to please their Creator on Rosh HaShana.'" If we refrain from blowing the shofar in deference to the ruling of our Sages, then we are surely able to achieve the same feeling of subjugation to God that is associated with the fulfillment of the mitzva of shofar. This subjugation of our hearts is what opens the gates of mercy and brings our favorable memory before the Almighty (see also *Meshekh Ḥokhma,* Lev. 23:24).

Rosh HaShana that falls on Shabbat is called "*yom zikhron teru'a*" – the day of remembrance of the *teru'a.* This means that we bring our memory before God not by blowing the shofar, but by recalling the sound of the shofar, by subjugating our hearts to the sovereignty of God. We conclude the *Shofarot* section of Musaf with the phrase, "for You listen to the sound of the shofar and heed the *teru'a* and there is none like You." God not only listens to the sound of the shofar, but also "heeds the *teru'a,*" meaning, He pays heed to the heartbreak and subjugation expressed by the *teru'a.* Only He who knows the human heart is capable of this; thus, "there is none like You."

“Sweeter than Wine”

> Judah b. Naḥman taught in the name of Resh Lakish, “‘God is elevated with the *teru'a*’ (Ps. 47:6) – When the Holy One, blessed be He, ascends to sit on the Throne of Justice, He ascends in justice, as it is written, ‘God is elevated with the *teru'a*.’ And when Israel take up shofars and sound the blasts, the Holy One, blessed be He, rises from the Throne of Justice and sits upon the Throne of Mercy, as it is written, ‘the Lord [is elevated] with the sound of the shofar,’ and He is filled with mercy for them and is compassionate towards them, and transforms the attribute of justice into the attribute of mercy for them.” (Leviticus Rabba 29:3)

“God is elevated” refers to the attribute of justice, while “the Lord [is elevated] with the sound of the shofar” refers to the attribute of mercy. We don’t fully understand these terms. What precisely are the attributes of justice and mercy, and how does the sounding of the shofar turn one into the other? In any event, what we have here is unusual: our Sages explicitly discuss the effect of a mitzva on the heavenly order, the divine attributes, an approach associated exclusively with the masters of Kabbala.

When Rosh HaShana falls on Shabbat, we content ourselves with the *Malkhuyot*, *Zikhronot*, and *Shofarot* blessings, and refrain from blowing the shofar. The Torah permits blowing a shofar when Rosh HaShana falls on Shabbat. But the Sages forbade this because they were concerned that a person who does not know how to blow may go to an expert to learn how, and he will end up carrying the shofar in the public domain – something that the Torah forbids on Shabbat.

Who were those Sages who had the authority to prohibit the sounding of the shofar on Shabbat based on such a far-fetched concern? *Midrash Sekhel Tov* (Gen. 22:18) says that it was the Men of the Great Assembly who decreed that the shofar not be sounded on Shabbat.

This was not their only decree aimed at preventing the violation of Shabbat. The Men of the Great Assembly were very sensitive about Shabbat observance, and forbade the carrying of objects that are *muktzeh*:

> Our Rabbis taught, "At first the Sages said, 'Only three utensils are permitted to be carried on Shabbat: a fig-cake knife, a soup-pot ladle, and a small table knife'..."
>
> R. Ḥanina said, "This mishna was taught in the days of Neḥemia b. Ḥakhalya, as it is written, 'In those days I saw in Judea some treading winepresses on Shabbat, and bringing in sheaves' (Neh. 13:15)." (Shabbat 123b)

The Men of the Great Assembly prohibited carrying any utensil on Shabbat except for the three listed in the *baraita*. But the *baraita* goes on to say that over time this decree was relaxed three different times, as more and more utensils were added to the list of permitted items. The question is: Why were the Sages so lenient about carrying household utensils which are useful only for satisfaction of material needs? Why weren't they also lenient about the shofar? Is transforming the attribute of justice into mercy not sufficiently important?

The answer is that the Sages understood that just as blowing the shofar affects the heavenly realm, so too the observance of the rabbinic decree not to sound the shofar on Shabbat can transform the attribute of justice into mercy.

What made the Sages confident that obedience to their decree has an effect on the heavenly order? The answer lies in the following statement of the Gemara:

> [R. Yehoshua] changed the subject and said, "Yishmael, my brother, how do you read the verse: 'for *dodekha* (your [masculine] love) is sweeter than wine' (Song 1:2), or 'for *dodayikh* (your [feminine] love) is sweeter than wine'?" He replied, "For *dodayikh* is sweeter." He said to him, "This is not so, as is proved by the following phrase: 'Your ointments [masculine] have a goodly fragrance.'" (Avoda Zara 29b)

From the Talmud Yerushalmi we see that this debate about how to read the word is directly relevant to the broader question of rabbinic authority:

> "For your love is sweeter than wine" – R. Ba b. Kohen said in the name of Bar Pazi, "Know that the words of the Scribes are dearer than the words of the Torah, for R. Tarfon, had he not said *Shema,* would only have violated a positive commandment, but because he violated the words of the School of Hillel, he deserved to die, based on 'Whoever breaks through a hedge, a snake shall bite him' (Ecc. 10:8)."
>
> R. Yishmael taught, "The words of the Torah include prohibitions and permitted acts; some are grave, while some are not. But the words of the Scribes – all of them are grave..."
>
> A prophet and a sage – to what may they be compared? To a king who sent two of his seals to the provinces. On one he wrote, "If he does not show you my signature and my seal, do not believe him," and on the other he wrote, "Even though he does not show you my signature and my seal, believe him." So too regarding a prophet it is written, "and he gave you a sign or a wonder" (Deut. 13:2). But here [regarding a sage]: "According to the law which they shall teach you" (17:11). (Yerushalmi Avoda Zara 2:7)

The words of the Sages are superior to those of a prophet, because the statements of the Sages must be accepted absolutely, while a prophet is required to give a sign.

Going back to the original discussion between R. Yehoshua and R. Yishmael, it seems that R. Yehoshua chose to discuss the specific verse from the Song of Songs because he wanted to make a point about rabbinic authority. In the Song of Songs, the Sages understood the man as representing God and the woman as representing the Jewish people. Because R. Yishmael read the word as "*dodayikh*," which is feminine for "your love," he concluded that this verse was God speaking to the People of Israel. According to him, the speaker is God, because the People of Israel are incapable of issuing decrees, and their words have no force. To this R. Yehoshua replied that the speaker in the verse is in fact the People of Israel; it is they who say to God, "for *dodekha* (Your love) is sweeter than wine"; they are praising God for endowing the Sages with authority. And this is how the talmudic passage ends:

> What is the meaning of the words, "for your love is sweeter than wine"? When R. Dimi came [from the Land of Israel] he explained it thus: "The People of Israel said before the Holy One, blessed be He, 'Master of the universe! Your love is more pleasant to me than the wine of Torah.'"

The Sages' decree even supersedes the way the world works. Our Sages teach that in a year in which the Jewish people do not blow the shofar on Rosh HaShana, they will be beset with troubles by year end. The Tosafot explain in the name of the *Halakhot Gedolot* that this principle does not apply if the people failed to blow the shofar because of Shabbat. In other words, there is a metaphysical principle that punishes the people's failure to sound the shofar. But when this principle collides with the rabbinic decree not to sound the shofar on Shabbat, the decree prevails.

We read in the Torah:

> I call heaven and earth to witness this day against you, that I have set before you life and death, blessing and curse…that you may love the Lord your God, and that you may obey His voice, and that you may cleave to Him. (Deut. 30:19–20)

The mitzvot are the means through which the People of Israel express their love for God. The observance of mitzvot is bound up with the love of God and with the awe of His majesty. On the verse, "O dry bones, hear the word of the Lord" (Ezek. 37:4), R. Yirmiya b. Abba says, "These were people who lacked the vitalizing fluid of good deeds" (Sanhedrin 92b). If you remove the element of love from the mitzvot, the desire to connect with God, to cleave to Him, and to walk in His ways, you turn it into something dry and lifeless.

This principle, which underlies all of the mitzvot, is what guided *Ḥazal* in their decrees. All of *Ḥazal*'s decrees reflect a desire to draw closer to God, to prevent the commission of the slightest sin that might erect a barrier between us and God. As a result, they had total confidence that they were implementing the will of God. They would issue their decrees, and the People of Israel, as it were, would declare to God, "The main thing is our love for You."

The essence of repentance also lies in renewed closeness to God, as Maimonides explains in Laws of Repentance:

> How exalted is repentance! Only yesterday he was separated from the Lord, God of Israel, as it is said, "Your iniquities were making a separation between you and your God" (Is. 59:2). He cries aloud and is not answered, as it is said, "When you make your prayers, I will not hear" (1:15). He performs mitzvot and they are flung back in his face, as it is said, "Who has required this at your hand to tread My courts?" (v. 12); "O, that there were even one among you that would shut the doors, that you might not kindle fire on My altar in vain; I have no pleasure in you, says the Lord of hosts, neither will I accept an offering at your hand" (Mal. 1:10).
>
> Today, the same individual is closely attached to the Divine Presence, as it is said, "And as for you who cleave to the Lord your God, you are alive, every one of you, this day" (Deut. 4:4). He cries and is immediately answered, as it is said, "And it shall come to pass that before they call I will answer" (Is. 65:24). He fulfills mitzvot and they are accepted with pleasure and with joy, as it is said, "for God has already accepted your works" (Ecc. 9:7). Better,

> they are eagerly desired, as it is said, "Then shall the offering of Judea and Jerusalem be pleasant to the Lord as in the days of old and as in ancient years" (Mal. 3:4). (*Mishneh Torah*, Laws of Repentance 7:7)

We say in our prayers, "Purify our hearts to serve You in truth." "In truth" means that our every word and every action should be sincere: that we serve God out of deep faith, out of love for Him, and out of a genuine desire to draw close and cleave to Him.

So too the Sages' decrees were motivated by a desire to draw close to God. That is why they are alluded to in the Song of Songs, which celebrates closeness to God and the desire for Him.

The Binding of Isaac

“Purify Our Hearts to Serve You in Truth”

Isaac asked Abraham, “Here is the fire and the wood, but where is the sheep for the sacrifice?”

He said, “My son – you will be the sacrifice.”

At that moment Abraham’s face changed. He said, “I am old, while he is young. Perhaps he will flee – what will then become of me?”

Isaac said to him, “Father, have no fear! May it be God’s will that my blood be accepted favorably – but bind me well, that I should not have to hold myself still. And when you return to Sarah, my mother, do not tell her suddenly, so that she will not harm herself: if she is standing on the roof – that she may not fall and die; if she is standing by the well – that she may not throw herself into it; or if she is holding a knife in her hand – that she may not kill herself with it.”

At that moment, Isaac assented verbally to his father’s wishes, but in his heart he thought, “Who will save me from my father? I have no one to help me but God, as it is written, ‘My aid is from the Lord, Maker of the heavens and the earth.’”

And the ministering angels said, “Come and see these two righteous ones: the father about to slay his son, and the son about

> to be slain – and neither one opposes the other." (*Avot DeRabbi Natan,* quoted in *Torah Shelema, Vayera* 92)

Ḥazal here seek to emphasize the humanity of Abraham. The dialogue between father and son brings the story to life and gives it a human dimension.

The Sages are teaching us that neither Abraham nor Isaac was an angel. The Mishna cites a prayer that supports the Midrash's reading of this event:

> He who answered Abraham at Mt. Moriah – may He answer you and listen to your cry on this day. Blessed are You, Lord, Redeemer of Israel. (Mishna Taanit 2:4)

We see that *Ḥazal* understood that Abraham prayed for God to cancel His decree, even though the text contains no hint of this.

Immediately we ask: Was it really Abraham's prayer that brought about God's intervention in the *Akeda*? Surely from the beginning God's intention was merely to test him, and there was never the slightest possibility that Abraham would sacrifice his son?

From the mishna we see that our Sages knew that the halting of the *Akeda* represented not only the realization of the divine will, but also a response to Abraham's human cry. Even had the divine plan not been to prevent the slaying, Isaac would have been saved by virtue of Abraham's prayer. In contrast to the story of Sodom, where Abraham argues with God, the emphasis here is on Abraham's prayer. Clearly, *Ḥazal* based themselves on a tradition that Abraham prayed, that he instituted a "prayer service" at that moment which has endured for generations.

Another midrash dramatically describes Abraham's prayer:

> "He placed him upon the altar" – Abraham's eyes gazing into Isaac's eyes, and Isaac's eyes gazing towards heaven. And tears fell from Abraham's eyes until he was swimming in tears.
>
> He said to him, "My son, since you have already expressed your readiness to relinquish your blood, your Creator will find a different sacrifice in your place."

> At that moment his mouth opened with a great weeping and he sighed a great sigh, and his eyes cast upward looking for the *Shekhina*. He lifted his voice and said, "I lift my eyes to the mountains; from where shall my help come? My help is from the Lord, Maker of the heavens and the earth" (Ps. 121:1–2). (*Yalkut Shimoni* 1:101)

Despite God's commandment to sacrifice his son, Abraham did not accept its finality; he prayed for his son. This midrash reveals Abraham's dual response to God's command. On the one hand, he was a loyal servant, eager to fulfill his Creator's word; on the other hand, he was a loving and compassionate father who could not control his feelings, and prayed for his son, pleading for his life to be spared.

We are familiar with the phenomenon of the suppression of any human or parental feelings while in the throes of religious ecstasy. In biblical times this found expression in the worship of Moloch, and in our times we see the same attitude in the response of our neighbors to the death of a "*shahid*." Had Abraham's test lacked this human dimension, the *Akeda* would not only lose its grandeur, but perhaps the whole episode would have been illegitimate and invalid.

The Gemara teaches:

> R. Yehoshua b. Levi said, "Why were they called the 'Men of the Great Assembly'? Because they restored things to their former glory.
>
> "Moses came and said, 'The great, mighty, and awesome' (Deut. 10:17).
>
> "Jeremiah came and said, 'Gentiles are high-stepping in His temple; where are His awesome deeds?' He did not say God was 'awesome.'
>
> "Daniel came and said, 'Gentiles are subjugating His children; where are His mighty deeds?' He did not say God was 'mighty.'
>
> "Then came the Men of the Great Assembly and said, 'The greatest expression of His might lies in His self-control, that He is patient with evildoers. And His awesome deeds are that, were

> it not for the awe of the Holy One, blessed be He, how could one nation continue to exist among the other nations?'"
>
> And how could the Rabbis [Rashi: Jeremiah and Daniel] deviate from a decree set down by Moses? R. Elazar said, "Because they know that God is truthful, so they would not be false with Him." (Yoma 69b)

"Where is His awesomeness?" "Where is His might?" Truth bursts forth with a shout, strong enough to change the wording of prayer. Truth is God's seal, and we are commanded to imitate His commitment to truth, even when it comes to our feelings.

Our Sages applied this approach in describing Abraham's fatherly feelings towards his other son, Ishmael. Even after God promises, "Your seed shall be called after Isaac," the Midrash (as quoted by Rashi) teaches:

> "Take your son, your only one."
>
> Abraham said to God, "I have two sons."
>
> God said to him, "Your only one."
>
> He said, "This one is the only son of his mother, and the other is the only son of his mother."
>
> God said, "Whom you love."
>
> Abraham said, "I love both."
>
> He said to him, "Isaac."

As Abraham stands and duels verbally with God, he is trying to obtain a role for his other son, Ishmael. He knows full well that God has decided that "your seed shall be called after Isaac," while Ishmael is the son of the handmaid. But he never forgets for a moment that Ishmael too is his son, and that he should see to him and his needs.

Truth is at the heart of our Rosh HaShana prayers. On this day we emphasize this attribute over and over: "For You are a God of truth, and Your word is true and stands forever," and we pray that God should "purify our hearts to serve You in truth."

We sound the shofar on this day, because it is a genuine sound – a simple sound, a cry emanating from the depths of the human heart. It is an honest and accurate expression of his heart's hidden recesses. The sound of the shofar emanates from a natural horn – not from a man-made musical instrument. For this reason it is forbidden to coat the shofar with gold or silver: so that the sound will be heard as is, with no "patina" or pretense.

According to tradition, one hundred shofar blasts are sounded on Rosh HaShana, "corresponding to the hundred sighs of the mother of Sisera," as we read (Judges 5:28), "Sisera's mother looks forth through the window and wails." This seems quite surprising: On Rosh HaShana, the Day of Judgment, a holy and awesome day, surely we have other events and images to focus on! Why specifically this memorial to the mother of Sisera? Indeed, there is nothing more genuine, more painful, than a mother crying over the death of her child. This is the symbol, the epitome.

On Rosh HaShana we pray that our prayers will not be uttered without sincerity, as empty words, but rather as expressions of inner truth, emerging from the innermost recesses of our heart. This is our wish not only for our prayers but for every aspect of our service of God. Indeed, "truth is the essence of Your word, and all Your righteous judgments are eternal" (Ps. 119:160).

Abraham's Dream for the Future

> R. Abahu said, "Why do we blow a ram's horn? God said, 'Blow a ram's horn before Me so that I will remember for you the binding of Isaac, and I shall consider as though you have bound yourselves before Me.'" (Rosh HaShana 16a)

> Abraham lifted his eyes and saw, and behold, behind him a ram caught in the thicket by its horns, and Abraham went and took the ram and offered it as a burnt offering in place of his son. Abraham called the name of that place "the Lord will see," as it is said to this day, "On the mountain the Lord will be seen."
>
> An angel of the Lord called to Abraham a second time from the heavens. He said, "'I have sworn by Myself,' says the Lord, 'that because you have done this thing, and you have not withheld your son, your only one – therefore I shall bless you greatly, and I shall increase your seed greatly like the stars of the heavens and like the sand that is upon the seashore, and your seed shall possess the gate of their enemies. And through your seed all the nations of the earth will be blessed, because you obeyed My voice.'" (Gen. 22:13–18)

Why does God repeat His blessing to Abraham? He already blessed him in his first revelation:

> I shall make you a great nation, and I shall bless you, and I shall make your name great, and you shall be a blessing; I shall bless those who bless you, while those who curse you I shall curse, and all the families of the earth shall be blessed through you. (12:2–3)

What does the second blessing add to the first? On the verse, "Behold, behind (*aḥar*) him a ram caught in the thicket by its horns," the Sages explain:

> What is the meaning of "*aḥar*"? R. Yitzḥak taught, "After all of these events, Israel will become caught up in sins and suffer troubles, but they are destined to be redeemed by the horn of a ram, as it is written, 'And the Lord God will sound the shofar' (Zech. 9:14)." (Genesis Rabba 56)

In order to understand the full significance of the *Akeda* and *Ḥazal*'s approach to it, we must note an additional point. The mishna states, "There were ten generations from Noah until Abraham" (Mishna Avot 5:2). Only ten generations had passed since God had declared, "The end of all flesh has come before Me" (Gen. 6:13). Immediately after the Flood, there was cause for hope on the horizon. But in Abraham's time, the world looked as though it had regressed to the time of the Flood, to a pagan world without a single believer in God. *Avraham HaIvri* (Abraham the Hebrew) was so called because "all the world was on one side (*ever*), and he was on the other" (Genesis Rabba 42:8). Just as Noah was the lonely man of faith in his generation – "for I have seen you to be righteous before Me in this generation" (Gen. 7:1) – so was Abraham in his.

Abraham's dream was to "perfect the world under the kingdom of God." He knew well that this process would last thousands of years, but he believed with all his heart that he and his descendants could realize this dream. At the same time, Abraham feared that it may be too late, that the world may already be destined for destruction, before the dream could be realized. God had promised Noah, "I shall not curse the land again because of man… nor shall I strike all living things again as I have done" (8:21). He had also promised, "Nor shall all flesh be cut off by the waters of a flood, nor shall there be another flood to destroy the land" (9:11). But there was no guarantee that the world would not bring about its own destruction. There was no guarantee against the appearance of a selfish generation that would seek to exploit the world's natural resources for its own benefit, leaving nothing for the generations to come. There was no assurance that the human race would not upset the balance of nature, irreversibly damaging the ozone layer, or releasing pollutants into the oceans, endangering all of mankind.

In order to repair the world, Abraham needed children to continue in his path. "Abraham and Sarah were old, full of days, and the manner of women had ceased from Sarah" (18:11). Abraham feared that Sarah's barrenness was a sign that there was no hope for the world, that his dream was an empty one.

But then one day his hope was rekindled: "the Lord remembered Sarah as He had said, and the Lord did for Sarah as He had spoken" (21:1). The divine promise, "Your seed shall be called after Isaac," was coming true; it was coming back to life in all its glory. Abraham could look ahead and see himself founding a nation that serves God and establishes His sovereignty in the world.

Even for Hagar, the future turned into something actual and important in the present. When she was in distress, she received a promise: "Arise; take up the boy and hold your hand to him, for I shall make him a great nation" (21:18).

Then comes the test of the *Akeda*. "Take your son, your only one, whom you love, Isaac, and go to the land of Moriah, and offer him up there as a burnt offering" (22:2). The test is immense, but it also had much broader significance for Abraham: the death of the great dream that he had harbored for so many days, months, and years – to establish a nation that will offer new hope to mankind and to the world.

The *Akeda* presents Abraham with the possibility that his great dream will disappear in an instant. Abraham will be remembered as a momentary burst of light in human history that leaves no lasting impression. Abraham accepts this. He raises no objection: What happened to Your promise, "I shall make you a great nation"? What about the blessing, "I shall make your name great, and you shall be a blessing"?

Indeed, "My thoughts are not your thoughts, and your ways are not My ways" (Is. 58:8). Before Abraham has had a chance to absorb the significance of the shattering of the dream, "an angel of the Lord called to him from the heavens, and said, 'Abraham! Abraham!' And he answered, '*Hineni* (Here I am)!'" (Gen. 22:11).

Abraham is speechless. All he can say is, "*Hineni*." In spite of everything, "Here I am." The angel commands, "Do not lay your hand on the boy, and do not harm him, for now I know that you are one who fears God, for you have not withheld your son, your only one, from Me."

Abraham sees the ram, takes it, and binds it on the altar. Looking at the ram that has been bound in place of his son, he understands that it is not the future that is being sacrificed, but the present. The wonderful prophecy of "The earth shall be full of the knowledge of the Lord as the waters cover the sea" (Is. 11:9) will one day come true, even if very far in the future. Even though "Israel will become caught up in sins and suffer troubles," at the end of days, "they are destined to be redeemed by the horn of a ram," as it is written, "And the Lord God will sound the shofar..." (Zech. 9:14).

For this reason, God repeats His promise:

> Therefore I shall bless you greatly, and I shall increase your seed greatly like the stars of the heavens and like the sand that is upon the seashore, and your seed shall possess the gate of their enemy. And through your seed all the nations of the earth will be blessed, because you obeyed My voice. (Gen. 22:17–18)

Abraham returns to his original dream. The terror has passed, and his anxieties have disappeared. Now, he is certain, the promise will be fulfilled:

> It shall be on that day that a great shofar will be sounded, and the lost ones will come from the land of Assyria and the forgotten ones from the land of Egypt. And they shall bow down to the Lord at the holy mountain in Jerusalem. (Is. 27:13)

The *Akeda* bears an important message for all generations. Even when it appears that one's dreams, hopes, and aspirations have shattered on the rocks of reality, do not despair! Individuals have the power to build worlds – if only they believe in themselves. I do not know if there were many generations that suffered such a sense of helplessness as our generation. Ours is a generation that survived the Holocaust – "a nation that is remnants of the sword," a generation that shortly thereafter had to stand, vastly outnumbered, and fight a war for its independence. It is a generation that, while meriting to witness the establishment of the state, could not then retire in peace and quiet. War followed war: the Sinai campaign, the Six-Day War, the War of Attrition, the Yom Kippur War, the Lebanon War, the war of rocks and Molotov cocktails, day by day, hour by hour.

In addition to the external threats to our security, we also face an internal, spiritual danger. The rate of intermarriage throughout the Jewish world continues to rise; the birth rate amongst the Jewish population is in decline. Many sectors of Jewish society are drawn to a vacuous culture of "eat, drink, and be merry, for tomorrow we die," a nihilistic lifestyle. Theirs is a culture devoid of commitment and responsibility. We have been promised a great future. But we are little people; it is not enough for us to know that the dream will be realized in the distant future. We want, here and now, that "the name of the Lord be exalted and sanctified in the world that He created as He willed. May He give reign to His kingship in your lifetimes and in your days, and in the lifetimes of all the House of Israel."

But all of this depends on us! At this time, we have an obligation to aspire to embody the character of Abraham: to believe in the power of individuals to change the world, to dream and to fight for a world that is more moral, more spiritual, more just. A world in which "every creation will understand that You have created it, and everything that is alive will declare, 'The Lord, God of Israel, is King, and His kingship has dominion over all!'"

The Faiths of Isaac and Ishmael

> And it came to pass after these things that God tested Abraham, and He said to him, "Abraham," and he answered, "Here I am." (Gen. 22:1)

What was the point of the *Akeda*? The great commentators all debated this question. One common view is that the *Akeda* represents the man of faith's blind obedience to God. This is an important foundation of service of God, but Maimonides offers a different perspective. He asserts that this was not the purpose of the *Akeda*, which actually had two other aims. One purpose was to demonstrate the level that monotheistic faith can attain:

> The account of Abraham at the *Akeda* comes to teach two great ideas that are principles of our faith. First, it shows us the extent of the love and fear of God… in order to show mankind how far one should go for the sake of love of God and fear of Him, inspired neither by hope for reward nor by fear of punishment, as we have explained elsewhere. (*Guide of the Perplexed* III:24)

In undergoing the test of the *Akeda,* Abraham sent a new message to the world: that he serves God not out of fear of punishment or fervent ecstasy, but out of love of God. Indeed, following the *Akeda,* all the peoples of the world saw that Abraham had been ready to slaughter Isaac in the name of his faith in God. The whole world knew that a person should be willing to sacrifice his life – or even the life of his only son – in the name of faith. According to Maimonides, this was Abraham's own intention: to demonstrate to the world "how far one should go for the sake of love of God and fear of Him."

We learn that religious experience and ecstasy are not the essence of serving God, but rather making a rational decision to fulfill one's obligation. Even when we repent, we should be motivated by reason, not a passing feeling. Real repentance grows out of thought, reason, and contemplation.

All his life, Abraham tried to publicize the faith of God in the world. Maimonides describes this activity:

> He began to stand and call out with a great voice to all of the people and inform them that there is one God in the world and He is to be served, and he would go from city to city and kingdom to kingdom and call and assemble people. (*Mishneh Torah,* Laws of Idol Worship 1:4)

Yet, Maimonides' explanation of the *Akeda* seems to contradict his own statement (Laws of Kings 10:2) that gentiles are not commanded in the mitzva of sanctifying God's name and are not required to give up their lives for their faith. Why then did Abraham have to publicize throughout the world the concept of one's readiness to die for his faith? Rav Kook addresses this and explains:

> When the divine illumination had to appear in its purity, it revealed itself via the powerful religious enthusiasm made manifest in the trial of the *Akeda,* which clearly demonstrated that passion and devotion to the divine reality need not be based on a knowledge of God clothed in the degrading garments of paganism

> in which the spark of divine goodness completely lost its way, but can be based on a pure apprehension of God.... This came to be through the decision of the *Akeda*, which remains a natural law for all generations: that even the delicate connection to that idea that transcends all aspects of the senses somehow penetrates the depths of the heart. (*Iggerot HaReiya* 379)

In light of this, we need to clarify the substantive difference between Abraham's faith and the faith of the pagans. The God of Abraham, Isaac, and Jacob is an abstract and unattainable God who has no image or bodily form and who cannot be conceived by human thought. The gods of Canaan, in contrast, were physical idols fashioned by human hands. The message of the *Akeda* lies not only in the readiness to sacrifice one's life for one's faith, as the other nations also were prepared for such sacrifice. Rather, Abraham's innovation was his readiness to sacrifice his son for a God who was not accessible through the senses. Naturally, the pagans believed that Abraham's faith lacked certainty. While they were able to touch their gods, bow down before them, and tend to them, Abraham had never seen his God.

Throughout this endeavor, Abraham was plagued by a nagging doubt: would the belief in an abstract God, who could not be grasped by the imagination of the masses, have the power to overcome the darker human inclinations towards injustice, violence, and destruction? In order to prove to the entire world that faith in a single God was capable of overcoming human nature, Abraham had to sacrifice his son at the command of that same abstract God. Only in this way could he make the ethical faith of God known among the nations, and demonstrate that this faith was genuine and strong, able to overcome natural feelings.

When the angel of God reveals himself a second time, it becomes clear that God does not desire human sacrifice, but the idea of self-sacrifice remained.

The second purpose of the *Akeda*, according to Maimonides, is the truth of prophecy and the certainty in the word of God that addresses man. The pagan world never knew what prophecy was, and the *Akeda* teaches the power of prophecy. Even though Abraham was promised, "Your seed shall be called after Isaac" (Gen. 21:12), when he was commanded to sacrifice his son on an altar, he moved quickly and calmly to fulfill the order. Had Abraham harbored any doubts about the authenticity of prophecy, he obviously would not have bound his son. Thus, Abraham proved that faith in the one God is absolute and free of doubt:

> The second purpose is to show how the prophets believed in the truth of that which came to them from God by way of prophecy. We shall not think that what the prophets heard or saw in allegorical figures may at times have included incorrect or doubtful elements, since the divine communication was made to them, as we have shown, in a dream or a vision and through the imaginative faculty.... If the prophets had any doubt or suspicion as regards the truth of what they saw in a prophetic dream or perceived in a prophetic vision, they would not have consented to do that which is unnatural, and Abraham would not have found in himself sufficient strength to perform that act, if he had any doubt. (*Guide of the Perplexed* III:24)

If Abraham or any other prophet had a doubt about the prophetic vision, "they would not have consented to do that which is unnatural, and Abraham would not have found in himself sufficient strength to perform that act, if he had any doubt." The willingness to sacrifice one's life is based on the absolute truth of the command and the certainty of the prophecy.

Did Abraham succeed in inculcating the message of the *Akeda*? To a large extent, the answer is yes. Christianity and Islam, the two dominant religions of the Western world, are both monotheistic, and are thus preferable to the pagan beliefs that preceded them.

But in reality the same difference that existed thousands of years ago between the faith of Abraham and the beliefs of the nations of Canaan remains today between our faith and that of the gentiles. The god of the Christians, as we know, is not abstract. Christianity believes in the "holy trinity," which places a human messiah alongside the transcendent God. The various denominations within Christianity understand this arrangement in different ways, but none of them believes in a completely abstract God.

In this regard Islam is much closer to Judaism. Maimonides, as we know, rules in his letter to Rabbi Ovadia the Proselyte that Muslims are counted among "the congregation of monotheists," and thus are not to be considered idolators.

On the other hand, there is an enormous difference between the Jewish concept of sanctification of God's name, and its Muslim counterpart. Like many fundamental beliefs of Islam, the belief in a hereafter was also borrowed from Judaism. But the Muslim version is substantially different from the hereafter that we believe in. We believe that in the World to Come,

> there is no body or physical existence, but rather only the souls of the righteous without any body, like the ministering angels… no eating nor drinking, nor any of all the things that human bodies need in this world. (*Mishneh Torah,* Laws of Repentance 8:2)

Muslims, on the other hand, believe in a physical paradise that awaits the righteous after their death. According to Muslim belief, the World to Come provides those who attain it with all the physical pleasures that they were unable to enjoy in this world. In contrast with the pure, spiritual, and elevated paradise in which we believe, Muslims expect that after death they will reach a place where they can realize their wildest and ugliest fantasies. In contrast to Christianity, Islam succeeded in blocking the human imagination from conceiving the abstract God as something tangible, but gave human imagination free rein in conceiving of the World to Come.

The difference between the original concept of the World to Come and the paradise that the Muslims imagine for themselves is of great significance, and has ramifications for our attitude towards their faith in general. It is true that Muslims believe in one God, but the goal of their service of Him is in order to reach the hereafter that they believe in. Muslim martyrs who are prepared to die in the fulfillment of their religious command do not sacrifice their lives for the sake of the unity of an abstract God, but to get to Paradise. They have turned the loftiest of commandments – sanctification of God's name – into a vehicle for the realization of their most vulgar urges. Their self-sacrifice is not for the sake of God, but for the sake of their own physical desires.

In addition to the desecration of the concept of sanctification of God's name, the belief in a physical paradise also causes horrifying acts that are themselves a desecration of God's name. Muslim spiritual leaders encourage murder, claiming that such acts publicize the name of the great God. But in fact they are encouraging their followers to sacrifice their lives in the name of the fulfillment of their physical desires.

Various midrashim provide lengthy and detailed descriptions of the three days preceding the *Akeda,* during which Abraham and Isaac walked together towards Mt. Moriah. For many years I searched among these dozens of midrashim that attempt to describe the conversation between the father and his son being led to slaughter, but not a single one mentions the paradise awaiting Isaac. This would seem rather strange: we would expect to read that Abraham reassured his son by promising that he would reach Paradise after his death. But not a single midrash makes such a claim.

This illustrates the vast difference between the self-sacrifice of Abraham and Isaac at the time of the *Akeda,* and the self-sacrifice of the sons of Ishmael today. Abraham went to sacrifice his son solely for the sake of the unity of God. He never imagined for a moment that the *Akeda* might benefit Isaac as a means of reaching Paradise, and did not entertain any illusions concerning the pleasures awaiting his son after his slaughter. A Jew does not wish to die in order to reach the World to Come, but he is prepared to give up his life for his Creator, without any expectation of a better life in the hereafter.

Jews have sacrificed their lives throughout the generations for the sake of God's name, following in the footsteps of Abraham and Isaac. In contrast, the Muslim martyrs of today sanctify the murder of others. Moreover, the Jews who sanctified God's name did so to glorify God, not for their own benefit, unlike the Muslims, who are promised a paradise of fleshly pleasures.

Although Muslims are considered members of "the congregation of monotheists," in the words of Maimonides, they have desecrated the concept of sanctification of God's name. Only we, the children of

Abraham, Isaac, and Jacob, sacrifice our lives when required to do so for the sanctification of His great name, and not for our own benefit. On this holy day (Rosh HaShana), we alone can cry out to the Creator of the universe, "Guardian of Israel, guard over the remainder of Israel…who declare, '*Shema Yisrael*.'" Only we have the right to plead to our Creator to have mercy on us and guard us from those who rise up against us to murder us:

> Guardian of the singular nation, guard over the remainder of the singular nation…who declare the oneness of Your name – "the Lord our God, the Lord is one."

Overcoming Mercy While Maintaining It: Abraham's Humanity

> R. Abahu said, "Why do we blow a ram's horn? God said, 'Blow a ram's horn before Me so that I will remember for you the binding of Isaac, and I shall consider as though you have bound yourselves before Me.'" (Rosh HaShana 16a)

We invoke the same idea in the *Zikhronot* section of the Musaf prayer on Rosh HaShana:

> May You recall…that [Abraham] bound his son Isaac upon the altar and overcame his mercy to perform Your will wholeheartedly…. So may Your mercy suppress Your anger.

In order to understand the significance of the phrase "overcame his mercy," it is necessary to look very closely at the act of the binding of Isaac.

On the surface, Abraham seems to accept the divine decree with silent submission. He is commanded to slaughter his son and, recognizing that nothing can stand in the way of a divine command, he nullifies his own will before the will of God. It appears that he suspends his feelings, his fatherly love, mercy, moral considerations. Everything stops, freezes, disappears before the divine command. "My heart is empty within me" (Ps. 109:22).

I think this interpretation is entirely mistaken. I believe that Abraham's love for his son neither disappeared nor dissipated. On the contrary – its intensity was a necessary condition for the *Akeda* itself. It is not for nothing that God emphasizes in commanding Abraham that he should slaughter the son "whom you love."

The warm relationship between father and son is strongly emphasized throughout the story:

> He took ... Isaac *his son* ... and placed them upon Isaac *his son* .... And Isaac said to Abraham, *his father*, and he said, "*My father*," and he said, "Here I am, *my son*".... "God will provide Himself with a lamb for the burnt offering, *my son*".... And he bound Isaac *his son* ... to slaughter *his son* ...

The essence of the *Akeda* lies precisely in that special loving relationship between father and son. Their love and affection magnifies the test, intensifies it, and expresses its uniqueness in contrast to the pagan offering of children to Moloch.

In *Ḥazal*'s teaching, and between the lines of the text itself, we find a further message: the patriarchs, the forefathers of the Jewish nation, are not angels. They are not depicted as performing miracles and working wonders. On the contrary, they are presented to us as human characters, in the loftiest sense: characters who are full of hesitations, emotions, and mixed feelings.

The image of Abraham as a "man of kindness" was not established through grand acts, but through daily acts of humanity: welcoming strangers into his home and hosting passersby who "prostrate themselves before the dust of their own feet" (Bava Metzia 86b). Abraham represents the kindness that is required for *tikkun olam* – perfecting the world. "For I know him, that he will command his children and household after him, and they shall keep the way of the Lord, performing righteousness and justice" (Gen. 18:19). Abraham is consistent in pursuing kindness and truth, even when this leads to confrontation with God

Himself, which takes more than a little audacity. At the same time – and perhaps specifically because of this consistency – God never shows displeasure with him, even when he negotiates with God to save the people of Sodom. Abraham speaks bluntly: "Far be it from You to do such a thing.... Far be it from You; shall the Judge of all the earth not perform justice?!" (v. 25), yet God does not get angry. He knows that Abraham is faithfully following His own path, "the way of the Lord, performing righteousness and justice." "Just as He is merciful and gracious, so you shall be merciful and gracious" (Shabbat 133b).

At times we find God when He is "a jealous and vengeful God" who even imposes difficult commands, such as "You shall leave no living being alive" (Deut. 20:16). Nevertheless, *Ḥazal* teach us that only the Thirteen Attributes of Mercy are the attributes of God. Actions that run counter to these do not reflect the attributes of God. We do not understand how the attribute of God's "goodness" can be reconciled with "a jealous God." All we know is that sometimes the world witnesses "angry" acts of God that way, but in any event, fury and jealousy are not a genuine reflection of God's attributes.

On the issue of moral sensitivity, we find in the Gemara:

> "And he [Saul] laid wait in the valley" (I Sam. 15:5) – R. Meni interpreted this to mean, [he argued] concerning affairs of the valley. When the Holy One, blessed be He, said to Saul, "Go and smite Amalek" (v. 3), he said, "If for a single life the Torah requires bringing the *egla arufa*, how much more so for all of these lives? And even if the people sinned, what was the sin of the animals? And if the adults sinned, what was the sin of the children?" A divine voice emerged and said to him, "Do not be too pious" (Ecc. 7:16). (Yoma 22b)

Rabbenu Ḥananel interprets:

> "'And he laid wait in the valley' – concerning affairs of the valley." In other words, the divine decree was difficult for him, and he said, "If, when a single corpse is found in the camp, an *egla arufa*

> is brought, then for all of these people whom we killed – how many more sacrifices must we offer to make atonement!"

According to Rabbenu Ḥananel, Saul was not disobeying God's command, but claiming that the *egla arufa* should be brought for all of the people that we killed. In other words, the rebuke to Saul – "Do not be too pious" – was not addressing the feelings of mercy that Saul expressed: these were legitimate. The criticism was aimed at the thought that offering lambs is sufficient to atone for sin. Saul is told that one should not try to assuage feelings of guilt by bringing sacrifices.

We see that it is legitimate to harbor feelings of mercy toward Amalek, even though as a practical matter one is still required to fulfill God's command to the letter.

Abraham represents humaneness, the attribute of mercy and kindness. Is it possible that upon receiving God's command to slaughter his son, all of this disappeared?

Ḥazal sensed this difficulty and resolved it by describing the arguments of Satan, and Abraham's response. This midrash presents Abraham's dilemmas, his anguish, his inner turmoil, his quandaries and questions:

> Isaac said to him, "Father, quickly perform God's will and burn me well and take my ashes to my mother and lay them there so she can see them and say, 'That is my son who was slaughtered by his father.' Father, what will become of you both in your old age?"
>
> He replied, "My son, we know that our death is close. He who comforted us until now will comfort us until we die."
>
> "And he placed him on the altar." Abraham's eyes gazed on Isaac and Isaac's eyes gazed at the heavens. Tears welled and fell from Abraham's eyes until the pool of tears was as tall as him. (*Yalkut Shimoni* 1:101)

This inner struggle not only magnified the test. It also reflects that Abraham followed in "the way of the Lord": "Just as He is merciful and gracious, so you shall be merciful and gracious." Armed with this attribute,

Abraham set off to perform God's command. God had commanded him, "Offer him up there as a burnt offering" – sacrifice Isaac, but not your instinctive feelings of kindness and mercy.

God seeks the attribute of kindness within us. "You have sought praise from those full of feeling, who set forth their cry, calling out supplication, awaiting pardon, and that is Your honor" (from the Yom Kippur service). God does not expect us to be angels or robots devoid of emotion, unfeeling, incapable of crying out. God seeks the person in whose heart rages the ongoing struggle between the obligation to perform the commandments of the King and his instinctive feelings of kindness and mercy.

Our statement in the *Zikhronot* prayer that "he overcame his mercy to perform Your will" expresses this message. Overcoming one's mercy – yes, but never erasing it altogether. For a moment it may be silenced by the voice of a divine command, but immediately thereafter it returns full force.

Like God, who even in His anger is tinged with mercy, so likewise is the attribute of Abraham.

"Caught in the Thicket"

> Abraham lifted his eyes and saw, and behold, behind him a ram caught in the thicket by its horns, and Abraham went and took the ram and offered it as a burnt offering in place of his son. (Gen. 22:13)

After the angel calls to Abraham and tells him, "Do not stretch forth your hand to the lad, nor do anything to him, for now I know that you are one who fears God," Abraham lifts his eyes. This is the third time that we find Abraham "lifting his eyes." The first was in Elonei Mamrei: "And he lifted his eyes and looked, and behold, three men were standing by him" (18:2). Then, on the way to the *Akeda*: "On the third day, Abraham lifted his eyes and saw the place from afar" (22:4). After the test of the *Akeda*, where does he lift his eyes? What is Abraham seeking now that the difficult experience is over?

Ḥazal explain that Abraham questioned the manner in which the *Akeda* concluded. Rashi quotes the Midrash:

> "Do not stretch forth" – to slaughter. He said to [the angel], "If so, then I came here for nothing! Let me inflict some wound on him and cause a small amount of blood to flow!"
>
> [Therefore] he said to him, "nor do anything to him" – do not inflict any blemish on him.

This exchange reflects the presumption that proving one's faith in God's unity requires some tangible action. In *Sefer HaKuzari*, the rabbi explains to the king of the Khazars that in the ancient world, such tangible evidence was essential:

> All nations were given to idolatry at that time. Even had philosophers come to the wise men of one nation, bringing proofs to the unity and sovereignty of God, those wise men would have been unable to dispense with images toward which they would address their prayers, and would have continued to teach the masses that the Divine Influence inheres in this image, which was distinguished by some miraculous feature. (*Kuzari* 1:97)

Thus, Abraham sought to draw a drop of blood from Isaac in order to create the sort of impression that arises from a tangible action, and thereby publicize belief in the one God. To this the angel of God responds, "Do not stretch forth your hand to the lad, nor do anything to him."

This command, "Do not stretch forth your hand to the lad, nor do anything to him," also greatly improved Abraham's inner confidence and resolve. The angel banished all the questions and visions which Satan had employed in his efforts to impede the journey to the *Akeda* – appearing, according to the Midrash, first as an old man, then as a young man, and then as a river. Abraham has now earned a new title: "for now I know that you are one who *fears God*."

This raises the question, what is unique about one who "fears God"? When he comes to Gerar, Abraham is shaken by the lack of "fear of God in this place," as if fear of God is something trivial and taken for granted. If Abraham had now been declared a man who "loves God," this would seem a great compliment, but what is the meaning of this "fear of God" that is recognized in the wake of the *Akeda*?

The *Akeda* demonstrates that fear of God can be achieved not only through tangible, physical actions, but also through abstract, spiritual service. Abraham demonstrated his self-sacrifice for his generation and for future generations, even though he did not raise his hand against the lad nor do anything to him. Rav Kook clarifies this idea further:

> When the divine illumination had to appear in its purity, it revealed itself via the powerful religious enthusiasm made manifest in the trial of the *Akeda,* which clearly demonstrated that passion and devotion to the divine reality need not be based on a knowledge of God clothed in the degrading garments of paganism in which the spark of divine goodness completely lost its way, but can be based on a pure apprehension of God. (*Iggerot HaReiya* 379)

The story of the *Akeda* teaches that we can make God King over the entire world in a manner that is pure and free of crude imagery.

The *Akeda* stands at the heart of Rosh HaShana, and it is mentioned during the Torah reading, the prayers, and in the liturgy surrounding the sounding of the shofar. The *Akeda* also alludes to another theme of Rosh HaShana – *Malkhuyot.* The halakha is that a blessing that makes no mention of God's sovereignty – i.e., one that omits the phrase "King of the universe" – is not considered a blessing. At the same time, the Tosafot rule that in the *Amida* prayer we do not expressly mention His sovereignty, but use a substitute:

> The Eighteen Blessings do not mention [divine] sovereignty.... Nevertheless, our invoking "the God of Abraham" corresponds to *Malkhuyot,* since Abraham made God King over the entire world, by making known His sovereignty. (Tosafot, Berakhot 40b).

Abraham's goal was to make God King over the entire world, and therefore the very mention of his name alludes to the expression "King of the universe." Maimonides (*Mishneh Torah,* Laws of Idol Worship 1:3) similarly explains that Abraham's aim was to establish a nation that knows God and reveals His sovereignty in the world.

The ram that replaces Isaac is caught by its horns in a thicket. Rashbam explains that Abraham understood that the reason the ram was entangled there was so that it could be sacrificed instead of Isaac. However, *Ḥazal* give this state of entanglement a symbolic interpretation:

> "Abraham lifted his eyes and saw, and behold, behind him a ram caught in the thicket by its horns" – This teaches that the Holy One, blessed be He, showed Abraham the ram freeing itself from one thicket only to become entangled in the next. The Holy One, blessed be He, said to Abraham, "In the same way, your descendants are destined to become entangled in their sins and caught up in troubles, and ultimately they will be redeemed through the horns of a ram, as it is written, 'And the Lord God will sound the shofar…'"
>
> Rav Huna b. Rav Yitzḥak taught that the Holy One, blessed be He, showed Abraham the ram freeing itself from one thicket only to become entangled in the next. The Holy One, blessed be He, said to Abraham, "In the same way, your descendants are destined to become entangled among the nations and caught up in troubles and dragged from one empire to the next – from Babylonia to Media, from Media to Greece, and from Greece to Edom. Ultimately, they will be redeemed through the horns of a ram, as it is written, 'And the Lord will be seen over them, and His arrow will go forth like lightning.'" (Leviticus Rabba, 29:10)

The Sages teach that we are still a long way from the complete fulfillment of Zechariah's prophecy, "And the Lord will be King over all the world." International and domestic "entanglements" still await us. The horn of the ram caught in the thicket reflects that even Israel, the nation chosen by God and the glory of creation, can become entangled. The shofar, made from a ram's horn and sounding the call of redemption, teaches that the process is not simple. Nevertheless, in the end, Israel will be redeemed through the ram's horn:

> And the Lord will be seen over them, and His arrow will go forth like lightning, and the Lord God shall blow the shofar, and shall move in the storm-winds of the south. The Lord of hosts shall defend them." (Zech. 9:14–15)

Studies in the *Akeda*

I

I wish to briefly address some of the questions arising from the story of the *Akeda*. This episode occupies a central place on Rosh HaShana. Rashi comments on the verse, "In the seventh month, on the first of the month, you shall have a Sabbath, a remembrance of sounding the shofar, a holy gathering" (Lev. 23:24):

> A remembrance of the verses of *Zikhronot* and the verses of *Shofarot*, to recall for you the binding of Isaac, in place of whom a ram was sacrificed.

We shall focus here on *Ḥazal*'s teachings and the view of Maimonides. The main questions pertaining are: Why did God want the *Akeda*? Did God entertain any doubt concerning Abraham's fear of God? What is unique about the story of the *Akeda* in a generation where the sacrifice of children to Moloch was an accepted norm of pagan worship? And is blind obedience to God the main message of the *Akeda*?

Along with these questions, which I will address below, there are additional issues of significance. In *Sefer HaKuzari*, Rabbi Yehuda HaLevi speaks of the perfected individual who is in complete control of all his emotional and intellectual faculties, to the extent that he controls not only his desires but also his imagination (an idea that I have not found espoused by any of his contemporaries). According to Rabbi Yehuda HaLevi, the *ḥasid* is meant to command his imagination to conjure images of such elevated occasions as the Revelation at Sinai and the *Akeda*:

> Thereafter, the pious person causes his imaginative power to conjure before his eyes, in imitation of the divine characteristic that is being sought, the most wonderful images that are preserved in his consciousness by means of the power of preservation, such as the Revelation at Mt. Sinai, and the episode concerning Abraham and Isaac at Mt. Moriah. (III:5)

If we are obligated to mentally picture the act of the *Akeda*, as the *Kuzari* suggests, we face a whole slew of new questions: How did Abraham react to the command? Was he able to reconcile himself to it, emotionally and intellectually? Did he accept it wholeheartedly, or with major doubts? What were those majestic and terrifying moments of the binding of Isaac like? Did Abraham and Isaac talk to each other as they walked together, and if so, about what? *Ḥazal* address these questions in their midrashim, and offer a range of different ideas.

To my mind, it is important first and foremost to emphasize one main point: according to all the descriptions offered by *Ḥazal*, Abraham never entertained for a moment the thought that the service of God entails human sacrifice. Abraham knew that this was the complete opposite of what God wanted. Moreover, in none of the midrashim have I found the slightest hint that Abraham sought, through the binding of his son, to attain life in the World to Come, in the spirit of the teaching, "Better one hour of beatitude in the World to Come than all of the life of this world" (Mishna Avot 4:17). There is not a single word about this in any of *Ḥazal*'s teachings on the *Akeda*.

II

The Midrash, and Rashi in its wake, note that Abraham proceeds towards the *Akeda* thoughtfully and soberly. In explaining why the journey to Mt. Moriah took three days, Rashi writes:

> "On the third day" – Why did he not see it immediately? In order that people could not later say, "The command shocked and confused him and muddled his thinking; had he had time to think about it, he would not have gone ahead with it." (Rashi, Gen. 22:4)

Had the *Akeda* not taken place on the third day, one might have concluded that Abraham acted out of a momentary lapse of his senses, out of a surge of religious ecstasy. Therefore he is delayed for three days, to teach us that he acted rationally. This point is emphasized by Maimonides:

> Had Abraham acted immediately upon receiving the commandment, he would have acted out of emotion, without reflection. But by acting several days after receiving the commandment, he acted out of genuine thought and reflection and consideration of the divine command and the love and awe of Him. There is no need to seek out any other idea that might have affected his emotions. For Abraham did not hasten to kill Isaac out of fear that God might slay him or make him poor, but rather to demonstrate to all how far one should go out of love and awe of God, not in the hope of receiving recompense and not for fear of punishment. (*Guide of the Perplexed* III:24)

Ḥazal emphasize Abraham's rationality in drawing a contrast between the *Akeda* and the worship of Moloch that was prevalent in the ancient world. The Torah teaches:

> To the Children of Israel you shall say, "Anyone of the Children of Israel, or of the strangers that sojourn in Israel, who gives of his seed to Moloch – he shall surely be put to death; the people of the land shall stone him with stones." (Lev. 20:2)

The Gemara explains:

> Rav Aḥa b. Rabba said, "One who caused *all* of his seed to pass [before Moloch] is exempt, as it is written, 'of his seed,' not 'all his seed.'" (Sanhedrin 64b)

The obvious question is, why should someone be exempt if he causes all of his children to pass before Moloch? Surely, if he is punishable for sacrificing one child, then he should be punished far more severely for sacrificing all of them! I believe that this teaching reflects a simple insight into human psychology: a person who sacrifices all his children to Moloch is mentally ill; he requires treatment, not punishment. Abraham sets off to sacrifice "all his seed," his only son whom he loves, Isaac, the essence of his dreams. This is even more striking in light of Maimonides' view that the purpose of the forefathers was to establish a nation that would know God and serve Him. And yet, Abraham is willing to sacrifice his only son, and thereby to destroy with his own hands his entire life's purpose. We cannot but conclude that the *Akeda* was carried out after careful consideration, on "the third day," not out of an uncontrollable urge, a momentary ecstasy, but after deliberation and thought.

Even the atmosphere of the *Akeda* provides none of the signs that indicate grand heroic acts. Unlike the worship of Moloch, there are no thundering drums or dancing throngs. Just father and son, no one else; even the "young men" accompanying them are left far behind. Just Abraham and Isaac, walking together, in silence.

III

Maimonides offers the following description of Abraham's awakening to divine service:

> After this mighty one was weaned, he began to explore with his mind. Though but a child, he began to think day and night, wondering, "How is it possible for this sphere to continue to revolve without having anyone guiding it and making it spin? Surely, it cannot revolve by itself!" He had no teacher, nor was there anyone to inform him. Rather, he was mired in Ur Kasdim among the foolish idolaters. His father, mother, and the entire nation were idol worshippers, and he would worship with them, but his mind was already exploring and gaining understanding.
>
> Ultimately, he achieved the way of truth and understood the path of righteousness through his accurate comprehension. He knew that there was one God who controlled the sphere and

> created everything, and that no other god exists. He knew that the entire world was mistaken, and that what caused them to err was their worship of the stars and images, which made them lose awareness of the truth.
>
> Abraham was forty years old when he became aware of his Creator. Once he knew, he began to present proofs to the inhabitants of Ur Kasdim and debate with them, telling them that they were not pursuing the path of truth. He smashed their idols and began to teach the people that it is fitting to serve only the God of the world. To Him alone is it fitting to bow, sacrifice, and offer libations, so that all the people in future generations would know Him. Conversely, it is fitting to destroy and smash all images, lest the nation err concerning them, like those people who thought that there was no God but those. (*Mishneh Torah*, Laws of Idol Worship 1:3)

Abraham's entire life constitutes a battle against the pagans who regarded human sacrifice as a proper form of worship. And now he is commanded by God to sacrifice his only son, contrary to all that he believes in. What went through Abraham's mind during those moments? We cannot know. We might imagine that he wondered, "How can I return home? How can I look people in the eye after having preached my whole life against human sacrifice?"

According to one of the midrashim, Sarah died after hearing about the *Akeda* (see Rashi, Gen. 23:2). In other midrashim, *Ḥazal* describe at length Abraham's deliberations prior to the *Akeda*. They do not describe him as setting out with a sense of exaltation and inner peace. According to some, Abraham suffered terrible inner struggles.

"Satan" who appears in the midrashim, confronting Abraham in order to prevent him from carrying out the *Akeda*, is in fact Abraham's own sense of morality, outraged by the command and urging him, "Do not stretch forth your hand to the lad." This understanding is expressed in the Midrash:

> Satan met him on the way and appeared to him in the guise of an old man. He said to him, "Where are you going?"

> He said, "To pray."
>
> Satan said, "Why would someone on his way to pray have fire and a knife in his hand, and carry wood on his shoulder?"
>
> He said, "In case we stay for a day or two, then we shall slaughter and cook and eat."
>
> Satan said to him, "Old man! Was I not there when the Holy One, blessed be He, said to you, 'Take your son…'? Will an old man like you then go and kill a son given to him at the age of a hundred?! Have you not heard the saying, 'That which he had, he threw away; now he asks from others'? And if you suggest that you might have another son – will you then obey the accuser, by destroying a life for which you will be held guilty by law?!"
>
> He said to him, "It was not the accuser, but the Holy One, blessed be He. I will not listen to you."
>
> Satan left him and took on the guise of a young man, and stood to the right of Isaac. He said to him, "Where are you going?"
>
> He answered, "To study Torah."
>
> Satan asked, "Alive or dead?"
>
> He said, "Can one study after he is dead?!"
>
> Satan said, "Unfortunate one, son of an unfortunate one! How many fasts did your mother fast until you were born; now this old man has lost his mind, and he is going to slaughter you!"
>
> He said: "Nevertheless – I shall not go against the will of my Creator nor against my father's command."
>
> Isaac then turned to his father and said, "My father, see what Satan said to me!"
>
> He said to him, "Pay no attention to him; he came only with the intention of wearing us down." (*Yalkut Shimoni* 1:101)

This is not a simple, easy story, but a sharp tale that emphasizes the humanity of the servant of God. Even the fear of God that fills his heart cannot blunt his humanity; even after the direct command from God, Abraham remains a loving father to his "only son whom he loves." The Midrash gives wonderful expression to this:

> "And he placed him on the altar." Abraham's eyes gazed on Isaac and Isaac's eyes gazed at the heavens. Tears welled and fell from Abraham's eyes until the pool of tears was as tall as him. He said to him, "My son, since you have already expressed your readiness to relinquish your blood, your Creator will find a different sacrifice in your place."
>
> At that moment his mouth opened with a great weeping and he sighed a great sigh, and his eyes wandered, seeking out the *Shekhina*. He lifted his voice and said, "I lift my eyes to the mountains; from where shall my help come? My help is from the Lord, Maker of the heavens and the earth" (Ps. 121:1–2). (*Yalkut Shimoni* 1:101)

Despite the explicit command to bind his son, Abraham is not resigned to the *Akeda*; he weeps for his son. The Midrash reveals Abraham's ambivalence towards God's command: on one hand, he is a loyal servant who hurries to fulfill the will of his Creator; on the other hand, he is a compassionate and loving father who cannot suppress his feelings and who prays for his son, pleading that his life be spared.

This midrash, describing Abraham's emotional prayer at the *Akeda*, is also reflected in halakhic practice. It used to be customary, on public fast days, to add extra blessings to the *Amida*, as we learn from the Mishna:

> In the first blessing, he concludes, "He who answered Abraham at Mt. Moriah – may He answer you and listen to your cry on this day. Blessed are You, Lord, Redeemer of Israel." (Mishna Taanit 2:4)

In the Torah we do not find that Abraham prayed or requested anything on Mt. Moriah. According to some midrashim, he pleaded for divine compassion with regard to future troubles. The Talmud Yerushalmi teaches:

> "He who answered our patriarch Abraham" – R. Bibi Abba taught in the name of R. Yoḥanan, "Abraham said to God, 'Master of the universe! You know that when You told me to offer up my son

> Isaac, I could have answered You and said, "Previously You told me, 'Your seed shall be called after Isaac' – yet now You say, 'And offer him up there as a burnt offering'?" But I did not do so, Heaven forbid; rather, I overcame my inclination and performed Your will. So may it be Your will, Lord my God, that when the descendants of Isaac my son are beset by trouble, and there is none to defend them, that You Yourself will be their advocate: "the Lord will see" – that You will remember in their favor the binding of Isaac their father, and be filled with mercy towards them.'" (Y. Taanit 2:4)

Clearly, this is not the plain meaning of the mishna. The plain meaning is that God answered Abraham's prayer and supplication that the decree be annulled, and told him, "Do not stretch forth your hand to the lad." This suggests that Abraham did not accept the divine decree, but rather cried out against the heavens: "Master of the universe, have mercy upon us and do not destroy us!" The Holy One, blessed be He, in His mercy, agreed and revealed His original intention, telling him, "Do not stretch forth your hand to the lad." For this reason, we ourselves pray, "He who answered Abraham at Mt. Moriah – may He answer us."

Thus, we have a solid tradition concerning Abraham's prayers at that time. Anyone familiar with the Sages could not imagine anything different: Could Abraham go off happily and gladly to bind his son? Abraham is still a human being, plagued with doubts, the doubts of a father who loves his son with all his being. He does not go with the hope of achieving life in the World to Come, or treasures. Rather, he does so in order to fulfill God's word, out of love for Him and fear of Him.

This humanity is also reflected in the midrashic description of Isaac. He too is depicted as a loving son, concerned for his parents' welfare, asking, "What will become of you both in your old age? How will you manage?"

> Isaac said to him, "Father, quickly perform God's will and burn me well and take my ashes to my mother and lay them there so she can see them and say, 'That is my son who was slaughtered by his father.' Father, what will become of you both in your old age?"

> He replied, "My son, we know that our death is close. He who comforted us until now will comfort us until we die." (*Yalkut Shimoni* 1:101)

According to a different midrash, a different thought occupied Isaac at that time:

> "When you return to Sarah, my mother, do not tell her suddenly, so that she will not harm herself: if she is standing on the roof – that she may not fall and die; if she is standing by the well – that she may not throw herself into it; or if she is holding a knife in her hand – that she may not kill herself with it."...
>
> And the ministering angels said, "Come and see these two righteous ones: the father about to slay his son, and the son about to be slain – and neither one opposes the other." (*Avot DeRabbi Natan*, quoted in *Torah Shelema, Vayera* 92)

Great nobility of spirit is embodied in Isaac's awesome expression of grace, kindness, and mercy. There is no promise of the World to Come, only his question – "What will become of you both in your old age?" and concern that the news be broken to his mother gently. This is a wonderful window into *Ḥazal*'s worldview. Abraham remains in all his humanity, full of doubts, struggling against his inner voices, praying and hoping, "Perhaps God will have mercy; perhaps He will be compassionate." Isaac too is concerned for his parents, and offers his own prayer.

IV

All of this brings us back to our original question: what is the point of this test? Rashi points out the difficulty presented by the story of the *Akeda*, and its message. In the wake of *Ḥazal*, he offers his own explanation:

> "For now I know" – From now on I will be able to answer Satan and the other nations, who question the special love that I have for you. Now I have an answer, as all can see that you are one who fears God. (Rashi, Gen. 22:12)

According to this explanation, the test of the *Akeda* is actually meant for the nations of the world. This is a very difficult answer. Maimonides suggests a different interpretation:

> The account of Abraham at the *Akeda* comes to teach two great ideas that are principles of our faith. First, it shows us the extent of the love and fear of God. Abraham is commanded to perform a certain act, which is not equaled by any surrender of property or by any sacrifice of life, for it surpasses everything that can be done and belongs to the class of actions which are believed to be contrary to human feelings. He had been without child, and had been longing for a child; he had great riches and honor, and was expecting that a nation should spring from his seed. After all hope of a son had already left him, a son was born to him. How greatly he must have delighted in the child! How intensely he must have loved him! And yet, out of his fear of God and his love for performing God's commandment, he thought little of that beloved child and set aside all his hopes concerning him, and consented to kill him after a journey of three days…to demonstrate to all how far one should go out of love and awe of God, not in the hope of receiving recompense and not for fear of punishment, as we have explained elsewhere. (*Guide of the Perplexed* III:24)

Still, we are left with a problem: God does not demand human sacrifice! Concerning the worshippers of Moloch, the Torah says, "For every abomination to the Lord, which He hates, they have done to their gods; for even their sons and their daughters they have burnt in the fire to their gods" (Deut. 12:31), and the prophet includes child sacrifices among the matters "which I did not command, not did I speak, nor did they arise in My mind" (Jer. 19:5). So how is it that "in order to demonstrate to all how far one should go out of love and awe of God," God commands Abraham to sacrifice Isaac? In order to make known to us the extent of love of God, is there really a need to command child sacrifice?

Rav Kook addresses this question in one of his letters:

> That profound devotion to idolatry on the part of primitive man, who viewed it as his be-all and end-all, until this devotion overcame even the natural compassion of parents for children and resulted in the establishment of the cruel sacrifice of both son and daughter as a fixed aspect of the service of the Moloch – this devotion is a dark, turbid consequence of the realization, hidden deep in the heart of man, that the divine reality is more precious than anything, and that even that which is most cherished and beloved of man is as naught in comparison with it. (*Iggerot HaReiya* 379)

Rav Kook adopts the view proposed by *Ḥazal*, based on the verse, "'And in every place incense is burnt and sacrifices are offered to My name, and a pure offering for My name is great among the nations,' says the Lord of hosts" (Mal. 1:11), that even the other nations – including idolaters – are really seeking God, but go about it in the wrong way. Behind the terrible cruelty of sacrificing their children to Moloch, which the Torah abhors and forbids in the strongest possible terms, is the recognition that "the divine reality is more precious than anything."

Rav Kook then goes on to write:

> When the divine illumination had to appear in its purity, it revealed itself via the powerful religious enthusiasm made manifest in the trial of the *Akeda*, which clearly demonstrated that passion and devotion to the divine reality need not be based on a knowledge of God clothed in the degrading garments of paganism in which the spark of divine goodness completely lost its way, but can be based on a pure apprehension of God.

The message of the *Akeda*, according to Rav Kook, is that one can achieve the same "passion and devotion to the divine reality" without tangible, pagan elements, but through faith in an abstract God.

Many years ago, I read Azriel Carlebach's book *India: A Travel Journal*. He describes a fascinating conversation with a guru in India. The latter claimed that Western culture had failed miserably, including its three great religions – Judaism, Christianity, and Islam. As proof he cited the events of the First and Second World Wars. And how did he explain this failure? He argued, "The reason is that you speak about abstract faith, about a God who has no human attributes. Therefore, people who believe in this God are capable of carrying out the most terrible atrocities. We, in India, have a human god, who is jealous and has desires, who has a body and a bodily form. Such a god can speak to us and educate us to be human."

What sort of faith did Abraham seek to disseminate in the world? Abraham engaged in an ongoing argument with the people of his generation. He claimed that God's way is "to perform righteousness and justice." The God who is not human demands of us human sensitivity and moral behavior. The Eastern religions, in contrast, ignore moral problems of justice and fairness. People die in the middle of the street, and no one says a word. The main thing is to have a religious experience, "connect" with the gods, and feel a spiritual high. One of my students once told me that it was only when he visited India that he could understand the power of the "inclination toward idolatry," that amazing religious experience. Look around and you can see the sheer force of worshipping a tangible god: in its name, thousands of people are willing to sacrifice their children, day after day, at any moment.

What about our own faith? Does it allow us to reach an advanced spiritual level of totality and devotion? Abraham establishes a one-time example: our faith can bring a person to the loftiest heights of self-sacrifice! Through the act of the *Akeda,* Abraham showed that even faith in a God "who has no body and no bodily form" can raise a person to such a lofty spiritual level that he is willing, for its sake, to sacrifice his son. This is the message of the test of the *Akeda*. Once Abraham demonstrated his willingness, the truth was revealed that God has no desire for human sacrifice. And therefore Abraham hears the voice of the angel of God, instructing him, "Do not stretch forth your hand to the lad."

It is this message that Maimonides seeks to convey. The entire story of the *Akeda* comes to teach us "the extent of the love and fear of God." Of course, it also becomes clear that this act, which represents "how far one should go," is not what God desires. The Holy One, blessed be He, the merciful and compassionate God, does not wish fathers to sacrifice their sons. God does not seek their death and does not require that we sacrifice them; on the contrary, "that they may live by them [God's commands] – and not die by them" (Yoma 85b).

Thus, the point here is not child sacrifice, but a completely different issue: how to persuade the world that it is possible to serve – with powerful religious passion – an abstract God who has no form. Is the appeal of this abstract faith doomed to a small, select group? Can only a tiny group of intelligentsia, capable of holding an abstract faith, cleave to God and His Torah, while the rest of the world remains stuck in a crude, tangible idolatry? This is the existential problem that God addressed with the command of the *Akeda*.

After Abraham demonstrated his willingness to sacrifice his son, it was clear to all that even abstract faith can bring a person to the highest level of fear of Heaven. Abraham did not understand this at first, and perhaps that is the reason that the three-day journey was necessary. Only after three days of walking "with Isaac his son" did he realize this was the great message that he was to convey to the world. Only then did he understand that he had been entrusted with the task of disseminating to the world the faith in God – a faith which, though not tangible in any way, could bring one to "the love and fear of God" to the point of giving up his life. Maimonides concludes with the words:

> And the angel said to him, "For now I know" – meaning that through this act, as a result of which you will be known as one who "fears God" completely, all of mankind will know the extent of fear of God.

V

According to Maimonides, the *Akeda* also holds another message: teaching the veracity of prophecy:

> The second purpose is to show how the prophets believed in the truth of that which came to them from God by way of prophecy. We shall not think that what the prophets heard or saw in allegorical figures may at times have included incorrect or doubtful elements, since the divine communication was made to them, as we have shown, in a dream or a vision and through

> the imaginative faculty. Scripture thus tells us that whatever the prophet perceives in a prophetic vision, he considers as true and correct and not open to any doubt; it is in his eyes like all other things perceived by the senses or by the intellect. This is proved by the consent of Abraham to slay "his only son whom he loved," as he was commanded, although the commandment was received in a dream or a vision. If the prophets had any doubt or suspicion as regards the truth of what they saw in a prophetic dream or perceived in a prophetic vision, they would not have consented to do that which is unnatural, and Abraham would not have found in himself sufficient strength to perform that act, if he had any doubt [as regards the truth of the commandment]. And in truth, it was proper that this lesson, of the *Akeda*, be taught through Abraham and Isaac, for Abraham was the first to teach the unity of God, to establish the faith [in Him], to cause it to remain among coming generations, and to win his fellow men for his doctrine, as Scripture says of him, "I know him, that he will command," etc. In the same manner as he was followed by others in his true and valuable opinions when they were heard from him, so also the principles should be accepted that may be learned from his actions, especially from the act by which he confirmed the principle of the truth of prophecy, and showed how far we must go in the fear and the love of God.
>
> This is the way we have to understand the accounts of trials: we must not think that God desires to examine us and to try us in order to know something that He did not know before. Far be this from Him; He is far above that which ignorant and foolish people imagine concerning Him, in the evil of their thoughts. Note this. (*Guide of the Perplexed* III:24)

Had Abraham entertained the slightest doubt as to whether God had really spoken to him and commanded him to slaughter his son, would he have bound him in order to offer him? And had God not commanded him, "Your seed shall be called after Isaac"? Therefore, Maimonides concludes, the *Akeda* comes to prove to the world that "whatever the prophet perceives in a prophetic vision, he considers as true and correct and not open to any doubt; it is in his eyes like all other things perceived by the senses or by the intellect."

As we know, prophecy occupies a central place in Maimonides' teachings. Not only is there one God, but He addresses and speaks to His creatures. Were it not for prophecy, the Torah could not have been given, and therefore "faith in prophecy precedes faith in the Torah" (III:45). This is the second message of the *Akeda*, and one of the central messages of Judaism. According to Maimonides (ibid.), this is also the deeper significance of the Holy of Holies: the Tablets of the Covenant symbolize the principle, "I am the Lord your God," while the cherubim symbolize prophecy. The divine voice emerges from between the cherubim and speaks to Moses, master of the prophets. In Maimonides' view, the institution of prophecy is the foundation of Judaism.

Maimonides asserts that there are two cornerstones of the Torah. One is the love of God, which we learn from Abraham, who sets out to fulfill God's will even though this entails the end of his dream to leave descendants who will become a nation with a great message for all of mankind. The second is the power of prophecy. Only the certainty of prophecy allows Abraham to carry out God's command. Abraham carries out the command to sacrifice Isaac, thereby teaching us that even faith in an intangible God can inspire a person with the same religious passion that seemed to exist only among idol worshippers.

This message has special significance in our generation. Our ancestors in previous generations served God with a simple, warm, passionate faith, without questions or doubts. In contrast, our religious experience is full of questions, conceptual and philosophical problems, and complex thinking. The message of the *Akeda* confronts us with a great challenge: we must prove that even in our complex world, one can achieve through faith the same religious fervor of Abraham and of preceding generations.

"The end of the matter, when all is said and done: fear God and keep His commandments, for that is the whole of man" (Eccl. 12:13). The "man" and his humanity are the essential condition for fear of God. The test of the *Akeda* reveals Abraham in all of his humanity, as a person and as a prophet, bearing a message of love and fear of the Creator, who has no body and no bodily form.

Shabbat Shuva

The *Teshuva* of Shabbat

> "Moses went and spoke these words to all of Israel" (Deut. 31:1) – The word "went" (*vayelekh*) always indicates rebuke, as it is written, "Go (*lekhu*), behold the works of the Lord" (Ps. 46:9). (*Tanḥuma, Vayelekh* 1)

The Midrash teaches us that what Moses conveyed to the Children of Israel was rebuke. However, the plain meaning of the text seems to follow Nahmanides' interpretation:

> To comfort them concerning his situation, telling them, "I am old, and you have no more use for me; moreover, God has commanded that I shall not cross over there. But do not fear and do not be afraid, for God will cross over with you; He shall not remove His Divine Presence from you on my account." (Nahmanides, Deut. 31:2)

These are calming, soothing words; why, then, does the Midrash view Moses' speech as one of rebuke?

Moses' words are indeed soothing words of farewell: "I am a hundred and twenty years old this day; I can no more go out and come in; also the Lord has said to me, 'You shall not cross over this Jordan'" (Deut. 31:2). However, there is also rebuke, in the form of thundering silence. The rebuke arises from the image of Moses who is no longer able "to go out and come in." Rashi explains, "I am not permitted to do so, for permission has been taken from me and given to Joshua."

The tragedy of Moses is, "But the Lord was angry with me for your sake" (3:26). Because of the actions of the Children of Israel, he is not permitted to enter the land. So Moses soothes the people, but his words also convey silent rebuke: you will be entering the land, but without me; I am prevented from entering because of your actions!

This relates to the character of the *teshuva* of Shabbat. The source for the mitzva of *teshuva* is, "Then they shall confess their sin which they have committed" (Num. 5:7). As we know, on Shabbat we do not say *Viduy*; what mode of *teshuva*, then, is appropriate for Shabbat? It seems that the *teshuva* of Shabbat is undertaken not through words – verbal confession – but rather through self-examination. In *Parashat Nitzavim* we are told, "and you shall take it to heart" (Deut. 30:1). Nahmanides maintains that this is an integral part of the commandment of *teshuva*:

> "For this commandment, which I command you this day – it is not hidden from you, nor is it far off" (Deut. 30:11) – "This commandment" refers to *teshuva*, for "you shall take it to heart... and you shall return to the Lord your God" is a mitzva that we are commanded to perform. (Nahmanides, Deut. 30:11)

The *teshuva* of Shabbat, then, is "thinking about them" – self-examination.

> And it shall be, when all these things have come upon you, the blessing and the curse which I have set before you, and you shall take it to heart among all the nations into which the Lord your God has driven you, and shall return to the Lord your God, and shall obey His voice according to all that I command you this day – you and your children, with all your heart, and with all your soul. (Deut. 30:1–2)

Again, the command, "you shall take it to heart," refers to *teshuva* through self-examination. The verses describe a consideration of why the nation is in exile "among all the nations into which the Lord your

God has driven you." *Haazinu* likewise demands, "Remember the days of old; consider the years of many generations" (32:7), and recounts traumatic events from Jewish history – "I will move them to jealousy with a non-people; I will move them to anger with a vile nation" (v. 21). The Torah commands that the song of *Haazinu* be written down, and the medieval authorities (*Mishneh Torah*, Laws of Torah Scrolls 7:1; *Sefer HaEshkol*) write that this command is the basis of the requirement that the entire Torah be committed to writing. The most important element, though, is this song of self-examination of the nation's past and present.

Teshuva involving examination of the fate of the Jewish people is especially significant at a time of redemption. We see in recent historical events some wondrous phenomena that demand that we engage in self-examination. Although God's hand is hidden, and we do not understand the meaning of the events, we must examine the state of the nation.

Examination of the state of the Jewish people is a component of communal *teshuva*. At the same time, "national" *teshuva* results from the *teshuva* of individuals. There is no separate reality of the nation without the individuals, and therefore the *teshuva* of the individual is an integral part of the national *teshuva*. The two processes are intertwined, and as *Ḥazal* teach, on Rosh HaShana we pass "like a flock of sheep" – each individual on his own, while at the same time "they are taken in in a single glance" (Rosh HaShana 18a); the totality is judged as a single entity.

The *teshuva* of the individual entails examination of oneself, of God's demands of him as an individual. This self-examination must take place within the person. When we examine things from without, we tend to attribute events and actions to external circumstances, but when one engages in self-examination, a person comes to the realization that "it is because my God is not in my midst that these troubles have befallen me" (Deut. 31:17). I must look to myself for the explanation.

Genuine self-examination requires plumbing the depth of evil and what leads to it, so that we can fix the causes of sin. *Parashat Vayelekh* teaches:

> Then My anger will burn against them on that day, and I will forsake them, and I will hide My face from them, and they shall be devoured, and many evils and troubles shall befall them, so that they will say on that day, "Are not these evils come upon me because my God is not in my midst?" And I will surely hide My face on that day for all the evils which they shall have perpetrated, in that they have turned to other gods. (vv. 17–18)

The commentators ask, why is it specifically *after* the stage of confession and realization that "God is not among us" that God responds by "hiding His face"? The *Shem MiShemuel* writes, in the name of his father, the *Avnei Nezer*:

> My father, our rabbi and teacher of saintly memory, explained that they will have done *teshuva* only for the actual transgression that caused the distancing of the Divine Presence, but not for the root of sin which brought about that transgression, for a slight transgression brings in its wake a more serious transgression. (*Shem MiShemuel, Vayelekh* 672)

In other words, it is not enough to say, "because my God is not in my midst"; a person has to try to uncover "the root of the sin which brought about that transgression." Examination of the deeper recesses of sin, and its causes, is an essential part of *teshuva*.

On the other hand, one also has to examine deeply the good that God bestows on us. Our challenge today is to muster all our energies, "'with all of your heart' – meaning, with both of your inclinations" (Berakhot 54a). The energy for building the nation depends on each and every individual. This is the meaning of the *teshuva* of Shabbat – a *teshuva* of self-examination that arises from the command, "you shall take it to heart."

R. Elazar b. Dordaya's Path to Repentance

> Return, O Israel, to the Lord your God; for you have stumbled in your iniquity. (Hos. 14:2)

Hosea's words are difficult to understand. The term "iniquity" refers to a sin committed deliberately, while the expression "stumbled" implies an unintentional act. The Gemara (Yoma 86b) addresses this and explains that repentance is so powerful that it transforms deliberate sins into unintentional ones. But this requires further clarification: how does this process work?

One may suggest an answer to this question based on the story of R. Elazar b. Dordaya:

> It was said of R. Elazar b. Dordaya that he did not leave out a single harlot in the world without patronizing her. Once, he heard there was a certain harlot in one of the towns by the sea who accepted a purse of dinars as payment. He took a purse of dinars and crossed seven rivers to get to her. When he was with her, she blew out a breath and said, "As this breath will not return to its place, so will Elazar b. Dordaya never be received in repentance."

> He went, sat between two hills and mountains and exclaimed, "Hills and mountains, plead for mercy on my behalf!"
>
> They replied, "Before we pray for you, we need to pray for ourselves, as it is said, 'For the mountains shall depart and the hills be removed' (Is. 54:10)."
>
> He exclaimed, "Heaven and Earth, plead for mercy on my behalf!"
>
> They replied, "Before we pray for you, we need to pray for ourselves, as it is said, 'For the heavens shall vanish away like smoke, and the earth shall wax old like a garment' (51:6)."
>
> He then exclaimed, "Sun and moon, plead for mercy on my behalf!"
>
> They replied, "Before we pray for you, we need to pray for ourselves, as it is said, 'Then the moon shall be confounded and the sun ashamed' (24:23)."
>
> He exclaimed, "Stars and constellations, plead for mercy on my behalf!"
>
> They replied, "Before we pray for you, we need to pray for ourselves, as it is said, 'All the hosts of heaven shall molder away' (34:4)."
>
> He said, "Then this depends on me alone." He placed his head between his knees and wept aloud until his soul departed. A heavenly voice called out, "R. Elazar b. Dordaya is destined for the life of the World to Come!"...
>
> Rabbi wept and said, "Some acquire eternal life after many years, some in a single hour." Rabbi also said, "Not only are penitents accepted, they are even called 'Rabbi.'" (Avoda Zara 17a)

This story is very strange. Why tell us that there was not a single harlot in the world whom Elazar had not visited? Why did he make such an immense effort to reach this one harlot? Such a sick obsession does not seem like a routine lustful desire, but seems to have some kind of message. Furthermore, how are we to understand the harlot's comment? And what is the point of Elazar's dialogue with the hills and mountains?

R. Elazar b. Dordaya seems to have been a man of great ambition who wanted to experience everything to the fullest. It was not enough for him to be a good Jew, but a Torah scholar. But he wanted to enjoy the pleasures of the world to the fullest and only afterward pursue his ambition in the realm of service of God. This is why he goes to every harlot in the world.

In fact, this last harlot understood that he was not an ordinary person. She understood that this man did not seek some momentary pleasure, like other people; he wanted to invest all of his energies in maximizing his experience of worldly pleasures, then move on to excel in other areas. She sensed that this person was not in his natural habitat and planned to abandon the sinful life after satisfying his ambitions in the realm of pleasure.

She told him that he will not succeed in returning to his old life after sinking into the depths of pleasure-seeking. She understood what he did not: someone who thinks to himself, "I will sin and then repent," becomes mired in the world of sin such that he can never return.

The Mishna (Yoma 8:9) says that one who says, "I will sin and then repent," is not afforded the opportunity of repentance. This does not mean that someone will prevent him from repenting. Rather, generally speaking, someone with such an attitude will never manage to bring himself to repent. Indeed, Maimonides lists one who says, "I will sin and then repent," as one of twenty-four things which prevent repentance (*Mishneh Torah,* Laws of Repentance, ch. 4). This is also the meaning of Hosea's statement: one stumbles, sinning unintentionally, but the sins gradually become more and more deliberate.

Hearing the harlot's statement, Elazar b. Dordaya understands his situation and suddenly feels lowly and miserable. His sins disgust him and he feels worthless. Feeling helpless, he turns to the great forces of nature – hills and mountains, heaven and Earth, sun and moon, stars and constellations. He thought their immense power could help him.

But his feelings of worthlessness were mistaken. Like many sinners, he fell prey to despair. In fact, when a sinner repents, he becomes loved by God, as Maimonides wrote:

> One who is penitent should not imagine that he is far below the level of the pious on account of the sins and transgressions that he performed. Not so! Rather, before God he is loved and

> adored as though he had never sinned. Moreover, his reward is great, because he tasted the taste of sin and was able to separate from it and subdue his inclination. (*Mishneh Torah,* Laws of Repentance 7:5)

Perhaps R. Elazar b. Dordaya believed that what caused him to sin were external forces beyond his control. So he turns to others for help. Only at the end he realizes that "this depends on me alone." He understands that he himself is the cause of his sins and that there is immense potential strength within him. So he makes a full repentance.

The sinner often sees himself as lowly and does not believe in the strength within himself. Similarly, Elisha b. Avuya thought that he could never repent. He heard a voice from "behind the heavenly curtain" proclaiming, "Return, wayward children – except for *Aḥer* [Elisha b. Avuya's nickname]!" (Ḥagiga 15a). The fact that no one heard this other than him proves that it was speaking directly to him. But he did not understand that the voice was calling to him, challenging him. In contrast, Elazar b. Dordaya, prompted by the words of the harlot, recognized that everything depended only on him. He assumed responsibility for his fate, galvanized his inner strength, and repented wholeheartedly.

When a sinner repents, he musters his strength for a positive outcome. His sins are not measured based on what he actually did, intentional acts, but based on how he started out, when he was still acting unintentionally. Someone like R. Elazar b. Dordaya, who finds the strength to make an about-face and renounce sin, transforms his deliberate sins into unintentional ones: "Return, O Israel, to the Lord your God; for you have stumbled in your iniquity."

Yom Kippur

"Who Purifies You": The Repentance of Yom Kippur

> For on this day He will atone for you to purify you, of all of your sins before the Lord you shall be purified. (Lev. 16:30)

> R. Akiva said, "Happy are you, Israel! Before whom are you purified, and who purifies you? Your Father in heaven." (Mishna Yoma 8:9)

In this verse and mishna we read about two processes of purification: God purifies Israel and Israel purifies itself. For which purification are we responsible? Rabbenu Yona explains:

> There is a positive commandment from the Torah that a person should rouse his spirit to repent on Yom Kippur, as it says, "Of all of your sins before the Lord you shall be purified." Accordingly, Scripture commanded us that we should purify ourselves before God with our repentance and He will atone for us on this day to purify us. (*Shaarei Teshuva* 2:14)

The novelty of Rabbenu Yona's statement is that there is a special commandment to repent on Yom Kippur; we are required to purify ourselves on this day.

On the other hand, God also purifies us on Yom Kippur. This raises the question, what is the nature of this special divine purification on Yom Kippur? To answer this, we will explore the idea of repentance.

Repentance is the central commandment of Yom Kippur, and Maimonides strongly emphasized its significance:

> Great is repentance, as it draws man close to God, as it says, "Return, O Israel, to the Lord your God" (Hos. 14:2).... That is to say, if you repent – you will cleave to God. Repentance brings closer the distant; yesterday he was despised by God, repudiated, distanced, and made disgusting, and today he is beloved and desired, close and a friend.... How great is the significance of repentance! Only yesterday he was separated from the Lord, God of Israel.... Today, the same individual is closely attached to the Divine Presence (*Mishneh Torah*, Laws of Repentance 7:6–7)

Even so, there is something fundamental that troubles us about repentance. Can we truly repent? We are troubled by the lament of Adam, who did not believe that he was capable of repenting. Adam said to God after the sin, "The woman whom you placed with me, she gave me the fruit and I ate it (*va'okhal*)" (Gen. 3:12). *Ḥazal* expounded upon this verse:

> "And I ate" (*ve'akhalti*) is not written here, but rather "and I will eat" (*va'okhal*) – I ate and I will eat. (Genesis Rabba 19:12)

Adam thought he would never be able to repent, for after being exiled from the Garden of Eden, he would certainly eat again from the forbidden fruit; he would surely sin again. In light of this, we ask ourselves, is there really any chance that we will not return to our own sins in the future? This question is especially acute in light of Maimonides' statement:

> And what is repentance? That a person should leave behind his sin and banish it from his thought and should resolve in his heart that

> he will not do it again … and he should regret the past … and the Knower of Mysteries [i.e., God] will attest about him that he will never return to this sin. (*Mishneh Torah,* Laws of Repentance 2:2)

Maimonides sets a high standard of certainty – that God will attest that the person will never return to that sin – but who can achieve such a thing?

The *Leḥem Mishneh* here notes that Maimonides does not say that the person will never sin again, but that one could bring witnesses "that he will never return to this sin," as though he were asking God to testify on his behalf. But this is also difficult: who has the nerve to ask God to bear witness that he will not return to the sin?

After *Viduy* on Yom Kippur, we say, "and strengthen our hearts that we should leave the path of evil," but is this sufficient? Is repentance effective if there is no certainty that the sin will not be repeated?

To answer this question, we must return to the words of Maimonides, and examine the apparent contradiction there. At the beginning of Laws of Repentance, Maimonides writes:

> How does one confess? He states, "I implore You, O Lord, I sinned, I transgressed, I committed iniquity before You by doing the following. Behold, I regret and am embarrassed for my deeds. I promise never to repeat this act again." These are the essential elements of confession. (1:1)

Maimonides writes something similar in the second chapter as well:

> And the Knower of Mysteries will attest about him that he will never return to this sin…. And he should confess verbally and say these things that he has resolved. One who confesses verbally without having resolved to abandon his sin is like one who immerses in a *mikve* while holding vermin in his hand, in which case the immersion is ineffective until he throws away the vermin. (2:2–3)

According to these two statements, the promise not to repeat the sin in the future forms an integral part of confession. Even so, later on in the same chapter, Maimonides writes:

> The confession which Israel customarily says is, "For we have all sinned," and that is the essence of confession. (2:8)

Here Maimonides records the standard formulation for confession and says nothing about making a resolution for the future. As we noted above, in the Yom Kippur service we do not commit not to repeat our sins. Rather, we pray "that we should not sin again."

To explain the words of Maimonides, we need to distinguish between the general commandment to repent and the repentance of Yom Kippur. In general, making a resolution for the future is an integral part of repentance. However, on Yom Kippur there is a special kind of atonement. The *Tanna'im* (Shevuot 13a) disagreed whether Yom Kippur atones only for those who repent, or even for those who do not repent. Maimonides rules that Yom Kippur only atones for penitents. However, it seems that there is a distinction between the repentance of Yom Kippur and repentance the rest of the year. During the year, we need to repent "by the book," which includes resolving not to sin again. However, on Yom Kippur, anyone who says, "we have sinned," is considered a penitent. It is true that this form of repentance lacks a true resolution for the future; however, the great power of Yom Kippur is that even this repentance is effective.

We asked about the nature of God's purification of Israel on Yom Kippur. The answer is that the repentance of Yom Kippur, though lacking a resolution not to sin again, is nonetheless accepted by God. God purifies all of us and enables us to be counted among the penitents, even though the process of repentance is not truly complete.

To be among the purified penitents on Yom Kippur, one's repentance must be sincere. *Ḥazal* expounded:

> "Listen to my song and hear my prayer from lips without deceit" (Ps. 17:1). "Hear my prayer" – that is the regular prayer; "from lips without deceit" – that is Musaf. What is written afterward? "From before You will come justice." (Y. Rosh HaShana 4:8)

Penitents are accepted and purified, as long as they speak sincerely.

***

The idea that God values repentance even when it is not complete is also evident from the story of Cain. The verse states, "And Cain went out from before the Lord" (Gen. 4:16). The Midrash says that Cain "deceived Heaven." Even so:

> Adam encountered [Cain] and asked, "How were you judged?"
> He said, "I repented and it was received."
> Adam began to weep: "This is the power of repentance and I did not know!" Immediately Adam stood and said, "A song of praise for the day of Shabbat: It is good to confess (*lehodot*, usually meaning "to thank") to the Lord…" (Ps. 92:1–2). (Genesis Rabba 22:13)

Adam says a song of praise for the day of Shabbat, and acknowledges that it is good to confess before God. Adam sees the insincere repentance of Cain, who deceived Heaven yet whose words were accepted. Now he understands that even partial repentance can be effective, and it too is accepted by God.

The question remains: How is it sufficient to say, "for we have all sinned"? Is there no requirement for a more comprehensive confession? The answer to this is based on a gemara in Yoma:

> Rav Huna said, "If a person sinned and then repeated the sin, it becomes permitted to him." Can a sin become permitted?! Rather, to him it feels like it is permitted. (Yoma 86b)

In other words, a person can lose control and then he cannot stop. The sin blunts his sense of commandment and as a result he begins to feel that every sin is permitted.

To combat such a comprehensive problem one needs to experience the giving of the Torah, which gives one an awareness of being commanded and a recognition of sin. Yom Kippur is the day on which the second tablets were received; it is the day on which we return to the Torah and to Him who gave us the Torah. Therefore, the basis for the repentance of Yom Kippur is the recognition of sin. To express this recognition, the statement "for we have all sinned" is sufficient. This is the essence of repentance on Yom Kippur.

This short statement of confession on Yom Kippur – "for we have all sinned" – reveals the individual's inner will. Maimonides discusses this in the context of a court's forcing a man to give his wife a *get*:

> If a person's evil inclination drives him to fail to perform a mitzva or to commit a transgression, and he was beaten until he performed the act he was obligated to perform, or until he distanced himself from the forbidden action, he is not considered to have been coerced. On the contrary, it is he who coerced himself by following his evil thoughts. Therefore, one who refuses to divorce [his wife], because he inwardly wants to be part of the Jewish people, he must want to perform all the mitzvot and avoid all the transgressions; it is only his evil inclination that drives him. Therefore, when he is beaten until his evil inclination has been weakened, and he says, "I want to [divorce]," he is considered to have performed the divorce willingly. (*Mishneh Torah,* Laws of Divorce 2:20)

We learn from this that there are two opposing wills within each Jew: the underlying desire "to be part of the Jewish people," "to perform all the mitzvot and avoid all the transgressions" and, on the other hand, the current desire to sin, which is brought on by the evil inclination. The real question is, which is the more authentic will: the deep desire to do good, or the passing urge to sin? The answer can be found in the Midrash:

> "I am black but comely, daughters of Jerusalem" (Song 1:5). "I am black" – in this world. "But comely" – in the World to Come. "I am black" – on weekdays. "But comely" – on Shabbat. "I am black" – all year long. "But comely" – on Yom Kippur. (*Yalkut Shimoni* 11:982)

This is the answer regarding a person's true will. On Yom Kippur, Israel's secret is revealed: their true desire is to do the will of their Father in heaven.

The relationship between Yom Kippur and the rest of the year is similar to the relationship between Shabbat and the rest of the week. On Shabbat nature returns to its original form and becomes beautiful again. Adam, who understood the power of partial repentance – like that of Yom Kippur – sang a song of praise for Shabbat, a song of praise for the inner desire that certainly seeks to do good. This inner desire is revealed on Shabbat, and even more so on Yom Kippur, which is called "*Shabbat Shabbaton.*"

On Yom Kippur we say a blessing that ends with the words, "and other than You, we have no king to pardon and forgive us." This is strange. Would we have thought that someone else could pardon us, making it necessary to emphasize that it is God who pardons and forgives us? The answer is that God not only pardons us, He descends to the depths of our desires as well. Only God knows that our inner desire is to do His will.

When one says on Yom Kippur, "for we have all sinned," he reveals that his desire is to do the will of his Creator, that he wishes to belong to the community of penitents, about whom it is said, "Who purifies you? Your Father in heaven."

Divine Sovereignty and Unity on Yom Kippur

> "For the day of the Lord is great and very terrible; and who can abide it?" (Joel 2:11) – this refers to Yom Kippur, when the Books of the Living and the Books of the Dead are sealed. (*Tanḥuma, Vayishlaḥ* 2)

God's sovereignty is a central aspect of Rosh HaShana, and this same theme still prevails on Yom Kippur. On Yom Kippur we continue to add to the third blessing of the *Amida* the affirmation of God's sovereignty in the world: "*Hamelekh HaKadosh*" ("the Holy King"). The judgment of man is fundamentally bound up with God's sovereignty. All of creation declares God as King and performs His will without question. Only man, possessing free choice, is able to rebel against the will of his Creator. Therefore, when God judges man's actions on the Day of Judgment, this is a manifestation of His sovereignty. God's sovereignty is the essence and focus of the day.

The verse, "Hear O Israel; the Lord our God, the Lord is one," reflects God's sovereignty (see Rosh HaShana 32b). When one declares God's unity, he also affirms God's sovereignty. The unity of God has two aspects, both of which are expressed in this opening verse of *Shema*. There is God's unity in and of itself, and there is God's unity as reflected in His sovereignty over creation. The former is difficult for us to conceive; it is reflected in the opening words of *Adon Olam*: "Master of the universe who reigned before any creature was created." Because God was King before He created us, this aspect of His sovereignty is not connected to us.

The other aspect of God's unity is His sovereignty over us. Here we are talking about the God who reveals Himself in our world. In this world quantities and numbers are very significant, so it is important to emphasize that God is one and not two (see *Mishneh Torah,* Laws of the Foundations of the Torah 1:7, that knowing this is a positive commandment). This aspect emphasizes that, because God is one, there is no constraint on His reign; there is no other power, even though we sometimes see phenomena in this world that seem mutually contradictory.

In our world, good and evil mix together, and it is often difficult to distinguish between them. Our world is a world of contradictions, which is the reason for the two goats on Yom Kippur – one sacrificed to God, the other sent to Azazel. The two goats are identical in appearance, height, and age, such that the human intellect cannot distinguish between them. The drawing of lots indicates which is to be sacrificed to God, and which is to be sent to Azazel.

There is an apparent contradiction between the unity of God in and of itself, and the next sentence in *Shema*: "Blessed is the name of His glorious kingdom for all eternity." "His glorious kingdom" describes divine sovereignty as we perceive it – which actually pales beside divine unity in and of itself. For this reason we say, "Blessed is the name of His glorious kingdom for all eternity," in a whisper. The Gemara elaborates:

> R. Yitzḥak said, "The school of R. Ammi taught that this may be compared to a king's daughter who caught a whiff of a fragrant dish. If she speaks [asking to taste it] she suffers disgrace; if she says nothing, she suffers deprivation. So her servants began bringing it to her in secret." (Pesaḥim 56a)

Throughout the year, the Jewish people are like the daughter of a king who smells a delicious dish. The aroma is less important than the food itself. We emphasize God's reign over us, while at the same time knowing that this pales in relation to God's oneness in and of itself. For this reason, we say, "Blessed is the name of His glorious kingdom...," in a whisper. On Yom Kippur, however, we say it out loud, because this is the essence of the day: God's unity as reflected in His sovereignty over us. Therefore we conclude the *Ne'ila* service by declaring, "Hear, O Israel; the Lord our God, the Lord is one," which includes both aspects.

God's sovereignty should extend "over the entire earth," and we – "a kingdom of priests and a holy nation" – are entrusted with making this a reality. We can see how everything that happens in the world is connected to Israel, and this is because human history is in fact a struggle over divine sovereignty. This struggle for divine sovereignty in the world cannot happen without the Jewish people. This is the meaning of the verse, "The saviors will ascend Mt. Zion to judge Esau's mountain, and the kingdom will belong to the Lord" (Ob. 1:21). Admittedly, we do not always see the connection between what is happening in the world and the struggle for divine sovereignty, but as we get closer to the Messianic Era, these connections become more apparent, and we see more clearly the centrality of Israel in the world.

In Psalms we read:

> Therefore we will not fear, though the earth change, and though the mountains are moved in the midst of the sea.... God is in the midst of her; she shall not be moved. God shall help her at the dawn of day. Nations raged, kingdoms were moved; He uttered His voice, the earth melted. (Ps. 46:3–7)

When we observe things happening in the world, we are certain that everything leads towards "the dawn" – the dawning of redemption and the revelation of God's unity. And then we pray that "God shall help her at the dawn of day" – so that everyone, every man, woman, and child, will understand the process leading to the unity of God.

King David concludes that chapter with the words, "Desist and know that I am God; I will be exalted among the nations, I will be exalted in the earth" (v. 11). What is the meaning of the order to "desist"? The Midrash teaches:

> The Holy One, blessed be He, said to Israel, "'Desist' from your evil deeds, and know that I am God." (Song of Songs Rabba 5:2)

The mending of our deeds is bound up with knowledge of God and His unity. Maimonides, in his *Eight Chapters* (ch. 5), writes that a person must subjugate all his physical powers so as to focus constantly on one single purpose: contemplation of God, to the extent that man is able to know Him. A condition for the perception and contemplation of God is the perfection of one's traits and behavior; these lead to a revelation of God's sovereignty in the world, in the sense of "I will be exalted among the nations; I will be exalted in the earth."

While the entire world trembles and shakes from the force of events in the world, Israel gathers in synagogues and *battei midrash* on Yom Kippur to declare, "Hear O Israel; the Lord our God, the Lord is one," and to add, "Blessed is the name of His glorious kingdom for all eternity."

"We Have Acted Without Knowing What We Did"

The order of our Yom Kippur prayers opens with the verse, "And all the congregation of Israel are forgiven, along with the strangers living in their midst, for they acted without knowing what they did" (Num. 15:26). According to the Rema (*Oraḥ Ḥayim* 619:1), this verse is to be repeated three times and, as with *Kol Nidrei*, it should be said while it is still day, since it pertains to the moments preceding Yom Kippur. Indeed, the connection between *Kol Nidrei* and Yom Kippur is an indirect one: a person cannot achieve complete repentance until he frees himself from the various vows and oaths which he has taken upon himself. It is man himself who is responsible for these, and they hinder his divine service. Thus, the actual prayer service of Yom Kippur commences with the above verse.

The use of this verse as the introduction to the prayer service raises two difficulties. First, as we know, the essence of Yom Kippur is our confession, where we say, "We have sinned, we have transgressed, we have committed iniquity." But this verse declares, "We have acted without knowing what we did." Why do we commence our prayers on Yom Kippur with a declaration that our transgressions were committed "without knowing what we did"? Second, *Ḥazal* explain that this verse refers to a *beit din* that erroneously permitted something pertaining to idolatry (see Rashi, v. 22). This situation, of course, is not relevant to us.

Nevertheless, it seems that this verse has a very important message for us. The paragraph in which it appears starts with the words, "If you err and do not observe all these commandments which the Lord has spoken to Moses" (Num. 15:22). Nahmanides writes:

> This is the sacrifice of one who transgressed the entire Torah, but unintentionally, such as one who went and joined one of the nations and acts like them, and does not want to be a member of the Jewish people at all. And all of this is done unintentionally, such as in the case of an individual, someone who was captured as an infant and raised among the nations, and in the case of a community, where they thought that the time for keeping the Torah had passed and it is not binding forever.... Or they say, as is written in *Sifrei*, "Did God not say that we should act and receive reward? Let us not act and not receive a reward." Or they forgot the Torah, like in the days of the wicked kings of Israel, such as Jeroboam, where most of the nation forgot Torah and mitzvot completely, and when the people of the Second Temple came in the Book of Ezra."

Nahmanides mentions dark periods when the Torah was abandoned or forgotten. Since the time of Nahmanides I do not know when the Jewish people faced such a situation, but in our generation we see it happening to an extreme degree. We can attest to a reality in which a community believes that "the time for keeping the Torah has passed," both in Israel and in Western lands. There are Jews – a great many – who believe that the Torah is no longer relevant in our day. The complicated reality of our times, with waves of *aliya* from the former Soviet Union, forces us to confront not only the argument that the Torah is no longer relevant, but also a situation in which the Torah has been completely forgotten. With all our excitement over the miracle of the Jewish national revival, we stand uncomfortable and incompetent in the face of a Jewish community double the size of the generation that left Egypt which has forgotten the Torah altogether, and yet is returning to the Land of Israel.

And we wonder: How is it possible that Jews who are returning to the land, who never in their lives have known anything Jewish, are returning to Judaism without a single act of accepting the Torah, of circumcision or immersion in a *mikve*? Judaism is not just an ethnic identity; it also has content and a religious message. What is the message that kept these people Jews? The verse speaks of "the strangers living in your midst" – but even a stranger surely knows something about his Judaism!

The Gemara teaches:

> A great principle is stated with respect to Shabbat: if a person forgets the essential law of Shabbat and performs many types of labor on many Shabbatot, he is obligated to bring only one sin offering. How might such a situation come about? If a child is taken captive among gentiles or someone converts to Judaism in the midst of gentiles and performs many forms of labor on many Shabbatot, he is obligated to bring one sin offering only. [Likewise] he is liable for one [sin offering] on account of [consuming] blood, one on account of *ḥelev*, and one on account of idolatry. (Shabbat 68b)

Rabbi Tzadok HaKohen of Lublin asks how someone could have converted among gentiles. If he knew nothing about Judaism, how could he convert? To this he responds:

> The essence of Judaism is to be called Israel, as it is written, "One shall say, 'I belong to the Lord,' another shall call himself by the name of Jacob, and another shall subscribe with his hand to the Lord and call himself by the name of Israel" (Is. 44:5). If he has nothing else but the fact that he is known by the name Israel – that is enough.... The Jewish people are bound together as a single people, and will not be separated to join themselves to the nations, to be part of them." (*Tzidkat HaTzaddik* 54)

Rabbi Tzadok teaches an important lesson. The fact that a person is a Jew sends a message to the entire world. The fact that a person declares he is a Jew, and declares the existence of the Jewish people – though people rise up in every generation to destroy it – is a major statement. This message proclaims to the entire world: there is indeed a God, the Creator of the world, as the prophet says, "You are My witnesses, says the Lord" (Is. 43:10). Even if those Jews do not know how to say *Shema*, their very existence declares, "Hear O Israel; the Lord our God, the Lord is one."

This is the most basic, fundamental principle of Yom Kippur: the idea that "we are Your nation and You are our God." Before we make an accounting of our good deeds and our failures, what we have done and what we have not done, there is an underlying principle that arises from the verse, "And all the congregation of Israel are forgiven, along with the strangers living in their midst, for they acted without knowing what they did." We gather and include all those unwitting sinners referred to by Nahmanides. This was true in every generation, and how much more so in a generation that witnessed the Holocaust and understands that even those who believe that "the Torah is no longer relevant" must be included as "unwitting sinners" and as part of the Jewish people.

This fundamental principle is important not only for those for whom being called a "Jew" is the sum total of their Judaism, but also for us. If we are judged strictly in accordance with our actions, who knows how the judgment will come out? However, we definitely have one point in our favor, and that is the spread of God's name in the world. We begin the holy day with this idea, with the achievement of "for Your sake we are killed all the day long; we are reckoned as sheep for the slaughter" (Ps. 44:23). All of our suffering is due to that testimony that we give concerning the existence of God.

There is another aspect of this that is worthy of mention. "One generation shall praise Your works to another" (145:4). Each generation praises God in a unique way. Each generation tells of God's miracles, recounting each new divine act in history. The Midrash teaches:

> R. Yitzḥak said, "In the year that the King Mashiaḥ will be revealed, all the kings of the nations will provoke each other.

> The king of Persia will provoke the king of Arabia, and the king of Arabia will go to Edom, to take advice from them. Then, the king of Persia will come back and destroy the entire world, and all the nations of the world will quake and be terrified and will fall on their faces, and will be seized by pains like birth pangs. And Israel will quake and be terrified and will say, 'Where can we go? To where shall we head?' And He will say to them, 'My children, do not be afraid! All that I have done has been solely for your benefit! Why are you afraid? Have no fear; the time of your redemption has arrived!'" (*Pesikta Rabbati* 36)

When the nations of the world quake and tremble in fright, it is only natural that the Jewish people also feel afraid, but God reassures us: "Do not be afraid!"

This speaks to a phenomenon that we have witnessed very recently, a worldwide phenomenon that caught us by surprise. Recently we lived under the illusion that the world is marching towards large multi-national confederations, with ethnic and national identities becoming less and less important. Nations were allying themselves with a regional superpower – the United States of America, Russia, and the European Union. In this environment there is a danger that Jews who forgot the Torah will also lose their basic identity of being called "Jew." If there are no Russians, no Lithuanians, and no Ukrainians, only Soviet comrades, then there is also no need for Jews. When the world is moving away from national identities, there is a danger that some people may think that there is no longer any need to emphasize that there are Jews.

And now – this illusion is crumbling. Currently, we see a growing trend to emphasize ethnic and national differences throughout the world, if I am not mistaken, even in the multi-cultural United States. Who knows if God is not bringing all of this about for the sake of Israel, for the Jewish people that must acknowledge its Jewishness. We must praise God for this help clarifying that we are Jews who bear God's name in the world and sanctify His name.

Our prayer service on this holy day includes the verse, "Please forgive this people's iniquity in the abundance of Your kindness, as You have forgiven this people from the time of Egypt until now" (Num. 14:19). This verse concerns forgiveness for the sin of the spies. Moses, in praying that God forgive the people, expresses his concern for *ḥillul Hashem* – the desecration of God's name that will result if the nations conclude, "It was because the Lord was not able to bring this people into the land which He swore to them that He has slain them in the wilderness" (v. 16).

The Torah reading for public fast days includes Moses' prayer following the sin of the golden calf: "Why should the Egyptians speak and say, 'In an evil [hour] He brought them out, to slay them in the mountains, and to consume them from the face of the earth.... Remember Abraham, Isaac, and Jacob, Your servants, to whom You swore by Your own self" (Ex. 32:12–13). The fear of *ḥillul Hashem* concerns us as Yom Kippur begins, reminding us that our main role is to sanctify God's name in the world.

Even if, Heaven forbid, we transgress, we cannot escape our destiny. The siddur of Avudraham explains the reason for reading the Book of Jonah at Minḥa on Yom Kippur:

> To teach the whole world that no one who has committed transgressions can escape from God, as it is written, "Where shall I go from Your spirit? Or where shall I flee from Your Presence? If I ascend up into heaven, You are there; if I make my bed in *Sheol*, behold – there You are" (Ps. 139:7–8). (*Siddur Avudraham*, Prayers of Yom Kippur)

A person can try to escape his destiny in life, but he cannot escape from God. Not everyone is as fortunate as Jonah to have God speak to him directly, "What do you mean, O sleeper?" and prevent him from fleeing his mission.

We need the purity and purification of Yom Kippur in order to return to ourselves, to return to our destiny and to the knowledge that our mission is to sanctify God's name in the world.

A Heavenly Voice on Yom Kippur

> It is a positive commandment from the Torah that a person rouse his spirit to repent on Yom Kippur, as it says, "that you may be purified from all your sins before the Lord" (Lev. 16:30). Accordingly, Scripture commanded us that we should purify ourselves before God with our repentance and He will atone for us on this day to purify us. (Rabbenu Yona, *Shaarei Teshuva,* ch. 11)

The mitzva of repentance on Yom Kippur is a special one, different from the mitzva of repentance during the year. Repentance of Yom Kippur leads not only to uplift and drawing close to God, but also a change in priorities. We reconsider what is really important in our lives.

The general mitzva of repentance is "that the sinner turns from his sin before God and confesses" (heading of Maimonides' Laws of Repentance). The repentance of Yom Kippur includes another dimension: purification. The usual process of repentance is a gradual one, accomplished a little bit at a time, while the repentance of Yom Kippur is like a person immersing himself in a *mikve* and emerging purified, all at once. The Midrash (Genesis Rabba 75:1) compares this to a chicken shaking off dust, in an instant leaving all its filth behind. That is the repentance of Yom Kippur, a repentance of purification.

Of course, this presents a difficulty: can a person be purified all at once, in a single day? A well-known *baraita* of R. Pinḥas b. Yair (Avoda Zara 20b) teaches that purity is achieved only after one has acquired the traits of prudence, alacrity, cleanliness, and abstemiousness. Ramḥal, in *Mesillat Yesharim* (ch. 16), defines the essence of purity as "perfection of one's heart and thoughts." How, then, can purity be achieved through an accelerated, one-time process? A person surely asks himself, "Is it possible that I – a mortal who comes from dust and will return to dust – can really stand and be purified before God?"

The answer is that on Yom Kippur God Himself comes to our aid: "For on that day He will forgive you, to purify you, that you may be purified from all your sins before the Lord" (Lev. 16:30). The Holy One, blessed be He, declares that if the Children of Israel wish to be cleansed, He will help them. In this verse the Torah sets down the purpose of this holy day: purification before God. This purification before God on Yom Kippur is both an obligation and a promise.

Yom Kippur is a day unlike any other. Needless to say, it is not like a regular weekday, but even among the holidays it is unique. The Midrash teaches:

> "The days in which they are to be fashioned, and for it too there was one of them" (Ps. 139:16) – R. Yehoshua said, "Out of the days that the Holy One, blessed be He, created, He chose one of them. And which is it? Yom Kippur, as it is written, 'Is not this the fast that I have chosen?' (Is. 58:6)." (*Tanḥuma, Bereshit* 28)

Elsewhere we find:

> The solar year comprises 365 days. The numerical value of *HaSatan* ("Satan") is 364, for Satan makes accusations throughout the year except on Yom Kippur. (Leviticus Rabba 21:4)

The uniqueness of Yom Kippur is reflected in different ways. For example, the Torah commands us to sound the shofar on Yom Kippur in a Jubilee year, thereby announcing the freeing of Hebrew indentured slaves. There is no more appropriate day for this blowing of the shofar than Yom Kippur. A servant whose ear has been pierced serves his master until the Jubilee year. *Ḥazal* criticize the willingness of the servant to attach himself in this way to his master and remain in his home, as we learn in the Gemara:

> [Why is the ear of the servant to be pierced?] The Holy One, blessed be He, said, "The ear that heard My voice at Mt. Sinai, when I said, 'For the Children of Israel are servants to Me' (Lev. 25:55) – and not servants of servants, but nevertheless this one went and acquired a master for himself – let that ear be pierced." (Kiddushin 22b)

Let us not forget that when the servant chose to have his ear pierced and remain in servitude, he had nothing of his own to eat, nothing to wear, and no place to sleep! Nevertheless, he is criticized for making himself a servant to a fellow Jew. He should have been ready to suffer hunger and deprivation, but remain a servant of God alone.

On Yom Kippur in the Jubilee year, even this servant goes free. However, just freeing him is not enough, for what will it help for him to be free if mentally he remains a servant? There is only one day in the year when he will be able to hear the true message of freedom: "'For the Children of Israel are servants to Me' – and not servants of servants." On Yom Kippur every Jew is required to hear that divine call: they are servants to Me, not to other servants.

A different heavenly voice that is heard on Yom Kippur is the one Elisha b. Avuya heard: the voice calling, "Return, return, O wayward children" (Jer. 3:22). The Talmud Yerushalmi recounts that R. Meir asked Elisha b. Avuya why he did not repent. The latter replies:

> I cannot.... Once I was passing before the Holy of Holies, riding on my horse on Yom Kippur, which fell on Shabbat, when I heard a heavenly voice emanating from the Holy of Holies and saying, "Return, children – except for Elisha b. Avuya, who knew My power, and yet rebelled against Me." (Y. Ḥagiga 2:1)

It is no coincidence that Elisha b. Avuya heard that heavenly voice specifically on Yom Kippur. On this day one hears great and meaningful voices, the voices of repentance.

What was Elisha b. Avuya's mistake? It seems that he misunderstood the meaning of the heavenly voice that said, "except for Elisha b. Avuya." The heavenly voice spoke for a reason; it was intended to rouse him to persist, to overcome, to make an effort. The heavens wanted Elisha b. Avuya to repent "mightily," in the sense of "let them cry mightily to God, and let them turn everyone from his evil way" (Jonah 3:8).

"Mighty" repentance can break down walls; it refuses to be relegated "outside the fence." The Gemara teaches (Pesaḥim 86b, according to some versions, see *Bei'ur Halakha* 170:5) that a guest must obey any instruction from his host, unless he tells him, "Leave!" The *Shelah* (*Shaar HaOtiyot, Emek Berakha* 23; cited also in *Peri Tzaddik, Miketz* 2) explains that, in a similar way, if a heavenly voice decrees, "Get out of My house" – the same message that Elisha b. Avuya heard – one should not obey, but rather enter, in repentance.

If a person is fortunate enough to open his heart on Yom Kippur, the heart beating in repentance and longing to return to God, then his heart will echo with that heavenly voice calling, "Return, return, O wayward children." But even someone who is heartbroken because he does not feel the atmosphere of the day, because his heart is closed to repentance – he should know that even broken-heartedness contains something of that same distant heavenly voice. That voice calls to him, "Go and call mightily to God," exert yourself, persist, and overcome, for His hand is outstretched to accept those who repent. One who is sad because he is not moved to repent should seek the gate of repentance that suits him – the gate of those who are in distress:

> When you are in distress and all these things have come upon you, in the latter days, if you turn to the Lord your God and obey His voice… (Deut. 4:30)

Through this gate passed one of the greatest sinners that ever lived – Menashe, king of Judea:

> So Menashe caused Judea and the inhabitants of Jerusalem to go astray, to do worse than the nations which the Lord had destroyed before the Children of Israel. And the Lord spoke to Menashe and to his people, but they would not listen. So that the Lord brought upon them the captains of the host of the king of Assyria, who took Menashe among the thorns, and bound him with fetters, and carried him to Babylonia. And when he was in affliction, he besought the Lord his God, and humbled himself greatly before the God of his fathers. And he prayed to Him and He received his entreaty, and heard his supplication, and brought him back to Jerusalem, into his kingdom. Then Menashe knew that the Lord was God." (II Chr. 33:9–13)

The Talmud Yerushalmi elaborates:

> When he saw that he was beset by troubles, there was not a single form of idolatry in the world to which he did not appeal.
>
> When none of this helped him, he said, "I remember that my father used to read me this verse in the synagogue: 'When you are in distress and all these things have come upon you, in the latter days, if you turn to the Lord your God and obey His voice, for the Lord your God is a merciful God, He will not forsake you, nor will He destroy you, nor forget the covenant of your fathers, which He swore to them' (Deut. 4:30–31). So I will read it; if He answers me, well and good; if not – then all gods are the same."
>
> And the ministering angels tried to close the windows [of heaven] so that Menashe's prayer would not rise up before the Holy One, blessed be He, and they said to God, "Master of the world – someone who has worshipped idols and placed an image in the Temple, shall You accept his repentance?" He said to them, "If I do not accept his repentance, then I am closing the door on all who seek repentance." What did God do? He bored a hole under His Throne of Glory, and heard Menashe's supplication.
>
> And this is as it is written, "And he prayed to Him and He received his entreaty, and heard his supplication, and brought him back to Jerusalem, into his kingdom." (Y. Sanhedrin 10:2)

When he hits bottom, Menashe remembers this verse and is fortunate to have God bore a hole under His Throne of Glory. This is the repentance that breaks through gates, the repentance of Yom Kippur, which brings with it purification: "that you may be purified ... before the Lord."

Every one of us should feel that "distress," both on the personal level and the national level pertaining to all of Israel. This sense of "when you are in distress" takes hold of us also with regard to the students of the yeshiva who perished. The Holy One, blessed be He, opens the gate to those who knock in repentance; let us therefore knock with all our hearts.

Fear and Joy

> R. Elazar b. Azaria explained, "'That you may be purified from all your sins before the Lord' (Lev. 16:30) – For sins between man and God, Yom Kippur brings atonement, but for sins between man and his fellow, Yom Kippur does not bring atonement until he pacifies his fellow."
>
> R. Akiva says, "Happy are you, O Israel! Before whom do you purify yourselves, and who purifies you? Your Father in heaven." (Mishna Yoma 8:9)

The Mishna suggests that there are two different ways to understand purification "before the Lord." R. Elazar b. Azaria explains that Yom Kippur brings atonement only for those sins which are "before the Lord" – i.e., transgressions of a religious character. R. Akiva explains that, since our purification is carried out by God and before God, it brings joy: "Happy are you, O Israel." There may be no difference of opinion here. R. Akiva may simply be pointing out another dimension of Yom Kippur – a dimension of joy that arises from our purification before God. In any event, these two interpretations illuminate the dual nature of this day.

On one hand, Yom Kippur is a day dominated by the fear of judgment. On the other hand, it also carries a note of joy; it is a day that demands songs of praise. *Ḥazal*'s teachings reflect both aspects. We find in the Gemara:

> The ministering angels said before the Holy One, blessed be He, "Master of the world, why do Israel not sing before you on Rosh HaShana and on Yom Kippur?" He answered them, "While the King sits upon the Throne of Justice and the Books of the Living and the Dead are open before Him, should Israel sing?" (Rosh HaShana 32b)

Indeed, Maimonides writes:

> We do not say Hallel on Rosh HaShana or Yom Kippur, for these are days of prayer and submission before God, and awe of Him, and fleeing to Him, and repentance and supplication and the asking of forgiveness. It is not appropriate in such circumstances to rejoice and be happy." (Commentary to the Mishna, Rosh HaShana 4:7)

Thus, the fear of judgment prevails over the sense of joy, and we do not say Hallel. Nevertheless, Maimonides writes:

> On Rosh HaShana and on Yom Kippur we do not say Hallel because they are days of repentance and awe and fear, not of great joy. (*Mishneh Torah*, Laws of Megilla 3:6)

A close reading of Maimonides reveals that there is some joy on Rosh HaShana and Yom Kippur, but it is not "great" joy. The Midrash states this even more explicitly:

> "The days in which they are to be fashioned, and for it too there was one of them" (Ps. 139:16) – This is the Day of Atonement for Israel, which is [a day of] great joy before Him who spoke and the world was created, and who gave it to Israel with great love.... Moreover, when God forgives Israel's sins, He is not grieved, but rather filled with great rejoicing. He tells the mountains and hills, the streams and the valleys, "Come and make a great rejoicing with Me, that I am forgiving the sins of Israel." (*Eliyahu Rabba*, ch. 1)

We have here a wondrous combination of two polar opposites: we do not say Hallel on Yom Kippur, but it is a day of great joy, a day on which it is appropriate to declare, "Happy are you, O Israel!"

Two more sources reflect the same contrast. *Midrash Tanḥuma* teaches:

> "For the day of the Lord is great and very terrible, and who can abide it?" (Joel 2:11) – This refers to Yom Kippur, when the Books of the Living and of the Dead are sealed. (*Tanḥuma, Vayishlaḥ* 2)

Man stands in judgment, and "Your judgments are a great deep" (Ps. 36:7) – he does not know what the verdict will be. Maimonides (*Mishneh Torah*, Laws of Repentance 3:5) emphasizes that the weighing of sins and good deeds is "carried out according to the wisdom of the Knowing God"; we are incapable of understanding this.

On the other hand, the Mishna teaches, "There were no better days for Israel than the fifteenth of Av and Yom Kippur" (Mishna Taanit 4:8). Here too the seemingly contradictory meanings of this holy day are combined: it is a holiday, but at the same time a "very terrible" day of judgment.

Concerning a communal sin offering, the Torah states:

> If you err and do not observe all these commandments which the Lord has spoken to Moses … and it shall be forgiven them, for it was without knowing, and they have brought their offering, a sacrifice made by fire to the Lord, and their sin offering (*ḥatatam*) is before the Lord, for acting without knowing what they did. (Num. 15:22–25)

Most of the commentators understand the word "*ḥatatam*" as a reference to the sin offering that is offered to God. However, it may refer not only to the sin offering but also to the sin itself. If this is so, then the verse is saying that "their sin is before the Lord." Standing before God usually has positive associations: the sacrifices are "for their favor before the Lord" (Ex. 28:38); Hannah declares, "I have poured out my soul before the Lord" (1 Sam. 1:15); and so on. In this verse, it seems that the standing before God is negative – the sin too was done before God, in the sense in which *Ḥazal* explain that Nimrod, described as a "mighty hunter before the Lord" (Gen. 10:9), aspired to rebel and cause others to rebel.

Since the sin is "before the Lord," the confession must be too. Maimonides teaches:

> If a person transgresses any of the commandments of the Torah, whether a positive command or a negative command, whether he transgressed willingly or inadvertently, when he repents and returns from his sin, he must confess before the blessed God. (*Mishneh Torah,* Laws of Repentance 1:1)

The sin is "before God," and our repentance too is "before God." These are two aspects that together are part of the dual nature of Yom Kippur.

Our aim on Yom Kippur is not just to evade the divine attribute of justice and God's anger, but to achieve purification before our Father in heaven. We must purify ourselves and repent, while at the same time waiting for God to purify us. In a famous poem, Rabbi Yehuda HaLevi writes, "I went out toward You, and I found You going out toward me." This is what we hope for: to purify ourselves and to be purified from Heaven.

Sometimes purification is not the result of repentance, but its catalyst. The most important part of the service of the High Priest on Yom Kippur involves his entry into the Holy of Holies to make atonement for the Temple itself. Only after he emerges does he confess over the scapegoat, which atones for the other transgressions. One would think that the order should be reversed: first he should atone for the nation's transgressions, and only afterwards enter the Holy of Holies. However, the Torah stipulates, "When he has made an end of atoning for the holy place, and the Tent of Meeting, and the altar, he shall present the live goat" (Lev. 16:20). It is by virtue of the purification inside the Holy of Holies that atonement can be achieved through the scapegoat.

The same is true for every individual who longs for some divine assistance even before he repents. There are two kinds of purification on

Yom Kippur: "For on that day He will forgive you, to purify you, that you may be purified from all your sins before the Lord" (Lev. 16:30). One is the purification achieved by man – repentance. In his *Mesillat Yesharim* (ch. 16), Ramḥal explains that the trait of purity means "perfection of one's heart and thoughts … so that a person leaves no room for the evil inclination in his actions." A person purifies his own thoughts, desires, and aspirations.

At the same time, there is also a special purification that comes only from God and that frees a person from his sins. Yom Kippur changes the situation in which "your iniquities have made a separation between you and your God" (Is. 59:2), and helps a person to repent, to turn over a new leaf, to extricate himself from the vicious cycle of sin. This is the meaning of the vision of Ezekiel:

> Then I will sprinkle clean water on you, and you shall be pure; from all your uncleanness and from all your idols will I purify you. I will give you also a new heart, and put within you a new spirit, and I will take away the stony heart out of your flesh, and I will give you a heart of flesh. (Ezek. 36:25–26)

On Jewish Faith During the Holocaust

> "For the day of the Lord is great and very terrible, and who can abide it?" (Joel 2:11) – This refers to Yom Kippur, when the Books of the Living and of the Dead are sealed. (*Tanḥuma, Vayishlaḥ* 2)

According to the Tosafot (Rosh HaShana 16b), the three books that are open on Rosh HaShana deal with one's fate in the World to Come. Nahmanides (*Torat HaAdam, Shaar HaGemul*), however, maintains that the judgment on Rosh HaShana and Yom Kippur concerns one's fate in this world. In our prayers we say that God regards every living thing, remembering it for life or for death; on Rosh HaShana it is written, and on Yom Kippur it is sealed.

In the verses that we say with the *Seliḥot* we emphasize the fear of the Day of Judgment, that great and very terrible day; "who can abide it?" We have a very real sense that "my flesh shudders for fear of You, and I am afraid of Your judgments" (Ps. 119:120). It is customary that on Rosh HaShana the *sheliaḥ tzibbur* adds the words, "O faithful God, as You prepare to pass judgment, were You to reach to the depths of judgment, who would ever be found righteous before You and acquitted by such judgment, O Holy One."

The fear of "the depths of judgment" is illustrated in a remarkable midrash. In *Parashat Mishpatim* it says, "You shall not afflict any widow or orphan. If you afflict them at all and they cry to Me, I will surely hear their cry" (Ex. 22:21–22).

The Midrash elaborates:

> "If you afflict them at all" – whether excessively or slightly… R. Yishmael and R. Shimon were being taken to their execution. R. Shimon said to R. Yishmael, "My teacher, my heart is pained since I do not know why I am being killed." R. Yishmael answered him, "Did anyone ever come before you in judgment, or with a question, and you kept him waiting while you finished your drink, or while you tied your shoe, or while you wrapped yourself in your tallit? The Torah says, 'If you afflict them at all' – whether excessively or slightly." At this, R. Shimon said to him, "My teacher, you have comforted me!" (*Mekhilta DeRabbi Yishmael, Nezikin* 18)

Rabban Shimon b. Gamliel is comforted when he understands that he deserved to be put to death. What was his sin? That he kept waiting someone who had come to ask him a halakhic question. As we know, God is exacting with *tzaddikim* to within a hair's breadth. Rabban Shimon is aware of this, and thanks R. Yishmael, telling him, "My teacher, you have comforted me."

The demanding nature of the attribute of justice heightens our sense of "My flesh shudders for fear of You." However, this sense comes only from fear of Heaven. *Ḥazal* taught, "'I am black' – all year long, 'but comely' – on Yom Kippur" (*Yalkut Shimoni* 11:982). Our special beauty on Yom Kippur comes from the fact that every one of us is at the pinnacle of fear of Heaven.

Yet, I have to ask – and I pray that I am not crossing a line – does the fear of divine punishment really lead to fear of Heaven? Rabbi Yisrael Salanter developed a system where fear of Heaven was based solely on fear of punishment, but it is fair to say that this approach did not last.

On Yom Kippur we seek to attain fear of Heaven, but it is not certain that fear of punishment, thinking about the Books of the Living and of the Dead that are opened, is the right way to go about it.

My friends, during the darkest time in Jewish history, the Holocaust, Jews saw with their own eyes that "some die without judgment" (Prov. 13:23). Not only individuals but millions died, as it were, without judgment. But something extraordinary happened: Jews who saw with their own eyes the murder of innocent babies, men, and women, whose children were snatched out of their arms, Jews who lost all hope of ever emerging alive from that hell – they all came together on Yom Kippur in the bunkers and prayed! What inspired them? Was it fear of judgment? These Jews experienced the worst concealment of God's face in history, yet they stood and cried out, as Job did: "Though He slay me, yet I will trust in Him" (Job 13:15).

Whatever else is true, for those Jews on that Yom Kippur, their fate in this world was of no concern. What, then, were they feeling and thinking as they prayed? The answer is to be found in the Mishna:

> R. Akiva said, "Happy are you, O Israel! Before whom are you purified; who purifies you? Your Father in heaven, as it is written, 'Then I shall sprinkle pure water upon you, and you shall be pure' (Ezek. 36:25), and it is written, 'The hope (*mikve*) of Israel is the Lord' (Jer. 17:13) – just as a *mikve* purifies those who are defiled, so the Holy One, blessed be He, purifies Israel." (Mishna Yoma 8:9)

R. Akiva was killed during a very dark time in Jewish history. For that very reason his words – "Happy are you, O Israel!" – are a source of inspiration for the entire Jewish people, even during the most difficult periods.

During the Holocaust, no one felt the fear of "who will live and who will die," but rather the exaltation of "Happy are you, O Israel." It was this feeling that made Jews declare, "May His great name be magnified and sanctified." I was fortunate that when I prayed on Yom Kippur there was already hope of being saved.[1] But even those who had no such

1. On Yom Kippur 5705 (1944), Rav Amital hid in a cellar in the city of Grosswardein while the Hungarian army was already preparing for the coming invasion by the Russian army. He was liberated from the labor camp on Simḥat Torah of 5705.

hope stood on Yom Kippur and prayed together with all of Israel, "And so place the fear of You, Lord our God, over all that You have made.... And so grant honor, Lord, to Your people."

What about us, will our entire experience of Yom Kippur be limited to the fear of judgment? Will we not feel the holy message that the Jews in the Holocaust left for us? That message demands that we pray for God's sovereignty. Our fear of judgment should not be based on fear of punishment, but on the fear that, Heaven forbid, we will be considered wicked before God. We must hear the call, "Before whom are you purified?" and be proud that it is God Himself who purifies us.

On the other hand, we cannot be indifferent to what is going on around us. That would involve lying to ourselves, and with lies one cannot stand before God. Ignoring the world is inhumane and un-Jewish. Even when things are most difficult, one is obligated to show concern for the individual and his fate. At the end of the Second Temple period, Rabban Yoḥanan b. Zakkai set out to save Judaism, so he requested, "Give me Yavne and its sages" (Gittin 56b). But, at the same time as he made this fateful request, with its profound consequences for the Jewish people, he also asked for a certain medicinal treatment for R. Tzadok, who had fasted forty years to prevent the destruction of Jerusalem. We see that, even at the most difficult and most important moments, the fate of every individual cries out to Heaven, and touches the heart of every Jew.

We need to understand that "the day of the Lord is great and very terrible, and who can abide it?" and, at the same time, to sincerely feel, "Happy are you, O Israel!"

Atonement and Purification

> R. Akiva said, "Happy are you, O Israel! Before whom are you purified; who purifies you? Your Father in heaven, as it is written, 'Then I shall sprinkle pure water upon you, and you shall be pure' (Ezek. 36:25), and it is written, 'The hope (*mikve*) of Israel is the Lord' (Jer. 17:13) – just as a *mikve* purifies those who are defiled, so the Holy One, blessed be He, purifies Israel." (Mishna Yoma 8:9)

The atonement of Yom Kippur is different from any other atonement. One who brings a sin offering or repents seeks to save himself from divine punishment, to save himself from the fate of Hell. The atonement of Yom Kippur comes not only to save a person from punishment, but also to purify him. The uniqueness of Yom Kippur lies in this dimension of purification.

What is repentance? The sinner abandons his evil ways, commits to wholehearted fulfillment of God's commandments, and strictly observes every precept. From his point of view, all is as it was. The same is true from the point of view of the Master of the universe, who shows compassion toward the penitent and accepts him with open arms. *Ḥazal* teach:

> "Lord, Lord" – I am He before one sins and I am He after one sins and repents. (Rosh HaShana 17b)

Seemingly, then, everything is back the way it was.

In truth, however, the reality is not so simple. Sin is an ongoing reality that creates a barrier between man and his Creator; "your iniquities have made a separation between you and your God" (Is. 59:2). Repentance breaks down the barrier created by the sin, but the distance between man and God remains. Although everything seems back the way it was, the heart senses that "there rose up a mountain between them" (Ḥullin 7b), between man and his Creator.

This is why the atonement of Yom Kippur is necessary. On Yom Kippur the individual returns to God and draws close to Him; this is the atonement that brings with it purification.

The Midrash teaches, "Were it not for Yom Kippur, the world would not exist" (*Pirkei DeRabbi Eliezer*, ch. 45). What does this mean? King David declares, "As for me, the nearness of God is my good" (Ps. 73:28). Divine service that lacks closeness to God cannot be sustained. This applies not only to the love of God, which is certainly based on closeness, but also to the fear of Him. For how long can a person fear God if the distance between them is so great? Rabban Yoḥanan b. Zakkai's wish for his disciples was, "May it be His will that you will fear Heaven like you fear mortals" (Berakhot 28b). Can a mortal king inspire fear from someone who is outside his control? The primary obstacle to attaining love and fear of God comes from feeling distant from Him.

The purification of Yom Kippur "renews our days as of old" and brings one closer to God, which heightens one's love and fear of Him. This is what the Midrash means that were it not for the purification of Yom Kippur, were it not for that sense of renewed closeness, the world could not exist.

What is "purity"? Purity means a cleansing of the heart so there is no barrier, nothing foreign that interferes. *Ḥazal* teach that every sin brings into existence an "angel of destruction." This angel exists not only in the upper worlds, but also settles in the recesses of the person's soul. The four types of atonement discussed in the Gemara (Yoma 86a) apply to different kinds of transgressions. But Yom Kippur adds the extra dimension of purification; it removes from the heart those foreign elements and "angels of destruction." The atonement of purification on

Yom Kippur comes to remove the defects left in our hearts by our sins; it removes the barrier between us and God. For this reason, the atonement of Yom Kippur is comprehensive: "for on that day He will forgive you, to purify you, that you may be purified from all your sins before the Lord" (Lev. 16:30). This atonement brings a person closer to God.

By virtue of the atonement of purification on Yom Kippur, there are no more destructive angels to interfere, blocking and distancing us from God. Atonement cleanses a person, as the Midrash teaches:

> "I am black but comely, O daughters of Jerusalem; like the tents of Kedar, like the curtains of Solomon" (Song 1:5). "Like the curtains of Solomon" – just as a garment that becomes soiled may be cleansed, so Israel, although they transgress, they return in repentance before God. (Exodus Rabba 23:10)

Maimonides too emphasizes:

> How exalted is repentance! Only yesterday he was separated from the Lord, God of Israel, as it is said, "Your iniquities were making a separation between you and your God" (Is. 59:2).... Today, the same individual is closely attached to the Divine Presence, as it is said, "And as for you who cleave to the Lord your God..." (Deut. 4:4). (*Mishneh Torah,* Laws of Repentance 7:7)

The purpose of the atonement of Yom Kippur is to achieve complete purification, which enables a person to achieve closeness to God and cleave to Him.

In reference to Yom Kippur, R. Akiva does not merely cite a verse that speaks of atonement for sin – "for on that day He will forgive you, to purify you, that you may be purified from all your sins before the Lord" (Lev. 16:30). He also brings verses that speak of a broader purification: "Then I will sprinkle pure water up on you, and you shall be pure; from all your uncleanness..." (Ezek. 36:25); "the hope (*mikve*) of Israel is the Lord" (Jer. 17:13). R. Akiva teaches us that on Yom Kippur we achieve a renewed bond – a pure, clear bond – with our Father in heaven.

Two Goats – Two Kinds of Atonement

In the Yom Kippur service we find two channels of atonement. The first involves the goat that is offered in the Temple, atoning for the defilement of the Temple; the second involves the scapegoat, to atone for "all the other transgressions in the Torah."

While these two channels are related, they are substantially different. The first goat, sacrificed in the Temple, atones for impurity caused in the most intimate of places, while the other goat atones for other transgressions.

These two channels are reflected in different dimensions within a person's heart. *Sefer Yetzira* discusses the concept of sanctity in the context of "*nefesh*," the essence of a person's soul. Just as there are physical locations that are sacred, and times that are sacred, so there is a sanctity in the innermost soul of man (see the introduction of the *Shelah* to Leviticus). There is a dimension in our soul that parallels the Holy of Holies. Every person has within him a place of aspirations, desires, and dreams: a place of concealed emotions.

In an ideal situation, a person's inner world remains pure, innocent, and genuine, and his innermost aspirations are for purity, integrity, sanctity, and knowledge of God. And if one's inner world is pure, then any sin that he commits is nothing more than a misstep that does not reflect his true essence. As the prophet says, "you have stumbled in your iniquity" (Hos. 14:2). Concerning such missteps, King David declared, "Happy is he whose transgression is forgiven; whose sin is covered" (Ps. 32:1). Happy is one whose sins do not characterize and define him.

The Midrash teaches:

> "I am black but comely, O daughters of Jerusalem, like the tents of Kedar, like the curtains of Solomon" (Song 1:5) – Just as a garment that becomes soiled may be cleaned and restored, so Israel soil themselves all year around with transgressions, but Yom Kippur comes and brings atonement. (*Yalkut Shimoni* 11:982)

In other words, the effect of the sin is external, so it can be cleansed and washed away.

However, sometimes impurity can seep in and contaminate the Holy of Holies. The inner "I" is affected when it becomes filled with pride and falseness, when the ambition to build a career comes at the expense of more important goals, when one desires the pleasures of the world rather than sanctity. God tells the prophet Ezekiel, "And behold, you are for them like a song for flutes by one who has a pleasant voice, and can play the instrument well, for they hear the words but they do not carry them out" (Ezek. 33:32). In other words, the people listen to the words of the prophet for their beauty, like the music of a flute, but they do not carry out God's will.

When a person's inner world becomes defiled, then sins are no longer occasional missteps, but rather a grave phenomenon that reflects a person's essence.

As we said, the process of purification and atonement is two-fold. First there is atonement for the Holy of Holies, for that innermost and holiest point. Only afterwards comes the next stage: "And when he has made an end of atoning for the holy place, and the Tent of Meeting, and the altar, he shall present the live goat" (Lev. 16:20). The atonement for sins only comes after the roots of sin have been remedied. That is how it was in the Temple, and so it is in the human soul: inner purification precedes the mending of one's actions. Before reciting *Viduy* we declare, "You know every secret since the world began." We acknowledge that God knows what is going on in our innermost soul; only after this we go on to list our sins.

In *Kitvei HaAri* it is written that Yom Kippur is the day of repairing our inner selves. A person's innermost soul is like the Holy of Holies, and we need to first examine our inner selves, our aspirations, our desires. Only afterward we seek atonement for our other transgressions.

"Your Face, O Lord, I Shall Seek"

> "Your eyes saw my unshaped flesh, for in Your book all things are written: the days also in which they are to be fashioned, and for it too there was one of them" [or, "and one of them was for Him"] (Ps. 139:16) – .... This refers to the Day of Atonement for the Jewish people, which is a great rejoicing before Him who spoke and the world came into being, who gave it to Israel with great love. (*Eliyahu Rabba*, ch. 1)

Yom Kippur is not part of the regular cycle of the year; it is a day that belongs "to Him," to God. A year includes 365 days, but one day stands out from all the others. In the Midrash we find:

> The solar year comprises 365 days. The numerical value of *HaSatan* ("Satan") is 364, meaning that Satan makes accusations throughout the year except on Yom Kippur. (Leviticus Rabba 21:4)

Three hundred sixty-four days of the year Satan accuses us of not behaving as we should. There is one single day – Yom Kippur – that breaks this cycle, when Satan is silent. Throughout the year we experience the routine of "sunrise, sunset." This routine also affects our relationship with

God: "Day by day they seek Me" (Is. 58:2); even seeking God becomes routine. Then Yom Kippur comes and breaks up the routine.

In *Midrash Eliyahu Rabba* there is an opinion that the special day that breaks the routine is Shabbat. Similarly, in *Yalkut Shimoni* (11:982) there are two interpretations of the verse, "I am black but comely" (Song 1:5). One states, "'I am black' – on weekdays, 'but comely' – on Shabbat," while the other proposes, "'I am black' – all year long, 'but comely' – on Yom Kippur.'" Just as Shabbat breaks the routine of the week, so Yom Kippur, which is *Shabbat Shabbaton,* breaks the routine of the year.

On Yom Kippur the High Priest brings all of the day's sacrifices himself, including both of the daily *tamid* sacrifices. In other words, even sacrifices which are not specifically related to Yom Kippur, but are part of the daily sacrificial service in the Temple, assume a special character on Yom Kippur. All of the day's sacrifices are disconnected from the routine and stand apart, by virtue of the High Priest.

For 364 days out of the year Satan makes accusations, because his power comes from routine. It is routine that erodes our consciousness that "the whole earth is filled with His glory." Routine imprisons us. On Yom Kippur we begin our prayers with *Kol Nidrei,* in which we seek to free ourselves from the prison of routine that confines us throughout the year. We need to free ourselves from the confinement of routine.

The shackles of routine affect our entire being. The *Shelah* (*Kitzur Shelah* 101) writes that at the end of the *Amida* one should say a verse that begins and ends with the letters corresponding to those at the beginning and end of his name, so that he will remember his name on the Day of Judgment. A person's name represents his true essence and the role that God intended for him. Jonah tried to flee from his destiny, and on Yom Kippur we read the Book of Jonah to remind ourselves that one cannot flee from God.

The flight from one's destiny and essence is also a form of prison. We are locked into certain presumptions concerning the lifestyle that is appropriate for us, even when it involves running away from God. On Yom Kippur we free ourselves from our shackles. On Yom Kippur in a Jubilee year, the indentured servants with pierced ears who stayed with their masters hear the liberating blast of the shofar, reminding them that "'The Children of Israel are servants to Me' (Lev. 25:55) – not servants of servants" (Kiddushin 22b). We too seek to hear the sound of that shofar on Yom Kippur, to throw off the shackles of our own servitude and go back to being servants of God rather than servants of servants.

Satan causes us to lose touch with our real "I." Our "I" is in exile, in the sense of "I was in the midst of the exile" (Ezek. 1:1). God calls to us, "Why, when I came, was there no man; [why] when I called, was there none to answer?" (Is. 50:2). We make no answer because we are subjugated to ourselves and the routine of our lives. With our own hands we have built the prison that confines us, a prison in which "their fear of Me is like the commandment of men learned by rote" (29:13). Yom Kippur is the time to extricate ourselves from that prison.

The *Viduy* of Yom Kippur should likewise be recited as a break from routine, which requires abasement before God. When reciting *Viduy* in the Temple, the High Priest would begin with "*Anna Hashem*," and the priests and the people would bow and prostrate themselves. Speaking God's ineffable name itself expresses abasement, after which one can make confession.

The crux of *Viduy* is acknowledging sin, as explained in the Midrash:

> "And they gathered together to Mitzpa, and drew water, and poured it out before the Lord" (1 Sam. 7:6) – Did they pour out water before God? Rather, it teaches that they poured out their hearts in repentance like water, and they said, "We have sinned to the Lord!"... So Samuel took up their case and said to God, "Master of the world! Is it not true that all You demand of a person is that he say before You, 'I have sinned'? Now Israel say before You, 'We have sinned' – how can You not forgive them?" (*Yalkut Shimoni* 11:103)

Viduy and saying "I have sinned" are an essential condition for finding God. The prophet declares:

> I will go and return to My place, until they acknowledge their offense, and seek My face; in their affliction they will seek Me. (Hos. 5:15)

Rashi explains:

> I will leave them alone and go back to heaven…until they acknowledge their offense – hold themselves responsible and admit their guilt.

Only when we are able to admit that we are guilty will we merit closeness to God, and not the abandonment of us by the Divine Presence, Heaven forbid.

Earlier in the same chapter in Hosea we read:

> They shall go with their flocks and with their herds to seek the Lord, but they shall not find Him; He has withdrawn Himself from them. (5:6)

God, as it were, has withdrawn and removed Himself from the Jewish people, but they do not despair; they go seek Him, in the sense of "I opened to my beloved, but my beloved had turned away and was gone; my soul failed when he spoke; I sought him, but I could not find him; I called him, but he gave me no answer" (Song 5:6). A time will come when we have to seek God. The need is so great that it is imperative to pray for His assistance: "Why, Lord, do You stand far off; why do You hide Yourself in times of trouble?" (Ps. 10:1). Still, it is difficult to sever ourselves from our worldliness, our animalistic nature; we seek God "with our flocks and with our herds." We need to know that unless we disconnect from our animalistic nature, we will not be able to find God; He will still withdraw Himself from them.

The High Priest begins with his own private *Viduy*, then goes on to confess for his fellow priests, and finally confesses the sins of all of Israel. The confessions start with the individual and conclude with the entire nation. A person must confess for himself, but at the same time should see himself as part of the community. This consciousness influences the entire world:

> R. Meir used to teach, "Repentance is great, for on account of an individual who repents, the sins of the whole world are forgiven, as it is said, 'I will heal their backsliding, I will love them freely, for My anger is turned away from him' (Hos. 14:5) – the verse does not say, 'from them,' but rather 'from him.'" (Yoma 86b)

A person who repents affects all of Israel, provided he is not content with his own personal purification, but also feels the pain of what is happening to the rest of the Jewish people, as did the High Priest.

The Torah commands:

> And now, write this song for yourselves and teach it to the Children of Israel; put it in their mouths, that this song may be a witness for Me against the Children of Israel. (Deut. 31:19)

The content of the song is the story of repentance: the sin, the punishment, and repentance. This process is relevant to every person, and therefore individuals are also required to write it. However, writing the song is not enough; we are required to write the entire Torah, as Maimonides teaches:

> It is a positive commandment for each and every Jewish man to write a Torah scroll for himself, as it is said, "And now, write this song for yourselves" – i.e., write down the Torah, which contains this song, because the Torah should not be written as separate passages. (*Mishneh Torah,* Laws of Torah Scrolls 7:1)

According to Maimonides, the original mitzva required writing only the song. But the Torah was not given in stages; similarly, a person cannot sever himself from the rest of the Jewish people. The story of one's personal repentance must be integrated and assimilated into the larger process of collective repentance, and the song must be written as part of the Torah in its entirety.

On Yom Kippur we are required to examine not only our major actions, but even our minor deeds. Nahmanides cites the Midrash:

> When Rabban Shimon b. Gamliel and R. Yishmael b. Elisha were incarcerated, they were sentenced to death. R. Yishmael wept.
>
> Rabban Shimon b. Gamliel asked, "Why do you weep? In a short time you will be sharing in the portion of the righteous, and still you weep?"
>
> He replied, "I weep because we are being executed like idol worshippers, fornicators, murderers, and desecrators of Shabbat."
>
> He said, "My teacher, perhaps you were once sitting down to a meal or sleeping when a woman came to ask you a question about her *nidda* status, whether she is pure or impure, and you told her, 'Wait until I have slept'? But the Torah says, 'You shall not oppress any widow or orphan.'" (*Torat HaAdam, Shaar HaGemul*)

These great rabbis were not punished for major matters, but for a slight offense to the dignity of a woman who came to ask a halakhic question. Even minor misdeeds can have major consequences. The Gemara says, "What is an instance of *ḥillul Hashem*? Rav said, 'If I took meat from the *shoḥet* and did not pay for it immediately'" (Yoma 86a). Every one of us can be held responsible for *ḥillul Hashem*, which even Yom Kippur does not atone for: only death atones. All for not paying the *sḥohet* on time. We are required to cause *kiddush Hashem*, as Maimonides writes:

> To the extent that everyone praises him and loves him and is jealous of his conduct, this is considered a *kiddush Hashem*, regarding which Scripture says, "And He said to me, 'You are My servant, Israel, in whom I will be glorified'" (Is. 49:3). (*Mishneh Torah*, Laws of the Foundations of the Torah 5:11)

On Yom Kippur we are required to repent for both major and minor things. We need to hear the sound of our beloved knocking, the inner voice that says, "Of You my heart said, 'Seek My face'" and to be able to respond to God, "Your face, O Lord, I shall seek" (Ps. 27:8).

Ne'ila

"Open for Me the Gates of Righteousness"

> I sleep, but my heart wakes: hark, my beloved is knocking, saying, "Open for me, my sister, my love, my dove, my undefiled; for my head is filled with dew, and my locks with the drops of the night." I have put off my coat; how shall I put it on? I have washed my feet; how shall I soil them? My beloved put in his hand by the latchet of the door, and my heart was thrilled for him. I rose up to open for my beloved, and my hands dripped with myrrh, and my fingers with flowing myrrh, upon the handles of the lock. (Song 5:2–5)

> This is as it is written in the Midrash. "'I rose up to open for my beloved, and my hands dripped with myrrh, and my fingers with flowing myrrh, upon the handles of the lock' (Song 5:5). 'I rose up to open for my beloved' – This alludes to Shaḥarit. 'And my hands dripped with myrrh' – This alludes to Musaf. 'And my fingers with flowing myrrh' – This alludes to Minḥa. 'Upon the handles of the lock' – This alludes to the *Ne'ila* prayer." (Rabbenu Baḥya, *Kad HaKemaḥ, Kippurim* [2])

The *Ne'ila* service adds an additional dimension to the prayers of Yom Kippur. Here we try to respond to God's "knocking," to open our hearts to the "Beloved" who has "put in His hand by the latchet of the door." The feelings of uplift experienced throughout the day are themselves the sound of the Beloved knocking at the door. Our feelings are not a response to the voice of the Beloved, but rather the voice itself. This is how the Holy One, blessed be He, asks us, "Open for Me, My sister, My love."

The disciples of both the Vilna Gaon and the Baal Shem Tov taught that the heavenly voice declaring, "Return, return, O wayward children" (Ḥagiga 15b), finds its way to the consciousness of every Jew who entertains thoughts of repentance.

In the words of the psalm, "Of You my heart has said, 'Seek My face.' Your face, O Lord, I seek" (Ps. 27:8). In our hearts we hear a voice that says, "Seek My face." Rashi explains that this voice issues at God's bequest:

> "Of You" – From You, in Your service, my heart says, "Seek" – all of you, all of Israel – "My face."

We are called to respond to that inner voice, and to reply, "Your face, O Lord, I seek." Of course, in order to hear the voice that issues from God, we have to peel away all of the outer layers and open our hearts.

Happy is the person who hears the voice of the Beloved declaring, "Return, return, O wayward children." But there are some who, like Elisha b. Avuya, also hear the closing words of that call: "Return, return, O wayward children – except for *Aḥer*" (Ḥagiga 15b). Elisha b. Avuya did not understand that this call was directed at him, challenging him to exert himself and repent. Elisha b. Avuya gave up. One who feels that his heart is deaf to that heavenly call, that he has no way of repenting, someone who is told, "Everyone should repent – but not you," must understand that this feeling is itself a call to exert special efforts and to lift himself to the point where he can repent.

> Open for me the gates of righteousness; I will go in to them, and I will praise the Lord. This is the gate of the Lord into which the righteous shall enter. (Ps. 118:19–20)

It is taught in the name of the Baal Shem Tov that a righteous person stands before the gate and pleads, "Open for me the gates of righteousness." The response that comes from heaven is, "This is the gate of the Lord" – you are standing before a locked gate, and this sense of gates being locked is itself "the gate of the Lord." This teaching discusses the righteous, but is also relevant to each and every one of us who stands at the climax of this holy day and pleads, "Open us a gate at the time of the locking of the gate."

In order to merit the opening of the gates of heaven, we have to open the gates of our heart. With the words of the prayer "Open us a gate…," we request divine assistance that will allow us to open our hearts – even just the tiniest opening:

> "My Beloved is knocking, saying, 'Open for me'" – R. Yissa said, "The Holy One, blessed be He, says to Israel, 'My children, open for Me just one opening of repentance, be it as tiny as the point of a needle, and I will open for you openings [so wide] that wagons and carriages could pass through.'" (Song of Songs Rabba 5:2)

We must open our hearts to our true identity, our true calling and destiny, instead of trying to run away from it as Jonah tried to run away from God. It is said in the name of the *Shelah* (*Kitzur Shelah* 101) that there is special merit in reciting a verse at the end of one's daily prayers that begins and ends with the same letters as one's own name, in order to remember one's name on the Day of Judgment. This teaches us the danger that a person may forget his name on the Day of Judgment; he may deny his true identity. Throughout the year, throughout one's life, a person can conceal his real "I," and present an artificial self, while the real "I" is in exile, in the sense of "I was in the midst of the exile" (Ezek. 1:1, and as Rav Kook explains the verse in *Orot HaKodesh* III:97).

But on the Day of Judgment and Yom Kippur, we try to identify our true nature, our inner essence. On the Day of Judgment and on Yom Kippur a person stands with his real name. Our efforts during *Ne'ila* need to express that true inner self.

King David declares:

> Hear the right, O Lord; attend to my cry, give ear to my prayer, from lips without deceit. Let my sentence come forth from Your Presence, let Your eyes behold the right. (Ps. 17:1–2)

The Midrash explains:

> Why does David mention these five things in this verse, and then conclude, "Let my sentence come forth from Your Presence"? David said, "Master of the world, if my judgment is concluded on Yom Kippur in the morning, I will not be able to stand [in prayer for the rest of the day]. Rather, after I say *Shema* and pray four prayers – then 'let my sentence come forth from Your Presence.'" (*Yalkut Shimoni* 11:670)

We should pray from the depths of our hearts and the inner chambers of our souls, and plead, "Purify our hearts to serve You in truth."

A New Prayer

> What is the source of *Ne'ila*? R. Levi said, "'Even if you make many prayers' (Is. 1:15) – from here we learn that one who prays at length is answered."... R. Hiyya taught in the name of R. Yoḥanan, R. Shimon b. Ḥalafta in the name of R. Meir, "'As she continued praying before the Lord' (1 Sam. 1:12) – from this we learn that all who pray at length are answered." (Y. Berakhot 4:1)

On Yom Kippur we add *Ne'ila* – an extra prayer service, over and above the regular prayer services. The essence of *Ne'ila* is that we "pray at length"; it is "an extra prayer" (Yoma 8b) – and all who pray at length are answered.

There are two aspects to prayer in general, and *Ne'ila* in particular. One is petition, asking God for our needs. The other is a request for closeness to God. In discussing *Ne'ila*, Maimonides emphasizes the first aspect:

> They instituted a prayer after Minḥa close to sunset on fast days only, in order to increase petition and pleading on account of the fast. This is called the *Ne'ila* prayer – as if to say that the gates of heaven are closed (*nin'alu*) along with the sun, which becomes hidden – since it is said only close to sunset. (*Mishneh Torah,* Laws of Prayer 1:7)

However, from other sources it would seem that adding additional prayers is improper. The Midrash teaches:

> Antonius asked Rabbi [R. Yehuda HaNasi], "Should a person pray all the time?"
>
> He answered him, "That is forbidden."
>
> Antonius asked, "Why?"
>
> He told him, "In order that one will not become irreverent towards the Almighty."
>
> Antonius could not accept this. What did R. Yehuda HaNasi do? He approached him early in the morning and said, "My lord!" After a while he came and said, "Emperor!" And a little later he came and said, "Peace be upon you, O king!"
>
> Antonius said to him, "How dare you insult the crown?"
>
> R. Yehuda HaNasi said to him, "Listen to what you just said. If you, a mortal king, react that way when someone asks after your welfare at every moment, then how much more so for a person to show disrespect to the King of kings, the Holy One, blessed be He, by disturbing Him all the time." (*Tanḥuma, Miketz* 11)

R. Yehuda HaNasi explains that someone who prays at length puts himself first, with his personal needs taking precedence. This shows disrespect toward the King of kings.

How, then, could our Sages have instructed us to add more prayers on Yom Kippur? The answer is that prayer can also express the second aspect mentioned above – seeking closeness to God. Petitioning God for our needs is simply a means of drawing closer to God. *Ḥazal* taught that God leaves the righteous in need because He desires their prayers, and the barrenness of our biblical matriarchs is explained in the same way (Genesis Rabba 45:4). In other words, prayer at length that is motivated by a desire for closeness to God is in fact praiseworthy, concerning which we are taught, "Would that a person would pray all day long" (Berakhot 21a).

In fact, praying at length solely for one's needs can also be legitimate. The Talmud Yerushalmi, Tractate Berakhot, draws a distinction in this regard between the prayer of an individual and that of a community. For the community it is permissible to pray at length. If praying at length is forbidden because it leads to irreverence towards God, then this distinction makes no sense. Therefore, it would seem that, according to the Talmud Yerushalmi, communal prayer is fundamentally different from the prayer of the individual. In the Zohar we find:

> Come and see: R. Shimon said, "The prayer of the many rises up before the Holy One, blessed be He, and He makes Himself a crown of that prayer, because it rises up in different ways and includes different shades. Since it comprises different shades, it becomes a crown and is placed upon the head of the eternal righteous One. But the prayer of an individual is not a composite; it rises in only one manner, and therefore the prayer of the individual is not assured of acceptance like the prayer of the community." (Zohar, *Vayishlaḥ* 167b)

In communal prayer, every person contributes his own special aspect, and the overall result is a grand, multi-colored crown. Communal prayer is not a tiresome repetition of the same request, but rather a magnificent crown with which God adorns Himself.

In the same way, prayer at length from a spiritually great individual is likewise desirable. *Ḥazal* taught (see Rashi, Gen. 30:8) that our matriarch Rachel prayed and pleaded to God for children. Moses too prayed "until he wearied Him" (Berakhot 32a), meaning that he offered endless pleading and supplication. This is unique to someone who is truly great – his prayer is like the prayer of a community, not like the prayer of an individual.

Nevertheless, the *Ne'ila* prayer has a special status. Even an individual praying alone on Yom Kippur says *Ne'ila* – as many of our friends serving in the army are doing. After all of the lengthy prayers and confessions of the day, *Ne'ila* is something different. Our feelings as we approach the end of the day, as our verdict is about to be sealed, have a special quality. The sense of broken-heartedness, of "in my distress I call upon the Lord" (Ps. 18:7), the feeling of a drowning man trying to reach the shore – all of this turns *Ne'ila* into a unique prayer. It is fundamentally different, not just a repetition of what we have already said.

Moreover, there is a special dimension to a prayer in which a person achieves complete repentance. Maimonides writes:

> Among the methods of repentance is for the penitent to constantly call out before God, crying and entreating... and changing his name, as if to say, "I am a different person, not the same one who committed those acts," and changing everything he does to the good and to the straight path. (*Mishneh Torah,* Laws of Repentance 2:2)

Someone who says, "I am a different person," is someone who has undergone change. Until now he prayed from one spiritual place, and now he prays from a different spiritual place, one that reflects his new state. One who prays *Ne'ila* is not the same person who prayed Shaḥarit, and therefore even if he prays alone, his prayer is nevertheless different and new.

Ne'ila is a new prayer, a prayer of repentance, a sincere seeking of closeness to God. Repentance as the day draws to a close, with the closing of the gates, is repentance that is "upon the handles of the lock."

Let us join to our prayers the prayers of our Jewish brethren who do not know how to pray, or who are unable to, and with these feelings of profound brokenness and yearning for closeness to God, let us approach the *Ne'ila* prayer.

"The Sound of My Beloved Knocking"

> This is as it is written in the Midrash, "'I rose up to open for my beloved, and my hands dripped with myrrh, and my fingers with flowing myrrh, upon the handles of the lock' (Song 5:5). 'I rose up to open for my beloved' – this alludes to Shaḥarit. 'And my hands dripped with myrrh' – an allusion to Musaf. 'And my fingers with flowing myrrh' – this is Minḥa. 'Upon the handles of the lock' – this is the *Ne'ila* prayer." (Rabbenu Baḥya, *Kad HaKemaḥ, Kippurim* [2])

If we study this profound midrash, cited by Rabbenu Baḥya, we find two messages. The first describes the sound of "the Beloved" knocking – the special appeal that the Holy One, blessed be He, makes to the Jewish people on Yom Kippur. This message is related to *Ḥazal*'s teaching in a different midrash:

> "I am black but comely, O daughters of Jerusalem, like the tents of Kedar, like the curtains of Solomon" (Song 1:5). "Black" – all year long, "but comely" – on Yom Kippur. (*Yalkut Shimoni* 11:982)

On Yom Kippur, we are in a different state than during the rest of the year. This state of "'comely' – on Yom Kippur" allows for a renewed bond between the Jewish people and the Master of the world.

The image of God waiting, as it were, outside of the locked door, begins with a knock:

> I sleep, but my heart wakes: hark, my Beloved is knocking, saying, "Open for Me, My sister, My love, My dove, My undefiled; for My head is filled with dew, and My locks with the drops of the night." I have put off my coat; how shall I put it on? I have washed my feet; how shall I soil them? My Beloved put in His hand by the latchet of the door, and my heart was thrilled for Him. I rose up to open for my Beloved, and my hands dripped with myrrh, and my fingers with flowing myrrh, upon the handles of the lock. (Song 5:2–5)

Throughout the year we hear "my Beloved knocking." God tries to enter our hearts, but we are lazy: "I have put off my coat; how shall I put it on? I have washed my feet; how shall I soil them?" We dismiss God's call; throughout the year we are too busy to hear the sound of His knocking. But on Yom Kippur the Holy One, blessed be He, embarks on a new initiative: "My Beloved put in His hand by the latchet of the door, and my heart was thrilled for Him." God gives us another opportunity on Yom Kippur. This is the first message in the midrash, focusing on God reaching out to the Jewish people.

The second message relates to our response. God makes an opening for us, and we seek to draw closer: Shaḥarit, Musaf, Minḥa, and – finally – *Ne'ila*. We need to make an opening, even just a tiny one; we need to open the gates of our heart.

"I rose up to open for my Beloved" – How does a person make an opening for God? King David says, "Lift up your heads, O you gates, and lift them up, you everlasting doors, that the King of glory may enter" (Ps. 24:9). All gates are open before the King of glory, the King of kings, so what is it that we must open? It seems that there is one place where the Holy One, blessed be He, wishes – as it were – to enter, and that is man's heart. We must open the gates of our hearts to the King of glory and allow Him to enter.

The heart, as a rule, is not always open. Throughout the year we have studied, heard, and read, but many of the lessons remain piled outside a heart that is shut tight. They say in the name of the rebbe of Kotzk concerning the verse, "And these things which I command you this day shall be *upon your heart*" (Deut. 6:6): "The words are placed *upon* the heart so that, at the right time, a time when the heart is open, they will be able to enter." So let us open our hearts and allow all those things to enter. We must respond to the knocking of the Beloved and open our heart to Him – before He turns away and is gone. If we open the gates of our heart, the gates of heaven will also be opened to those who knock in repentance.

Throughout the day we have engaged in repentance and confessions, and we hope with all our heart to see the gate open. We long to hear words of appeasement from the Holy One, blessed be He. Our Sages included as part of the *Amida* the formula, "the King who pardons and forgives our iniquities and those of all His people, the House of Israel, and makes our guilt pass away, every single year." Five times over the course of the day we repeat this blessing, and we seek to open the gates.

It is told of Rabbi Levi Yitzḥak of Berditchev that he was once the *sheliaḥ tzibbur* for *Ne'ila,* and when he reached the conclusion of the blessing, "the King who pardons and forgives," he stopped, saying nothing for a long time. The congregation waited tensely in silence, until Rabbi Levi Yitzḥak suddenly called out, "Blessed are You, Lord, the King who pardons and forgives our iniquities and those of all His people, the House of Israel, and makes our guilt pass away, every single year, King of all the earth, who sanctifies Israel and Yom Kippur." After Yom Kippur was over, his disciples asked him what had happened. Why did he stand silently, and what caused him to suddenly break his silence? Rabbi Levi Yitzḥak replied that he had seen a grave accusation against the Jewish people in heaven, and the gates of forgiveness and atonement were about to be locked. He therefore interrupted his prayer and stopped. "I tried to defend our holy nation, Israel," he explained. "I wept, I cried, but I could not change the decree. Then I remembered something that had happened in our home when I was a young boy.

"In those days my mother, of blessed memory, kept a special cupboard for candies, out of reach of our little hands. But sometimes, when we really wanted something sweet, we had a trick that always worked. We would stand in front of the cupboard where we knew that she had hidden the candies, and we would start to say, 'Blessed are You, O Lord our God, King of the universe, through whose word everything came to be.' And then my mother had no choice; she had to let us eat some of the candy, for otherwise our blessing would have been uttered in vain.

"And so," Rabbi Levi Yitzḥak concluded, "I did the same thing today. When I saw that there was a very grave accusation against Israel in heaven, and there would be – Heaven forbid – no forgiveness for Israel, I began to say the blessing, including God's name: 'the King who pardons and forgives our iniquities.' We can rely on the Master of the world that He will forgive our iniquities and not allow our blessing to have been said in vain!"

Let us also offer genuine and heartfelt prayer to the King who forgives our iniquities; let us desist from the oppression that is in our hands, and return to performing wholeheartedly the statutes that God desires, and may the Holy One, blessed be He, hear our prayers and accept us in complete repentance before Him.

Opening of the Gates of the Heart

"Our Father, our King – open the gates of heaven to our prayers." This is a constant request, quietly underlying all our prayers on Yom Kippur and growing especially intense as we reach *Ne'ila*. Together with this request to open the gates of heaven, we make another request: to open the heart of the community and of each individual: "Open for Me, My sister, My love, My dove, My undefiled; for My head is filled with dew, and My locks with the drops of the night" (Song 5:2).

Rabbenu Baḥya writes:

> This is as it is written in the Midrash, "'I rose up to open for my beloved, and my hands dripped with myrrh and my fingers with flowing myrrh, upon the handles of the lock' (Song 5:5) – 'I rose up to open for my beloved' – this alludes to Shaḥarit; 'and my hands dripped with myrrh' – an allusion to Musaf; 'and my fingers with flowing myrrh' – this is Minḥa; 'upon the handles of the lock' – this is the *Ne'ila* prayer. (*Kad HaKemaḥ, Kippurim* [2])

The Midrash tells us that we must exert ourselves to open the gates of our heart, and each of the prayer services of the day contributes towards this goal. The final prayer, *Ne'ila,* is the closest to the realization of this mission – the opening of the gates.

In the Talmud Yerushalmi (Berakhot 4:1) the *Amora'im* debate whether praying at length is desirable and proper only for the community as a whole, or also for the individual. The halakhic conclusion is that there is benefit even from the lengthy prayer of the individual, since God desires his prayer too: "Let me hear your voice, for your voice is sweet and your countenance is comely" (Song 2:14), and "would that a person would pray all day long" (Berakhot 21a).

On Yom Kippur praying at length plays an important role in a person's relationship with himself. The lengthy prayer helps to open the gates of one's heart to our Father in heaven. Praying at length also contains an element of struggle. Our patriarch Jacob gave to Joseph "that which I took from the hand of the Emorite with my sword and with my bow" (Gen. 48:22), which Onkelos translates, "with my prayer and with my entreaty."

In our prayers to God, it is essential that we pray from a position of humility and meekness: "A poor man speaks entreaties" (Prov. 18:23), "a prayer of the afflicted when he faints, and pours out his heart before the Lord" (Ps. 102:1). At the same time, when a person prays with the aim of opening the gates of his heart, he needs to engage in a mighty struggle, "with my sword and with my bow," to cause the gates of his heart to open.

In Minḥa on Yom Kippur we read the Book of Jonah. Avudraham explains the reason for this custom:

> To teach the whole world that no one who has committed transgressions can escape from God, as it is written, "Where shall I go from Your spirit? Or where shall I flee from Your Presence? If I ascend up into heaven, You are there; if I make my bed in *Sheol,* behold – You are there" (Ps. 139:7–8). (*Siddur Avudraham,* Prayers of Yom Kippur)

Jonah tried to run away from God but nearly drowned at sea: "And there was a mighty tempest in the sea, so that the ship seemed likely to be wrecked" (Jonah 1:4). Like Jonah, we too have a sense that the Children of Israel are facing the threat of being wrecked, Heaven forbid. And yet, at this critical time – to our shame – we go down into the bowels of the ship, lie down, and go to sleep. We flee from our destiny, even at such a fateful time!

On this great and holy day we hear a heavenly voice proclaiming, "Return, return, O wayward children!" (Jer. 3:14). Elisha b. Avuya heard the same heavenly voice, but thought that it was not addressing him. The disciples of the Baal Shem Tov asked (see *Degel Maḥaneh Efraim, Vayikra*), if we cannot hear the heavenly voice, why does it call upon us to repent? The answer is that this heavenly voice represents the thoughts of repentance that are always present in our hearts. On Yom Kippur we are able to hear them; on Yom Kippur we express our desire to repent.

But it is important to know that even someone who hears the heavenly voice calling for repentance will not always accept upon himself to perform God's will and to fulfill his destiny in the world. A person may respond to the demand, "What do you mean, O sleeper? Arise, call upon your God" (Jonah 1:6), and even start confessing, acknowledging that "for my sake this great tempest is upon you" (v. 12), but sometimes the very confession itself is a sort of running away. Even someone who repents may lack the courage to acknowledge, "I am not fulfilling my destiny; I am fleeing from it."

In order to truly fulfill our destiny, we must truly experience the earthquake, the great storm, the sense that "I cried to the Lord out of my distress, and He answered me; from out of the belly of *Sheol* I cried, and You heard my voice" (2:3). In the mighty battle of prayer, we must open that which is locked in our hearts, stop running away, and return to God wholeheartedly.

Like the Prayer of an Infant

Jewish prayer contains many different elements: prayer substitutes for the Temple sacrifices, it is "service of the heart," it anchors man's loftiest emotions, and also enables us to contemplate the greatness of God. These elements underlie all of our prayers, but it seems that *Ne'ila* represents one main principle: "additional pleading and petition" (*Mishneh Torah*, Laws of Prayer 1:7). The Talmud Yerushalmi (Berakhot 4:1) states that the essence of *Ne'ila* is to pray more. One of the sources for the importance of offering additional prayers is the example set by Hannah:

> And it came to pass, as she prayed at length before the Lord, that Eli watched her mouth. And Hannah spoke in her heart; only her lips moved, but her voice was not heard, and Eli thought she was drunk. (I Sam. 1:12–13)

Hannah's request of God was clear and organized, but as she extended her prayer, it changed form, becoming wordless and soundless. For this reason, it seems, Eli believed her to be drunk.

When one says the fixed text of a prayer, it can be difficult to hear the voice of the heart, emerging from the depths: "The heart is deceitful above all things, and grievously weak; who can know it?" (Jer. 17:9).

Only the Master of the world, who "searches the heart, trying the inward parts" (v. 10), can interpret what is in our hearts. At the inauguration of the Temple, Solomon asks that God hear the prayer of Israel in times of war, drought, famine, and so on. After listing all these various situations, he asks:

> Whatever prayer and whatever supplication is made by any man, or by all Your people, Israel, *who shall know every man the plague of his own heart*, and spread forth his hands towards this house – then may You hear, in heaven, Your dwelling place, and forgive, and do, and give to every man according to his ways, whose heart You know – *for You, only You, know the hearts of all the children of men.* (1 Kings 8:38–39)

What does this last prayer add to the earlier prayers? It seems that there are prayers and wishes that a person himself is unable to express in words. Only God knows the import of such unspoken thoughts – "for You, only You, know the hearts of all the children of men."

Thus, there is an unformed prayer that cannot express in words the feelings of the person; it may be compared to the crying of an infant, who cannot express in words what pains him. The Responsa of the Rivash (no. 157) records that Rabbi Shimshon of Chinon, after studying the mystical secrets of the Torah, would pray like a newborn infant.

The Hasidim told a similar story concerning the Baal Shem Tov. One year, he prayed with great fervor during the High Holidays. Suddenly, he had a vision that a certain Jew in a different city prayed with even greater fervor than himself. The Baal Shem Tov travelled to that city to visit this Jew. He asked him, "Do you study much Torah?" The Jew answered, "No." The Baal Shem Tov then asked him, "Do you know how to pray?" The man answered, "No." The Baal Shem Tov made another attempt to understand: "What did you do during the High Holidays?" The man answered, "Rabbi – I don't even know the whole alphabet. I only know the letters from *aleph* to *yud*. When I entered the synagogue I saw everyone standing and praying with great fervor. I said, '*Aleph, beit, gimmel…*' until I reached the letter *yud*. Then I said, 'Please, God, join the letters that I have said into words and sentences of prayer, and please accept them with love.' I said this with all my might over and over again."

We do not truly know the proper set of priorities when it comes to our needs and those of the Jewish people. Therefore we pray like an infant who cries and cannot express its wants and needs, and we ask God to compose the proper and appropriate prayers.

The Gemara recounts:

> Our Sages taught, "When R. Eliezer fell ill, his students came to visit him. They said to him, 'Rabbi – teach us the proper path, which will give us life in the World to Come.'
>
> "He said to them, 'Protect the dignity of your fellows, keep your sons from philosophic speculation, and set them at the feet of Torah scholars. And when you pray, know before whom you stand. Through this you will earn life in the World to Come.'" (Berakhot 28b)

What was R. Eliezer trying to teach his disciples when he told them, "When you pray, know before whom you stand?" It seems that he meant, "When you pray, don't look for all sorts of special, original *kavanot*. It is enough that you know before whom you stand; then your prayer will be like the prayer of an infant, and that will earn you life in the World to Come."

The *Ne'ila* prayer was instituted for all public fast days, but on Yom Kippur it has special significance; it is said at the climax of the day, at the moment of atonement, "as it grows dark" (Tosefta Yoma 4:17). The *Shelah* writes:

> The pinnacle of Yom Kippur is *Ne'ila*… for the atonement of Yom Kippur occurs at the end of the day. And the Men of the Great Assembly established at that time to say, "And You, Lord our God,

> have given us with love this Yom Kippur fast, to be the end, the pardon, and forgiveness of all our iniquities, that we may end the oppression that is in our hands." (*Shelah,* Ḥullin, *ner mitzva* 54)

At this auspicious hour, the very pinnacle of Yom Kippur, may our prayer be like the prayer of an infant.

"Upon the Handles of the Lock"

> This is as it is written in the Midrash: … "'I rose up to open for my beloved' – this alludes to Shaḥarit; 'and my hands dripped with myrrh' – an allusion to Musaf; 'and my fingers with flowing myrrh' – this is Minḥa; 'upon the handles of the lock' – this is the *Ne'ila* prayer." (Rabbenu Baḥya, *Kad HaKemaḥ, Kippurim* [2])

The original verse describes four different stages. The first is, "I rose up to open for my beloved" – an awakening of a desire to seek the beloved. The second stage is, "my hand dripped with myrrh" – the need to prepare for this encounter, with the kind of preparations that have a sweet perfume. The third stage is, "my fingers with flowing myrrh" – referring to the need to perfume not just the hands generally, but to apply myrrh specifically to the fingers; this means that one is obligated to pay attention even to the finer details of one's conduct. The fourth stage is, "upon the handles of the lock" – only after the proper preparation can we lay our hand upon the handle of the lock. Only one whose actions smell sweet is ready for an encounter with the Presence of God.

"I rose up to open for my beloved" – The purpose of the prayers of Yom Kippur is to open our heart to God. All year long we are like the maiden – "I sleep, but my heart wakes" – and the Divine Presence pleads, as it were, "Open for Me, My love." Unfortunately, we are unmoved: "I have put off my coat, how shall I put it on?"

But at the time of *Ne'ila,* we seek to open the gates. Not only the gates of heaven are opened, but also the gates of the heart. When the heart is locked, the heavens are also locked. The keys to the gates of heaven are in our hands and in our hearts.

At Minḥa on Yom Kippur we read the Book of Jonah. Avudraham explains the reason for this custom:

> To teach the whole world that no one who has committed transgressions can escape from God, as it is written, "Where shall I go from Your spirit? Or where shall I flee from Your Presence? If I ascend up into heaven, You are there; if I make my bed in *Sheol,* behold – You are there" (Ps. 139:7–8). (*Siddur Avudraham,* Prayers of Yom Kippur)

The Midrash teaches:

> "But Jonah rose up to flee to Tarshish from the presence of the Lord" (Jonah 1:3) – Was he then fleeing from before God? Is it not written, "Where shall I go from Your spirit? Or where shall I flee from Your Presence?"... Rather, Jonah said, "I shall leave the Land of Israel, where the Divine Presence does not reveal itself." (*Yalkut Shimoni* 11:549)

Jonah is supposed to bring the people of Nineveh to repent, but he tries to run away from his destiny by fleeing to a place where he cannot receive prophecy. We, like Jonah, flee from before God; we try to run away from our purpose. We think small: "Tell me what my duty is, and I will do it" (Sota 22b). We are not prepared to do anything beyond our minimum obligation.

On Yom Kippur we need to listen to the call of the ship captain: "What do you mean, O sleeper? Arise, call upon your God" (Jonah 1:6). It is important to remember that sometimes a person turns to God, but at the same time also runs away from Him; he runs away from his destiny. We read the Book of Jonah on Yom Kippur to know what our purpose is in this world.

At the time of *Ne'ila* we identify with Jonah:

> The waters compassed me about, the weeds were wrapped about my head. I went down to the bottoms of the mountains; the earth with her bars closed on me forever; yet You have brought up my life from the pit, O Lord my God. (2:6–7)

As we approach *Ne'ila,* as we "arise to open for the Beloved," we still need a small push to open our hearts. Let us make a supreme effort so that all the things we have learned, all the lessons that are "placed upon our hearts," will enter the heart. If we open the gates of our heart, God will fulfill His promise and open the gate to those who knock in repentance.

"The Lord is near to all those who call upon Him" (Ps. 145:18). *Ne'ila* opens with "a praise by David," a psalm arranged in alphabetical order. We use all the letters in our search for a way to express our desire for closeness to God. We seek the words which will allow us to have "the Lord near."

In a special *piyyut* for *Ne'ila,* we say, "You have separated man from the outset; You have recognized him, had him stand before You. For who can tell You what You are to do, and even if one proves righteous – what can he give You?" Maimonides' version of this prayer starts, "*But* You have separated man from the outset." Even though "the preeminence of man over the animals is nothing, for all is but a fleeting breath," and even though we say, "What are we? What are our lives?" we still say – according to Maimonides – "*But* You have separated man." We need to recognize that "but," the essential difference between animals and man, who is the ultimate purpose of Creation.

We should be proud of that difference, proud of the role that the Holy One, blessed be He, has entrusted to us. But with this pride, concern: we need to recognize the gravity of that mission; "know before whom you stand."

Ne'ila

The time of *Ne'ila* is a time of favor for knocking on the gates, for opening our hearts. Let us make the most of this final hour of the Ten Days of Repentance, about which it is said, "Seek the Lord while He may be found" (Is. 55:6).

"I Pour Out My Plea to Him"

"Open us a gate at the time of the locking of the gate." During *Ne'ila* we ask that the Holy One, blessed be He, open us a gate, and at the same time we ask that He open our hearts to His Torah: "Open my heart to Your Torah, and let my soul pursue Your commandments." For His part, God asks of us, "Open for Me just one opening of repentance, be it as tiny as the point of a needle" (Song of Songs Rabba 5:2). All of the prayers of this day depend on the opening of our hearts, and this is the time: *Ne'ila.*

The first requirement for *Ne'ila* is removing our heart of stone. In the words of *Ḥazal*:

> Ḥizkiya taught, "A man's prayer is not heard unless he makes his heart soft like flesh, as it is written, 'And it shall be that every new moon… all flesh shall come to bow down to the ground before Me, says the Lord' (Is. 66:23)." (Sota 5a)

We need our heart to be free of hardness and closedness, a heart that is open to receive criticism and advice, to absorb knowledge and fear of God. If a person "makes his heart like flesh," his prayer is heard, but if his heart lacks this softness, then it is closed, and all the talk about opening the heart is worth nothing. We pray that our heart opens, so that we will not see, Heaven forbid, the realization of the prophecy, "I will meet them like a bear that is bereaved of her whelps, and I will rend their closed heart" (Hos. 13:8).

The *Tanna'im* disagree about the order of prayer: should the petition for our needs precede our praise of God, or should praise come first?

> R. Eliezer says, "A person first asks for what he needs and then prays, as it is written, 'A prayer of the afflicted when he faints and pours out his heart before the Lord' (Ps. 102:1). 'Plea' refers to prayer, as it is written, 'And Isaac went out to plead in the field' (Gen. 24:63)."
>
> R. Yehoshua says, "First he should pray and only afterwards ask for what he needs, as it is written, 'I pour out my plea before Him, I declare my trouble before Him' (Ps. 142:3)." (Avoda Zara 7b)

Rashi explains that the *Amida* prayer is considered, in this context, "prayer," and not a request for what we need. Elsewhere (Berakhot 31a), however, Rashi writes that the *Amida* prayer has two components: it starts with praise for God (the first three blessings) and then turns to requests for our needs. We see that asking for our needs is integral to the *Amida* prayer!

It seems that we can distinguish between two types of asking for our needs. Sometimes, such a request is an end in and of itself. However, there is a higher level, in which we ask for what we need as a means to connect to God. *Ḥazal* teach that our matriarchs were barren because God "desires their prayers" (Genesis Rabba 45:4). Such prayer is a request for our needs, but its essence is seeking contact and closeness with God.

In Tractate Avoda Zara, Rashi addresses the question of individual needs, and such needs are indeed unrelated to the *Amida* prayer. But in Tractate Berakhot, he is talking about the needs expressed in the *Amida* prayer, which are a means of achieving closeness to God.

"A prayer of the afflicted when he faints (*ki yaatof*) and pours out his heart before the Lord" (Ps. 102:1). The Targum translates the term "*yaatof*" as "weary" or "weak." Though he is weary of praying, he nevertheless pours out his petition before God. This may also be an allusion to *Ne'ila*, which is said at the end of the day, as Yom Kippur draws to a close.

Either way, the prayer of the afflicted is a prayer of pouring out feeling. We do not focus on our own private wants and needs, but rather seek to pour out our feelings before God. The pouring out of feeling should be spontaneous, emanating from the depths of the heart, with no structure or style: "I pour out my plea before Him, I declare my trouble before Him."

How can we pour out our feelings spontaneously when the text of the prayer is fixed and final? The answer is that the inner emotion which we bring to prayer is what gives it that dimension of "pouring out feeling." Prayer that issues from a sense of broken-heartedness is the pouring out of feeling before God. This does not require saying specific words; it is a prayer like the crying of an infant who does not know what he wants, but knows that he lacks something, and his parent will hear his cry and satisfy his need. The Responsa of the Rivash (no. 157) records that Rabbi Shimshon of Chinon, after he studied the mystical secrets of the Torah, would pray like a newborn infant.

The gates of the Sanctuary are about to be locked! At this time one more service is required of us; one more entry into the Holy of Holies, just as the High Priest would enter to bring out the pan and the censer, knowing that when he emerged, all that would remain in the Holy of Holies were the Tablets of Testimony in the Ark. Let us also open our hearts, and take out whatever does not need to be there. In our hearts there will remain, with God's help, only the Tablets of the Covenant, and the covenant with God will remain there in its purity.

The Prayer of the Broken-Hearted

> This is as it is written in the Midrash, "'I rose up to open for my beloved' – this alludes to Shaḥarit; 'my hands dripped with myrrh' – an allusion to Musaf; 'and my fingers with flowing myrrh' – this is Minḥa; 'upon the handles of the lock' – this is the *Ne'ila* prayer." (Rabbenu Baḥya, *Kad HaKemaḥ, Kippurim* [2])

In past years we spoke about the verse, "The Lord is near to all those who call upon Him, to all who call upon Him in truth" (Ps. 145:18); we noted that we turn to the Holy One, blessed be He, in a truth that is subjective, a human truth. However, no matter how hard we try to interpret the words, "call upon Him in truth," as something easy and accessible, ultimately there is still a condition: God is nearby, but only if we call upon Him *in truth*. However, there is another verse that speaks of God's nearness without any conditions: "The Lord is near to those who are broken-hearted, and He saves those who are of a contrite spirit" (34:19). When a person has a broken heart, there is closeness to God with no conditions.

In Solomon's prayer at the inauguration of the Temple, we find:

> Whatever prayer and whatever supplication is made by any man, or by all Your people, Israel, who shall know every man the plague of his own heart, and spread forth his hands towards this house. (1 Kings 8:38)

Every individual "who shall know every man the plague of his own heart" is counted as one who is broken-hearted. The "spreading forth of hands," with a profound experience and awareness of the aching heart, is a manifestation of God being "near to those who are broken-hearted."

In our *Seliḥot* we said, "Lord, God of Israel, You are just, O God of pardon; with sorrowful and broken heart we have come to entreat You, and with brokenness of spirit." It seems that in this generation, after the Holocaust, the entire Jewish people is included in the category of the "broken-hearted." Even after the wondrous miracle and great sanctification of God's name that was wrought by the establishment of the State of Israel, we still have enemies who threaten to annihilate the Jews. By the grace of God, who gives us the strength to succeed in battle, we have the ability to fight and to defend ourselves, but who knows, Heaven forbid, what cost in blood this may entail – may God have mercy. So there is certainly good reason to stand before God with a broken heart.

Although God is "near to those who are broken-hearted," there is a condition: the person has to feel broken-hearted; he cannot stand in prayer with an arrogant heart. King Solomon declares, "An abomination to the Lord is anyone who is proud in heart" (Prov. 16:5). The same message echoes in the Gemara, in the words of Ula:

> Every man who is haughty... is considered as though he had built a high place for worship (*bama*), as it is written, "Cease from man, although his breath is [still] in his nostrils, for what (*bameh*) is he to be accounted of?" (Is. 2:22) – read not "*bameh*" but "*bama.*" (Sota 4b)

Haughtiness is like building an idolatrous altar. One who builds a private altar for himself, not content with sharing in the communal worship, is someone who is haughty and conceited – the opposite qualities from a broken and humble heart.

The *haftara* of Yom Kippur teaches just how close God really is to the broken-hearted, "with him who is contrite and of humble spirit" (Is. 57:15). The Gemara comments on this:

> Rav Huna and Rav Ḥisda [disagreed]. One said that it means, "the contrite are with Me [God]," while the other said it means, "I [God] am with the contrite." The more reasonable view is the latter interpretation, as the Holy One, blessed be He, disregarded all the mountains and hills and brought His Divine Presence down to Mt. Sinai, but did not elevate Mt. Sinai [up to Himself]. (Sota 5a)

Rashi explains that "the contrite are with Me" implies that God raises the contrite individual up to the level of dwelling with God, so that he dwells "with Him." "I am with the contrite" means that God brings His Divine Presence down to dwell with the individual.

Ascending to dwell with God is beyond our comprehension: who can dwell with God? On the other hand, God descending, as it were, to dwell with the contrite of spirit makes sense, and we are capable of conceiving it, since this is indeed what God does. And if the Holy One, blessed be He, is so close to us, then let us make the most of the opportunity and pray wholeheartedly!

> "He heeds the prayer of the destitute and does not despise their prayer" (Ps. 102:18) – R. Yitzḥak explained that this refers to our generations, which have no king, no prophet, no *Urim VeTumim*; all they have is prayer. King David implored God, "Master of the world – do not despise that." (*Yalkut Shimoni* 1:551)

If we wish our prayer to be heard, that God will "not despise" our prayer, then we must fulfill the words of Ḥizkiya in the Gemara there: "Hizkiya said, 'A man's prayer is not heard unless he makes his heart like flesh'" (Sota 5a). Rashi explains: "'Like flesh' – which is soft, and not like stone, which is hard."

This is a general requirement that we soften our hearts towards every person: between man and his fellow, between husband and wife, between parents and children, between teachers and students, between the giver of charity and its recipient. Our heart must be soft like flesh, not hard like stone. If there is no softness in a person, then his heart is closed, and all the talk about opening the heart will be worth nothing. Moreover, we need to beware the prophecy of Hosea: "I will meet them like a bear that is bereaved of her whelps, and I will rend their closed heart" (Hos. 13:8).

"The Lord is near to all who call upon Him, to all who call upon Him in truth." Today, in the generation after the Holocaust, we are all "broken-hearted." Therefore God is near to all of us. May He have compassion on us, hear our prayer, and seal us for a good, long life, and for peace.

Afterword

Philosophical and Educational Themes in Rav Amital's Discourses for the High Holidays

Rabbi Yehuda Gilad

> We took sweet counsel together, and walked to the House of God in company. (Ps. 55:15)

What is the secret of the tremor that we felt, as students at Yeshivat Har Etzion, with the approach of the *Yamim Nora'im*? How does one explain the magic that touched our hearts as we listened to the simple and wondrous *siḥot* of the rosh yeshiva, Rav Amital *zt"l*, during the month of Elul and the *Yamim Nora'im*? What was the delicate spirit that wafted between the words, causing the innermost fibers of the soul to tremble?

Was it the description of the elderly patriarch Abraham, stretching forth his hand to take up the knife and slaughter his son, while at the same time crying to the heavens, "I lift my eyes to the mountains; from where shall my help come?" Or perhaps the image of him "swimming in tears"?

Was it the image of Isaac addressing his father in such human terms, asking, "What will become of you both in your old age?" Or rather, perhaps, the cry, "Then this depends on me alone!" emanating from R. Elazar b. Dordaya in the depths of despair, which mixed with the hundred sobs of the mother of Sisra, fearful for the fate of her son, and mingled with the cry, "I am the man who has seen suffering," conveyed in the warm voice of our own teacher, Rav Amital?

Whatever the key, it is impossible to recreate the electric atmosphere in the *beit midrash* of Yeshivat Har Etzion during Rav Amital's *siḥot* for the *Yamim Nora'im*, or during the prayer services that he led. Something of it no doubt left an impression in the hearts of the listeners, like an ancient melody that stirs the depths of the heart.

However, besides the uplifting spiritual experience, there was also profound Torah, and we must not forget this. This collection of *siḥot* is an attempt to fill the letters and words printed on the page with the Oral Torah that echoes in our memory. Oral teachings may not be committed to writing – but at the same time, "this is Torah, and we need to learn it."

I attempt below to define some of the central themes running through the spiritual and educational philosophy of my teacher and father-in-law, Rav Amital, as reflected in his *siḥot* for the *Yamim Nora'im*.

Rav Amital would frequently repeat the maxim, "A person should always be God-fearing." In order to be God-fearing it is necessary, first and foremost, to be a "*mentsch*." Moreover, his interpretation of the concluding verse of Ecclesiastes – "The end of the matter, when all is said and done: fear God, and observe His commandments, for that is the whole of man" – was that "man" – meaning, being humane – is an essential prerequisite for fear of Heaven. The lofty level achieved by Abraham, God's beloved, in the test of the *Akeda* – "Now I know that you are one who fears God, seeing you have not withheld your son, your only son, from Me" – did not come at the expense of his humanity. Rav Amital emphasized that the story of the *Akeda* is not a simple story free of difficulties, but a sharp expression emphasizing the humanity of the servant of God.

Rav Amital's treatment of the story of the *Akeda* is a perfect example of the novelty of his spiritual philosophy. As we know, commentators have been perplexed by Abraham's silence during this episode. In contrast to his cry, "Will the Judge of all the earth not perform justice?" and the fierce negotiations concerning the fate of Sodom, Abraham's mute obedience during the *Akeda* cries out to the heavens. Some scholars view this negatively (mainly outside of the world of the *beit midrash*, although there are echoes of this view in some ancient *piyyutim*), while others praise Abraham for it. Along came Rav Amital and explained that according to the prevailing view among *Ḥazal*, which is also reflected in halakha, Abraham was not silent at all! The Mishna in Taanit provides that on a public fast day, additional blessings are recited as part of the *Amida*, including "He Who answered Abraham at Mt. Moriah – may He answer you and listen to your cry on this day. Blessed are You, Lord, Redeemer of Israel." Likewise, we recite in our *Seliḥot*, "He Who answered our father Abraham at Mt. Moriah – may He answer us." Rav Amital asked, but nowhere in the Torah do we find mention of Abraham having prayed or asked for anything on Mt. Moriah! His answer was, there are midrashim that describe Abraham's prayer; indeed, we must assume that he prayed, for how could he not have?!

In my opinion this represents a revolutionary approach to understanding the story of the *Akeda*. The story is usually viewed as the clearest expression of the superhuman quality (some would say, the inhuman quality) demanded of a servant of God in an extreme situation of self-sacrifice for the sake of *kiddush Hashem*. In Rav Amital's view, inspired by Rav Kook, the episode conveys a supremely humane message. The greatness of the man of faith is reflected not in the suppression of his feelings, but rather – on the contrary – it is the harsh doubts and grappling on the road to fulfilling God's command that reflect the most desirable path for a servant of God.

Furthermore, Rav Amital made explicit mention of current events, thereby revealing something of the educational motives, *inter alia*, underpinning this idea: "We are familiar with this phenomenon of suppressing all human or fatherly feelings while in the throes of religious ecstasy. In biblical times this found expression in the worship of Moloch, and in our times, we see the same attitude in the response of our neighbors to the death of a '*shahid*.'" It was so important to Rav Amital to emphasize the huge difference between the noble act of Abraham and the abominable acts of those concerning whom we say, "He has not made our portion like theirs, nor our lot like all of their multitudes." Indeed, he went so far as to state that "had Abraham's test lacked this human dimension, the *Akeda* would not only lose its grandeur, but perhaps the whole episode would have been illegitimate and invalid"!

This reveals one of the foundations of Rav Amital's thought. There are approaches that see uprooting the human dimension and suppressing it before God's will as the pinnacle of serving God and fear of Heaven. By suppressing one's lowly human side, man can achieve true closeness to his Maker. This sense of closeness to God gives a person an uplifting, purifying spiritual experience. However, this uplifting experience is, by its nature, disconnected from everyday life and the moral challenges that it brings. Rav Amital viewed this as a great danger.

The purpose of the selection of Abraham is described by God: "For I know him, that he will command his children and his household after him, and they shall keep the way of the Lord, to do justice and judgment, that the Lord may bring upon Abraham that which He has spoken of him" (Gen. 18:19). The "way of the Lord" is "to do justice and judgment," and the opposite must also be true: a path that does not lead a person to justice and judgment in everyday life is not the way of the Lord! For this reason, Rav Amital presents us with an approach that seeks and finds fear of Heaven here in this world. It is specifically through our humanity, with all its doubts, pains, and deficiencies, with all the moral challenges that it entails, that we embody the fear of Heaven. The encounter between God and man takes place in the human realm. Man may indeed be required to subordinate his will to the will of God, but he will find himself doing so with questions, uncertainties, and prayers. What God desires most is the heavenly expanses that open up from within man's inner turmoil and from among the fragments of his broken heart.

Rav Amital would often quote the comment of Rabbi Menaḥem Mendel of Kotzk on the verse, "And you shall be holy men unto Me": God says, "Holy angels I have in droves up in heaven; it is holy men – holy with a human holiness – that I seek."

This path is both easier and more difficult. On one hand, it is easier, because a person feels comfortable with himself, with his humanity, and this approach reassures him: "It is not in the heavens, nor is it over the sea ... for the matter is very close to you, in your mouth and in your heart, to perform it." On the other hand, this path is also more difficult and demanding. Sometimes it is easier to ascend to the heavens than to bring the heavens down to Earth. Disconnecting from the here and now allows for an overpowering religious experience that can carry a person to lofty spiritual heights. In contrast, the demand that we be holy people, filled and motivated by human holiness, demands hard work, honesty, pure motives, ethical standards, and morality within a complex and challenging world which generally is not accompanied by uplifting experiences of spiritual exultation.

"Purify our hearts to serve You in truth." It would seem that the fear of falseness, of what is superficial and alien, motivated Rav Amital and drew him, again and again, toward a primal, authentic simplicity. Rav Amital invites us to discover the depth of simplicity, the simple shofar blast that emanates from the innermost depths which is so necessary in our complicated world. As Rashi teaches in his comment on the Mishna in Rosh HaShana, "The shofar of Rosh HaShana is a straight (literally, "simple") antelope's horn." The reason is explained in the Gemara: that matters of prayer require simplicity.

In one of his *siḥot* Rav Amital cites the testimony about Rabbi Shimshon of Chinon who, having studied all the proper kabbalistic *kavanot* for prayer, prayed a simple prayer "like an infant." Between the lines we detect a subtle reservation about delving into the kabbalistic sphere. He seems to be concerned about the disconnection from the experience of living a simple, human life of divine service as well as the sense of superiority that might develop as a result.

Rav Amital greatly loved the teaching of the *Sefat Emet* on the verse, "How beautiful are your footsteps in sandals (*bane'alim*), O prince's daughter!" The excitement and enthusiasm is at its best when it is safely and securely concealed (*bane'alim* = locked away). Making it public cheapens it, sometimes even distorts it. Pure, clean divine service belongs in the inner recesses of the psyche. Its heart beats quietly within; its voice is not heard.

For this reason, Rav Amital repeatedly cites *Ḥazal*'s teaching, "One's prayer is not heard unless he makes his heart like flesh." As Rashi explains, "'Like flesh' – which is soft, and not like stone, which is hard."

After praising this quality of softness and tenderness, Rav Amital concludes with the wish "that our prayers be like the prayer of an infant."

Another central element in Rav Amital's teachings relates to the relationship between the individual and the community, the personal and the communal. In his *siḥot* for the month of Elul, Rav Amital would cite *Ḥazal*'s teaching in Tractate Rosh HaShana, "This teaches that the Holy One, blessed be He, wrapped Himself like a *sheliaḥ tzibbur* and showed Moses the order of prayer." From this wondrous image of God wrapped in a tallit Rav Amital drew two messages about how one should pray. The wrapping in the tallit represents the de-emphasis of the ego. Excessive preoccupation with "I" and "me" borders on arrogance, and petitions aimed solely at the needs of the individual are compared in the holy Zohar to the barking of a dog.

At the same time, a person must beware of the other extreme of self-abasement. Each one of us is a *sheliaḥ tzibbur* and needs to feel the communal responsibility that he bears. Every person who stands in prayer in the synagogue is also a *sheliaḥ tzibbur* for all of Israel – including those who never set foot in a synagogue, even during the *Yamim Nora'im*.

"I dwell amongst my people," declares the Shunamite woman, and from her we learn that the prayer of the individual is in its proper place only when it is part of the prayer of the community.

The authenticity in Rav Amital's *siḥot*, their genuineness, captured the hearts of his listeners. One of the reasons is the feeling that Rav Amital integrated the private, individual realm with communal and national concerns. His personal background as a survivor of the Holocaust finds expression here and there in his *siḥot*, as he shares his thoughts of that dark time and the implications for us today.

In one of his *siḥot* Rav Amital cites the verse, "The Lord is near to those who are broken-hearted," and comments that "after the Holocaust, the entire Jewish people is included in the category of the 'broken-hearted.'" The footsteps of redemption and revival also resounded in his heart, without obscuring the abyss left by the Holocaust. The Holocaust and the rebirth of Israel, the two most dramatic events in Jewish history since the destruction of the Temple, play a central role in Rav Amital's teachings – both as a private individual, a sensitive soul, a survivor of that terrible conflagration, and as a leader, educator, and public intellectual with a well-developed sense of history.

Rav Amital was wedded to a complex religious worldview. His demand for profound simplicity in man's relationship with God was light years away from a simplistic religious view. After the Holocaust, any simplistic approach to divine providence in the world is a dangerous pretension. Concerning his own feelings during that time, Rav Amital wrote, "I saw before my eyes the hand of God, but I did not understand its meaning." This complex experience of confronting the secret of God's Presence, full of faith and non-comprehension at the same time, was clearly evidenced in Rav Amital's *siḥot* during the *Yamim Nora'im* in his words, in his silences, and in the space between them.

Rav Amital's students joke that a new *berakha* was instituted in our *beit midrash*: "who sanctified us with His commandments and commanded us to hear the cry of an infant." Rav Amital recounted over and over the story of the *Admor HaZaken* who once rebuked his son for having been so immersed in his study that he failed to hear the crying of an infant in his cradle. In the *siḥot* for the *Yamim Nora'im* too, in between the discussion of *Selihot*, the prayers, and the shofar, there is the unmistakable sound of the infant crying.

We cannot conclude our discussion without mentioning Rav Amital's electrifying leading of the prayers on the *Yamim Nora'im*. His *siḥot* were delivered before or during the prayer services and the sounding of the shofar. The depth, simplicity, honesty, and naturalness flowed seamlessly from his *siḥot* to his prayers and from his prayers to the *siḥot*, until it seemed at times that they had merged together.

The *siḥa* preceding *Ne'ila* had its own special status. As the gates of heaven were closing, before pouring out his heart before his Creator, Rav Amital would sing, with a special melody, the words of the midrash on the verse in Song of Songs: "I sleep, but my heart wakes: hark, the sound of my beloved knocking, saying, 'Open for me, my sister, my love, my dove, my undefiled, for my head is filled with dew, and my locks with the drops of the night.'... I rose up to open for my beloved, and my hands dripped with myrrh, and my fingers with flowing myrrh, upon the handles of the lock."

What is that "sound of my beloved knocking?" Rav Amital would ask, and his answer was that those feelings of uplift that we experienced throughout the day are themselves the sound of our Beloved knocking. It is not from the expanses of the infinite that the Beloved calls to His bride; it is not from the distant heavens that the Holy One, blessed be He, is revealed to man; but rather from within the fragments of his own broken heart: "The Lord is near to all who call upon Him, to all who call upon Him in truth."

The fonts used in this book are from the Arno family

Maggid Books
The best of contemporary Jewish thought from
Koren Publishers Jerusalem Ltd.